Turning | Points
IN WORLD HISTORY

The Cold War

Derek C. Maus, *Book Editor*

Daniel Leone, *President*
Bonnie Szumski, *Publisher*
Scott Barbour, *Managing Editor*

**GREENHAVEN
PRESS®**

THOMSON
————★————™
GALE

San Diego • Detroit • New York • San Francisco • Cleveland
New Haven, Conn. • Waterville, Maine • London • Munich

Cover credits: © David and Peter Turnley/CORBIS
Library of Congress, 61, 68, 151
National Archives, 116, 136

LIBRARY OF CONGRESS CATALOGING-IN-PUBLICATION DATA

The Cold War / Derek C. Maus, book editor.
    p. cm. — (Turning points in world history)
Includes bibliographical references and index.
ISBN 0-7377-1415-8 (pbk. : alk. paper) — ISBN 0-7377-1414-X (lib. : alk. paper)
    1. Cold War. 2. Europe—Politics and government—1945– . 3. World politics—1945– . 4. United States—Foreign relations—Soviet Union. 5. Soviet Union—Foreign relations—United States. I. Maus, Derek C. II Series. III. Turning points in world history (Greenhaven Press).
D843 .C57724 2003
909.82'5—dc21   2002023168

Printed in the United States of America

Contents

a diplomatic tool in relation to the Soviet Union. By mid-1946, however, the global situation had changed significantly, and demonstrating the potential threat of the bomb to the Soviets became an important element in diplomatic intimidation.

Despite some misgivings about their use at Hiroshima and Nagasaki, atomic bombs were generally perceived in a positive light by Americans at the outset of the Cold War, whether as a political bargaining tool to control the Soviets or as a military option in actual conflicts such as the Korean War.

Chapter 2: Cold War Hot Spots: Confrontation in the Nuclear Age

The Korean War of 1950–1953 was the first major conflict that directly tested Truman's containment policy of preventing communism from gaining further territory. The test, though, came not only from the military enemies in North Korea and China, but from internal opponents such as General Douglas MacArthur, who claimed that Truman's policy was too timid.

The fervent anticommunism of the early 1950s in the United States was a cultural response to the perceived invulnerability of the Soviet Union. Because it was widely felt that this archenemy could not be directly attacked, the best alternative was to find and persecute Communist sympathizers in the United States.

The superpowers seemingly came close to direct military conflict twice in the early 1960s, in Berlin and Cuba. Both crises were aggravated by Soviet-U.S. misunderstanding, deception, and bluffs that exaggerated the willingness of both countries to go to war.

Foreword

Certain past events stand out as pivotal, as having effects and outcomes that change the course of history. These events are often referred to as turning points. Historian Louis L. Snyder provides this useful definition:

> A turning point in history is an event, happening, or stage which thrusts the course of historical development into a different direction. By definition a turning point is a great event, but it is even more—a great event with the explosive impact of altering the trend of man's life on the planet.

History's turning points have taken many forms. Some were single, brief, and shattering events with immediate and obvious impact. The invasion of Britain by William the Conqueror in 1066, for example, swiftly transformed that land's political and social institutions and paved the way for the rise of the modern English nation. By contrast, other single events were deemed of minor significance when they occurred, only later recognized as turning points. The assassination of a little-known European nobleman, Archduke Franz Ferdinand, on June 28, 1914, in the Bosnian town of Sarajevo was such an event; only after it touched off a chain reaction of political-military crises that escalated into the global conflict known as World War I did the murder's true significance become evident.

Other crucial turning points occurred not in terms of a few hours, days, months, or even years, but instead as evolutionary developments spanning decades or even centuries. One of the most pivotal turning points in human history, for instance—the development of agriculture, which replaced nomadic hunter-gatherer societies with more permanent settlements—occurred over the course of many generations. Still other great turning points were neither events nor developments, but rather revolutionary new inventions and innovations that significantly altered social customs and ideas, military tactics, home life, the spread of knowledge, and the human condition in general. The developments of writing, gunpowder, the printing press, antibiotics, the electric light, atomic energy, television, and the computer, the last two of which have recently ushered in the world-altering information age, represent only some of these innovative turning points.

Each anthology in the Greenhaven Turning Points in World History series presents a group of essays chosen for their accessibility. The anthology's structure also enhances this accessibility. First, an introductory essay provides a general overview of the principal events and figures involved, placing the topic in its historical context. The essays that follow explore various aspects in more detail, some targeting political trends and consequences, others social, literary, cultural, and/or technological ramifications, and still others pivotal leaders and other influential figures. To aid the reader in choosing the material of immediate interest or need, each essay is introduced by a concise summary of the contributing writer's main themes and insights.

In addition, each volume contains extensive research tools, including a collection of excerpts from primary source documents pertaining to the historical events and figures under discussion. In the anthology on the French Revolution, for example, readers can examine the works of Rousseau, Voltaire, and other writers and thinkers whose championing of human rights helped fuel the French people's growing desire for liberty; the French *Declaration of the Rights of Man and Citizen*, presented to King Louis XVI by the French National Assembly on October 2, 1789; and eyewitness accounts of the attack on the royal palace and the horrors of the Reign of Terror. To guide students interested in pursuing further research on the subject, each volume features an extensive bibliography, which for easy access has been divided into separate sections by topic. Finally, a comprehensive index allows readers to scan and locate content efficiently. Each of the anthologies in the Greenhaven Turning Points in World History series provides students with a complete, detailed, and enlightening examination of a crucial historical watershed.

Introduction

Despite its superficial simplicity—two countries, each with giant armies, facing off in a test of will to determine whose ideology is superior—the Cold War is by its very nature an extremely difficult period in world history to understand. The fact that it has ended relatively recently compounds the difficulty of looking back on it with an objective eye, especially since many of its prominent figures are still in the public eye. For instance, the leaders of both the former Cold War rivals at the start of the year 2002 have direct ties to the Cold War. Russia's president, Vladimir Putin, was an officer in the KGB, the Soviet Union's intelligence agency and secret police, and U.S. president George W. Bush is the son of George H.W. Bush, who was president during the final years of the Cold War and who also served as head of the CIA, the KGB's American counterpart, for a year in the 1970s. The Cold War itself may be over, but the political careers of those who came of age during the Cold War will continue for several decades to come, a factor that can make looking back at the period with clear hindsight somewhat difficult.

Nevertheless, it is important to attempt to do so since a lack of consensus still exists on what lessons, if any, the Cold War has taught the world. A poll conducted in January 1990 by CBS News and the *New York Times* indicated that more than three-quarters of the Americans surveyed (77 percent) believed that neither side had won the Cold War, and only 14 percent answered that the United States and its allies had done so. Given that this poll was conducted immediately after most of the Communist regimes in Eastern Europe had fallen (along with the Berlin Wall) and that the leaders of the two superpowers had recently declared the Cold War officially over, these numbers may seem somewhat surprising since the oft-cited "fall of communism" would seem by definition to have also been a victory for those who opposed communism. Historians have carried on a lively debate since that time in an effort to clarify the lasting meaning of the Cold War for future generations, but they have not necessarily come any closer to achieving a consensus than their peers did in the immediate aftermath of the Cold War.

Without a doubt, the Cold War represents a watershed period in human history if only because it marked the first time in our collective existence that we developed the power to end that existence almost instantaneously. The questions surrounding the legacy of the Cold War, however, deal not only with issues surrounding nuclear weapons but also with a wide variety of policy measures that leaders on both sides felt were justified in taking in the name of defending their nation's values. Part of an objective after-the-fact assessment of the Cold War certainly involves congratulating those who made the right moves in the high-stakes game of political chess that was the Cold War. However, another part arises from philosopher George Santayana's famous warning in *The Life of Reason* that "those who cannot remember the past are condemned to repeat it." The Cold War was not fought without mistakes, and learning from those mistakes is crucial for living in as implicitly dangerous a time as the atomic age.

Perhaps the best perspective for approaching the task of uncovering the Cold War's meaning comes from George Kennan, whose Long Telegram helped to set the Cold War in motion in 1946. Writing in an October 28, 1992, editorial in the *New York Times*, he advised that the fortunately peaceful resolution to the long standoff between the United States and the Soviet Union was "a fit occasion for satisfaction but also for sober reexamination of the part we took in its origin and long continuation. It is not a fit occasion for pretending that the end of it was a great triumph for anyone."

A Brief History of the Cold War

Even as World War II drew to a close, the alliance of necessity among the United States, Great Britain, and the Soviet Union began to collapse. Although military victory over the remaining two legs of the Axis—Germany and Japan—was virtually assured as of early 1945, the shape of the postwar world was still unclear. It was an irreconcilable difference of opinion on this issue—or, more accurately, the wide range of issues that were involved in determining the postwar world—that rapidly shifted the nature of global politics from open military conflict, as had been the case since the late 1930s, to a more covert and indirect ideological conflict between the capitalist nations of the West and the Communist nations of the East. Dubbed "the Cold War" by American journalist Walter Lippmann in 1947, this state of relatively abstract hostility—occasionally lapsing into actual combat, usually between so-called client states of the two sides—lasted until the late 1980s or early 1990s, when the collapse of the Communist governments in Eastern Europe and the dissolution of the Soviet Union effectively ended the basis for the conflict.

Despite widespread claims by journalists, historians, and politicians that the demise of communism indicated that the West had "won" the Cold War, the unique nature of this protracted showdown requires considerably closer examination before any such claims can be justified. Because of the development and rapid proliferation of nuclear weapons, the Cold War marked the first period in human history in which warfare between two powerful opponents could potentially not only redraw political boundaries and change the balance of power but also conceivably destroy the entire planet in the process. Because of this fact, the Cold War was based on something of a paradox. Leaders on both sides frequently argued that communism and capitalism could not coexist, which guaranteed an opposition as the two sides attempted to establish their influence around the globe. However, unlike during World War II, when military confrontation was used by the Allies to subdue the rise of fascism, the possibly dire consequences of any direct conflict between the two superpowers demanded that the two sides avoid attacking one another to settle their differences. Thus, the Cold War became a nearly fifty-year war of words and wills, as both sides aggressively tried to promote and protect their respective ideologies at home and abroad while always remaining aware of the repercussions of pushing the limits too far.

A Hot War Turns Cold

Historians disagree about the exact starting date of the Cold War. Unlike World War I, which was directly triggered by the assassination of the Austrian archduke Francis Ferdinand on June 28, 1914, or World War II, which began with the German invasion of Poland in September 1939, there was neither a single military action nor a formal declaration of hostilities to mark the beginning of the conflict. Despite the lack of overall consensus, most studies of the Cold War identify the period from late 1943 through early 1946 as being of the greatest importance in establishing the bipolar world that existed during the Cold War. As the threat posed by the Axis steadily decreased during the final two years of World War II, the former allies found themselves increasingly free to focus once again on ideological differences that had divided them before the rise of fascism. The subsequent division of the world into two hostile spheres of influence was under way almost before the ink was dry on the peace treaties that ended World War II.

A conference held at Tehran, Iran, in November and December 1943 was only the first in a series of meetings between the leaders of the three great Allied powers—U.S. president Franklin Roosevelt, British prime minister Winston Churchill, and Soviet premier Joseph Stalin—during the final two years of World War II. Initially, these meetings were intended to help coordinate the Allies' operations against the Axis. For example, one of the main purposes of the meeting at Tehran was to inform Stalin of the British and American plan to invade occupied France during the coming summer—what would become the D day invasion on June 6, 1944—and to synchronize that attack with the Soviet counteroffensive against the Germans in the east. However, the three leaders also began planning, with increasing urgency, the political state of the postwar world.

At Tehran, the three leaders limited themselves to a relatively abstract discussion of such issues as what, if any, influence the liberating countries should have in the territories over which they gain control. These issues became considerably less abstract as such liberation became a reality in subsequent months. By the time of the February 1945 conference in the Soviet Black Sea resort city of Yalta, the Allied leaders were formulating plans for the mutual occupation of Germany after its ultimate defeat, which was now only a matter of time. They also agreed not to challenge each other's authority in areas that had already been occupied. For example, British and American forces would remain in control of Italy, and Soviet forces controlled most of the sections of Eastern Europe that had previously been in German hands. Both sides outwardly insisted that such occupied areas—with the notable exception of Germany—would be allowed to establish their own elected governments as soon as possible, but the respective spheres of influence established by the agreement at Yalta would remain essentially the same for the next forty-five years.

The leaders of the three main Allies—with Harry Truman replacing Roosevelt and Clement Attlee replacing Churchill—met once more, this time in the German city of Potsdam in late July and early August 1945. The war in Europe had ended, and the military focus had turned to the war in the Pacific, where victory for the Allies was increasingly certain, but the costs of achieving that victory were still unclear. The division of Europe that had taken place in principle at Yalta was put into writing by agreements signed at Potsdam. Although the notion of self-determination for occupied territories was still in theory the guiding principle, both sides used the vagueness of the Potsdam accords in the immediate postwar years to press for the creation of sympathetic governments in the countries over which they had influence.

This practice helped rapidly create Eastern and Western blocs of nations, which were dominated by the military, political, and/or economic might of the Soviet Union and the United States, respectively. These two blocs were separated initially by a demilitarized and collaboratively occupied Germany, but that separation ended when Germany was severed into two distinct parts in 1949. The former Soviet zone of occupation became the Communist-run German Democratic Republic, and the zones previously occupied by France, Great Britain, and the United States became the Federal Republic of Germany. In sum, the three major wartime conferences among the Allies helped set the stage for the Cold War by dividing the continent of Europe into two distinct halves.

The Role of the Atomic Bomb

Another part of the discussions at Yalta was already obsolete by the time of the Potsdam Conference six months later. At Yalta, Stalin had agreed to have Soviet troops enter the war in the Pacific as soon as the war in Europe was concluded. Given that a difficult and costly invasion of Japan still seemed necessary at that time to end that phase of the war, this was widely viewed as a gesture of continued good relations among the Allies. By late July, though, the strategic situation had changed dramatically with the successful test of an atomic bomb by a team of scientists working for the United States in the top-secret Manhattan Project. The bomb was tested on July 17, 1945. On July 24, Truman casually informed Stalin at Potsdam that the United States had a "new weapon of unusual destructive force."[1] Stalin, by all accounts, registered little reaction. On July 26 the Allies issued an ultimatum to Japan, demanding either unconditional surrender or total destruction. This ultimatum was now backed with Truman's atomic ace-in-the-hole rather than the threat of Soviet entry into the Pacific theater.

British and U.S. attitudes toward Soviet participation in the final push against Japan had changed dramatically by the time of the Potsdam meeting. This was not just because of the bomb but also because of the different attitudes that

Truman and Roosevelt had regarding the Soviets. Truman was much less inclined to work with the Soviets than Roosevelt had been; accordingly, he adopted a much harder line toward U.S.-Soviet relations upon taking office in April 1945. With the atomic bomb in his possession, Truman did not feel compelled to offer the Soviets even a symbolic share in the defeat of Japan. As historian John Lewis Gaddis notes,

> It quickly became clear to the few who knew this secret [of the atomic bomb's existence] that Stalin's assistance in defeating Japan would not be needed after all. The Potsdam Conference . . . saw a distinct cooling in Anglo-American enthusiasm for Soviet entry into the Pacific war. When that event finally took place on 8 August, two days after the destruction of Hiroshima, it came across as an undignified scramble on Stalin's part to salvage an unexpectedly unpromising position.[2]

Other historians have even gone so far as to claim that the use of the atomic bomb, especially on Nagasaki, was done as much to force Japan's surrender as to threaten the Soviets by demonstrating the possible consequences of opposing the United States's postwar plans. In the years immediately following the war, Truman was frequently accused of engaging in "nuclear diplomacy" by either explicitly or implicitly threatening the use of atomic bombs against the Soviets or their allies in a number of situations. His ability to do so was dramatically reduced, though, when the Soviets successfully tested their own atomic bomb on August 29, 1949, thereby touching off the nuclear arms race that for many was the defining characteristic of the Cold War.

The Divisions Widen

The split between the United States and the Soviet Union was not yet guaranteed at the start of 1946, but developments over the next two years virtually assured an extended period of antagonism between the two countries. Not only was Truman siding openly with the more anti-Communist voices in his government, but Soviet actions in the rest of the world seemed to justify the opinions of those who believed that peaceful coexistence with the Soviets was impossible.

In February 1946 diplomat George Kennan—then stationed at the U.S. embassy in Moscow—sent what came to be known as the Long Telegram back to Truman in Washington. In this document, Kennan asserted that his observations of Stalin and his government had led him to the conclusion that the Soviet Union was not interested in any form of cooperative existence with the United States. Although Kennan did not explicitly argue that U.S. policy should follow the same course with regard to the USSR, he did claim that the "problem of how to deal with this force is undoubtedly the greatest our diplomacy has ever faced and probably the greatest it will ever have to face."[3]

Truman's solution to this diplomatic problem was to avoid direct confrontation with the Soviets in regard to their internal politics but also to oppose the Soviets wherever and whenever he felt that they were seeking to expand their influence. Not only did Truman consistently press Stalin to live up to the agreement made at Yalta to allow free elections in the countries of Eastern Europe—especially Poland—but he also objected to perceived Soviet expansionist overtures in Southeast Asia and parts of Europe, such as Greece and Turkey. In March 1946 Truman angrily accused Stalin of being deliberately slow in withdrawing Soviet troops from Iran—where they had been stationed during the war to protect vital oil fields from capture by the Germans—in an effort to influence the local government and perhaps even annex the country to the Soviet Union. Truman threatened to bring the issue up before the newly created United Nations Security Council before the Soviets finally agreed to withdraw. This was the first, but hardly the last, occasion on which an American president acted to "contain" the spread of communism, and by the next year, such a policy officially became that of the nation.

At the same time, Soviet attitudes toward the West were becoming similarly defensive in tone, reacting to ostensibly imperialist behavior by the United States. As historian Richard Crockatt notes,

Nikolai Novikov [an official in the Soviet embassy in Washington, D.C.], writing in September 1946, pictured an America bent on "world domination." Reactionaries had displaced those within the Democratic Party who advocated cooperation with the Soviet Union, the development of a far-flung military base system indicated the "offensive nature" of American strategy, and the United States and Britain were establishing what amounted to a condominium to divide up the world "on the basis of mutual concessions."[4]

The rhetoric contained in such public pronouncements as Churchill's famous Iron Curtain speech in February 1946 and the dismissal of more moderate politicians such as Secretary of Commerce Henry Wallace—who had argued openly for making peace with the Soviets—from Truman's administration seemed to support Novikov's position. Its effect in Soviet circles was comparable to that of Kennan's Long Telegram in that it hardened the conviction that conflict with the West was inevitable, given the supposedly insatiable desire of capitalism to expand its reach. This attitude helps explain why Stalin declined to allow Eastern Europe to participate in the economic revitalization program (the Marshall Plan) that the United States proposed in 1948, especially since its formulator, Secretary of State George Marshall, was an outspoken anti-Communist. Both sides spent much of 1946 convincing themselves that their opponent was preparing for an all-out assault on their values and way of life.

The Truman Doctrine and Beyond

When Truman stepped before a joint session of Congress on March 12, 1947, to announce that "it must be the policy of the United States to support free peoples who are resisting attempted subjugation by armed minorities or by outside pressures,"[5] he left little doubt that he intended to oppose the expansion of communism vigorously. His position soon became known as the Truman Doctrine, a term that hearkened back to the first half of the nineteenth century, when the Monroe Doctrine explicitly stated the U.S. policy of forcefully opposing outside intervention in the countries of the Western Hemisphere. The ostensible occasion for Truman's declaration was the announcement by the British that

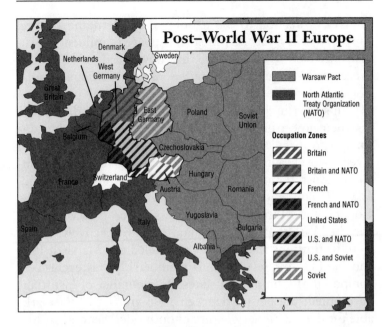

Post–World War II Europe

Denmark
Netherlands
West
Germany
Sweden
Great
Britain
East
Germany
Poland
Soviet
Union
Belgium
Czechoslovakia
Switzerland
Hungary
France
Austria
Romania
Yugoslavia
Spain
Italy
Bulgaria
Albania

Warsaw Pact

North Atlantic
Treaty Organization
(NATO)

Occupation Zones

Britain

Britain and NATO

French

French and NATO

United States

U.S. and NATO

U.S. and Soviet

Soviet

they could no longer afford to economically support anti-Communist forces in the ongoing civil war in Greece. Perhaps fearing that the Soviets would see this as an opening to increase their influence in the region, but also readily understanding the rhetorical opportunity it presented to him, Truman pledged U.S. economic aid not only to the Greeks and their immediate neighbors in Turkey but also to all countries that wanted to resist "outside pressures"—by which he meant *Communist* pressure, of course.

The process Truman had set in motion with his speech in 1947 was gradually refined into actual national policy over the course of the next three years, eventually being put into official form in 1950 in a document called National Security Council Resolution 68, or NSC 68. This document argued for a massive military buildup to defend against the predicted aggression of the Soviets and reinforced Truman's idea that the nation had a moral obligation to stop the advance of communism. The establishment of the Marshall Plan in 1948 and of the North Atlantic Treaty Organization (NATO) in 1949 allowed Truman to put his money (and his guns) where his mouth was, giving direct economic aid and military protection to the nations of Western and Central Europe that lay outside the Soviet sphere of influence. Truman intended to keep them that way and devoted an unprecedented share of the resources of the traditionally isolationist United States to assuring this.

Not surprisingly, the Soviets responded in kind, solidifying their power in the Eastern European countries by continuing to install explicitly Communist governments (e.g., Czechoslovakia in 1948) or removing any remaining non-Communist remnants within already established regimes (e.g., Poland and Hungary). They also established the Council for Mutual Economic Assistance (COMECON) and the Warsaw Pact in 1949 and 1955, respectively. These were institutions that directly paralleled the Marshall Plan and NATO, except that their membership was exclusively composed of Communist states. As a number of historians have noted, the period between 1946 and 1950 is remarkable for the reactionary nature of both sides' actions. As historian Wilfried Loth points out,

> The conflict between East and West was no longer understood simply as a power-political struggle for spheres of influence and security requirements, but increasingly in terms of a battle for survival between two opposing social orders and life-styles. As a result of this ideological polarisation, the actual diversity of political life was increasingly lost to view . . . [and] each crisis of mutual relations which resulted from this incipient organization process . . . led to an intensification of this polarisation.[6]

In essence, both sides had convinced themselves so fully of the reality of a two-sided world by the late 1940s that they viewed their own actions not in rational terms of balancing cause and effect (i.e., the establishment of NATO *caused* the establishment of the Warsaw Pact, or the establishment of the German Democratic Republic *caused* the establishment of the Federal Republic of Germany) but more as justification of their paranoia concerning their opponents' intent (i.e., the establishment of NATO proved the aggressive intentions of the West, which required the defensive establishment of the Warsaw Pact, which was in turn viewed as an aggressive gesture by the West, and so on).

Such a system maintained a perilous equilibrium as long as neither side *actually* made an aggressive move against the other since that would require an equally aggressive response. Maintaining this balance became the great challenge of the remaining four decades of the Cold War, a prospect made all the more challenging as the arms race intensified and made all-out nuclear holocaust the potential endpoint of any military escalation. Both sides needed to maintain a defensive posture to convince their respective populations that they were serious about protecting their national values, but both sides also understood the dangers of crossing the line and engaged in a number of indirect means of conducting their conflict that stopped short of outright "hot" war.

Early Challenges to the Cold War Order

This system was challenged almost as soon as it was established by growing tensions in Germany and Southeast Asia. In June 1948 Britain, France, and the United States accelerated the pace of their plans to unite their occupied territories in Germany economically in preparation for the creation of a new West German federal state. The Soviets, who were opposed to all efforts to create a West German state that would implicitly be friendly to the United States and its allies, responded by blocking all transportation routes into their zone of Germany, which included the city of Berlin. Since Berlin had also been divided into separate zones of occupation among the four countries, this left more than 2 million people cut off from supplies of food, fuel, and other necessities.

Stalin's goals were either to force the Western allies to abandon their plans for the new federal state altogether or at least to force them to leave West Berlin entirely, thereby allowing the Soviets to create an East German state completely under its control. The two sides traded heated rhetoric and looked for a diplomatic settlement to the standoff. At the same time, the U.S. and British militaries began airlifting supplies into Berlin, a move that not only provided for the needs of Berliners during the blockade but also played well back in the United States. Newsreel footage of German children waving at planes dropping food parcels into the encircled city helped further convince the American populace that Truman's grave pronouncements about Soviet malice were true.

Loth explains to what extent both sides wished to avoid war over Berlin, though, no matter how symbolically important an issue the blockade was:

> It was not clear at first for how long provision for over two million Berliners could be carried out from the air. In addition, there was a widespread fear that the Soviet Union could block even the air route. In fact this fear was unfounded, since Stalin was not prepared on account of the foundation of a Western state, however contrary to Soviet interests, to risk a war that would be bound to end with the destruction of the Soviet Union. The myth of Soviet strength, however, led most Western politicians to overlook how risky and how close to the limits of the feasible this Soviet manoeuvre really was. [U.S. governor in Berlin Lucius] Clay, who did not share belief in this myth, repeatedly urged breaking through the blockade of the motorways with tanks, but was repeatedly rebuffed by his government out of fear of an armed conflict. Hardly anyone wanted war on account of Berlin: not in the USA and definitely not in Europe.[7]

The Soviets eventually relented in May 1949, but the lack of resolution in the conflict created two separate German states in the immediate aftermath of the blockade. Both of these became independent nations by the mid-1950s and represented, politically and symbolically, the clear division of Europe into two hostile camps. The reunification of Germany in 1990 was one of the clearest signs that the Cold War had ended.

Korea had been divided after World War II much as Germany had. Soviet and American troops landed on the Korean peninsula in August and September 1945, respectively, to liberate it from Japanese occupation. Both quickly set up friendly governments to administer the areas that they controlled. The two zones of occupation were separated by the thirty-eighth parallel, which ran roughly through the center of the peninsula. By 1948 the United States and the Soviet Union had each sponsored the creation of competing Korean states. Kim il-Sung became premier of the People's Democratic Republic of Korea in the north, and Syngman Rhee took over as president of the Republic of Korea in the south. Neither side recognized the sovereignty of the other, though, and Kim's outspoken desire to reunify Korea under his control quickly clashed with Rhee's desire to repel the spread of communism in Asia. Because they closely echoed the U.S. policy of containment, Rhee's goals received the support of General Douglas MacArthur, commander of U.S. occupation forces in Japan and a fervent anti-Communist. This support increased after the establishment of the Communist People's Republic of China in October 1949 seemed to herald the rapid expansion of communism in the region.

Armed conflict between the two Koreas along the thirty-eighth parallel had already been taking place before 1950, but it was the North Korean invasion of South Korea in June 25, 1950, that engulfed the entire peninsula in what would become the first large-scale "proxy war" of the Cold War. North Korea received extensive economic and military assistance from the Communists—from China to a greater degree than from the Soviet Union—and South Korea received massive aid from the United States to defend itself. Although this aid was ostensibly from the United Nations—MacArthur was appointed commander of UN troops in Korea in July 1950—the United States was the unquestioned political, economic, and military force behind the UN at this time. For example, 90 percent of the nearly six hundred thousand UN troops initially sent to Korea in 1950 were from the United States.

A substantial number of the actual combatants on either side were not Korean, especially after November 1950, when large numbers of Chinese troops drove MacArthur's UN troops back from their positions near the Yalu River, which formed the border between China and North Korea. According to the U.S. Department of Defense, nearly 5.7 million U.S. soldiers would eventually serve in Korea and almost forty thousand were killed. No official figures on Chinese involvement have been released, but estimates range from hundreds of thousands to several million troops. In effect, the two sides were waging their larger ideological battle using other countries to stand in their place in a military conflict.

After several substantial advances by both sides, the war eventually reached a relative stalemate, which MacArthur proposed breaking by launching an all-out offensive, including invasions and potential nuclear strikes in China itself. Truman disagreed with MacArthur's strategy and also disapproved of the general's open advocacy of nuclear warfare. Truman removed MacArthur as commander in Korea on April 11, 1951, a move that backfired politically when MacArthur, still revered by most Americans as a war hero from World War II, went before Congress on April 19 and stated his strong anti-Communist position there. The backlash against Truman's perceived weakness cost him, and he decided not to run for reelection in 1952. Former general Dwight D. Eisenhower was elected, in part because of his promise to end the war in Korea. An armistice was finally signed in July 1953 and the two Koreas remained separated, as they have ever since, by a narrow demilitarized zone running nearly along the thirty-eighth parallel.

The Eisenhower Years

Within months of assuming the presidency, Eisenhower was faced with a change of power in the Soviet Union. After nearly thirty years in power, Stalin died on March 5, 1953. A brief struggle ensued among a number of possible successors, but eventually Nikita Khrushchev assumed power in the Soviet Union. Khrushchev began making overtures toward the West that were not as hostile as those of his predecessor, even at times making outright, if not necessarily consistent, calls for peaceful relations between the two superpowers. The new Soviet leadership immediately tried to distance itself from the Stalinist past and actively began renouncing the "excesses" of the previous three decades. Stalin himself was posthumously denounced by Khrushchev in a speech at the Twentieth Party Congress in 1956, an occasion that seemed to herald a dramatic change in Soviet society. Many in Eisenhower's administration, especially Secretary of State John Foster Dulles, remained skeptical, and the mood of the country in general was still too consumed with the extreme anti-Communist sentiment stirred up by Senator Joseph McCarthy's House Un-American Activities Committee (HUAC) to trust Khrushchev's motives.

Eisenhower's two terms in office were a mixed bag in terms of East-West relations. A number of developments caused a general uncertainty in the United States, both in terms of governmental policies and larger cultural attitudes. McCarthy's fall from grace in 1954 caused some public reevaluation of the motives behind the ardent opposition to communism. McCarthy had begun his campaign in 1950 with the intention of exposing "Communist infiltrators" and spies within the government. The "red scare" that his statements produced had seemed justified in 1950 and 1951, when high-profile spy cases like those of Alger Hiss and the Rosenbergs disclosed the apparent presence of Soviet spies in sensitive areas (although the validity of both cases was questioned). As McCarthy broadened his probe to seek out Communists within the arts, the entertainment industry, and the military, his tactics were increasingly questioned. He was eventually discredited for conducting a witch hunt, a metaphor taken from *The Crucible*, a play by Arthur Miller, himself one of McCarthy's targets. Miller's play had indirectly compared McCarthy's methods to those of the witch trials in Salem, Massachusetts, during the American colonial period. Miller argued that both used popular paranoia instead of actual evidence to indict individuals of nonexistent crimes.

The development of more potent nuclear weapons also added a new dimension of insecurity to the Cold War world. The United States successfully tested the world's first hydrogen bomb on Elugelab atoll in the South Pacific on November 1, 1952. This weapon by itself was more powerful than the total of all of the conventional bombs dropped by all combatants during World War II and represented a dramatic shift of power in the Cold War. The shift was not long-lasting, however, as the Soviets tested their first hydrogen bomb in August 1953. As had been the case with earlier developments, both sides interpreted this technological advance as further evidence of mounting preparations for an offensive and justified their own rapid buildup of such weapons by citing the other side's nuclear capability. By the end of the 1950s, Great Britain had joined the H-bomb club (China and France would follow suit during the 1960s), and both the United States and the Soviet Union had a nuclear stockpile large enough to render the planet uninhabitable. The implications of such unparalleled destructive force made even some former advocates of nuclear weaponry, such as Winston Churchill, change their minds. The United Nations even established a Disarmament Commission in 1952 that sought to demilitarize the world in general and to eliminate nuclear weapons specifically. Although this particular effort met with little success, it presaged the much larger disarmament movement of the 1970s and 1980s. As nuclear stockpiles expanded during the 1950s and 1960s, their strategic value began to diminish (since their use by either side would virtually assure complete destruction) and the idea of nuclear weapons as deterrents began to take shape on both sides.

Finally, the often unpredictable and contradictory nature of Khrushchev himself made it difficult for U.S. leaders to determine what course to take with regard to the Soviet Union. Crockatt describes the seemingly paradoxical character of the Soviet leader as follows:

> An advocate of "peaceful coexistence," he also made dramatic and bellicose pronouncements about the irreconcilable nature of the conflict between East and West and took pride in parading Soviet achievements—such as its impressive economic growth rates in the mid-1950s and the launch of [the world's first artificial satellite] Sputnik [in 1957]—which seemed to suggest that the Soviet Union was capable of beating the West at its own game. Moreover, while Khrushchev announced to an astonished Party Congress in 1956 that Stalin had committed grave errors and that much of his legacy must be repudiated, later the same year, he ordered Soviet troops into Hungary to suppress an uprising which was fuelled by his own de-Stalinization speech.[8]

Strident anti-Communists like Dulles and John F. Kennedy, then a senator from Massachusetts, focused on Khrushchev's more provocative aspects, such as his famous "We will bury you" comment (one of Khrushchev's frequent economic boasts that was perceived by many Americans as a military threat) or his speech before the United Nations in 1960, during which he angrily banged his shoe on the podium.

At best, Khrushchev was an enigmatic leader who tried to balance a somewhat idealistic and often cooperative world-view with the reality that he also needed to appease hard-liners within the Communist Party in order to retain power. At worst, he was a master of deceptive propaganda, speaking publicly about cooperation and peace while actively supporting Communist insurrections in Asia, Africa, and Latin America. In either case, Khrushchev's inconsistent personality helped contribute greatly to what were arguably the most tense years of the Cold War, 1959 through 1962.

Khrushchev and Kennedy Square Off

Even before Kennedy defeated Eisenhower's vice president, Richard Nixon, in the 1960 presidential election, relations between the superpowers had become more strained. On January 1, 1959, Fidel Castro had led a successful revolution in Cuba and quickly aligned himself with the Soviets, who provided his fledgling regime with substantial economic aid. This action established a seemingly hostile government within ninety miles of the United States's southern shore and quickly became a source of tension. Even as the two super-powers made friendly gestures toward one another—Khrushchev and Nixon exchanged official visits in 1959—their proxies fought one another in Southeast Asia and Africa, where growing numbers of independence movements created new opportunities for both sides to gain influence.

The presidential campaign between Nixon and Kennedy was filled with anti-Communist rhetoric, which intensified after the Soviets disclosed on May 7, 1960, that they had shot down an American U-2 spy plane over their territory and captured its pilot, Gary Francis Powers, who had admitted to spying for the United States. Eisenhower and Khrushchev had

Europe During the Cold War

Denmark

Netherlands

Britain

Berlin

East
Germany

Poland

Belgium

USSR

Luxembourg

West
Germany

Czechoslovakia

Switzerland

Austria

Hungary

France

Italy

Romania

Yugoslavia

Spain

Soviet-Controlled
Eastern Europe

Albania

been scheduled to meet in Paris to sign a treaty banning atmospheric tests of nuclear weapons, but the U-2 incident destroyed the mutual trust that had been emerging between the two leaders, and the conference never took place. The two presidential candidates took the opportunity to distance themselves from Eisenhower's seemingly failed efforts at cooperation with the Soviets, and Kennedy narrowly defeated Nixon in the election, in part due to his strategy of instilling fear of a "missile gap"—a supposed Soviet superiority in nuclear-tipped missiles that could threaten the United States—into voters. This gap turned out to be nonexistent, but it had been an effective tool in convincing voters that the candidate with the toughest stance against the Soviets would be the best choice. Kennedy's inaugural address in January 1961 left no doubt that he fit that role:

Let every nation know, whether it wishes us well or ill, that we shall pay any price, bear any burden, meet any hardship, support any friend, oppose any foe to assure the survival and success of liberty. . . . To our sister republics south of our border, we offer a special pledge—to convert our good words into good deeds—in a new alliance for progress—to assist free men and free governments in casting off the chains of poverty. But this peaceful revolution cannot become the prey of hostile powers. Let all our neighbors know that we shall join with them to oppose aggression or subversion anywhere in the Americas.[9]

The mild overtures toward peace that Kennedy made later in the same speech were largely overshadowed by the gauntlet he threw down to the Soviets over Cuba, which would help bring the Cold War to perhaps its greatest climax.

Within months of taking office, Kennedy intensified the ideological rivalry with the Soviets. First, he sponsored an attempted invasion of Cuba by a military force composed of U.S.-trained Cuban exiles in April 1961. The so-called Bay of Pigs invasion was a disaster, and Castro's reputation grew dramatically as a result, although the invasion had failed more because of the ineptitude of the invaders than due to the skill of the Cuban defensive tactics.

In August of the same year, the still unresolved issue of the divided city of Berlin again took center stage. In order to stop emigration from Communist countries through West Berlin, Khrushchev ordered a dividing wall built between the two halves of the cities. In principle, this act violated the agreement on cooperative administration of the city that dated back to the end of World War II, but neither side was willing to push the issue. The Berlin Wall, one of the most potent symbols of the Cold War, had been erected, and Kennedy's opposition to it was more rhetorical than political, leading Khrushchev to believe that Kennedy lacked resolve.

This perception contributed to a general increase in potentially provocative behavior by the Soviets, culminating in the early fall of 1962, when the United States and the Soviet Union came face to face with each other over the issue of Soviet missile installations in Cuba. When satellite photos indicated that the Soviets were preparing to place intermediate-range missiles in Cuba, Kennedy ordered a total naval blockade of Cuba to prevent the importation of further weapons. Khrushchev first claimed that the missiles were purely defensive, designed to help Cuba repel another invasion like that which took place at the Bay of Pigs. He then pointed out that the United States had similar installations in Turkey that were as much a threat to the Soviet Union as the missiles in Cuba were to the United States. Khrushchev refused to withdraw the missiles, and Kennedy considered several options, including an all-out invasion of the island. After several tense days, Khrushchev agreed to withdraw the missiles in Cuba, but both sides had now experienced the possible scenarios leading to a nuclear war firsthand, even if, as individuals on both sides have maintained, no one ever seriously considered using them. The Cuban Missile Crisis helped bring the dangerous reality of nuclear diplomacy into clear focus for both sides. In doing so, it indirectly spurred nearly two decades of relatively warmer relations between the United States and the Soviet Union.

The Age of Treaties and Détente

Within a year of the Cuban Missile Crisis, there were signs that both sides had decided to pull back from the brink of nuclear war. Not only had they signed the Limited Nuclear Test Ban Treaty in August 1963—a symbolic first step toward reversing the monumental acceleration of the arms race that had taken place over the past decade—but their rhetoric toward each other had also softened considerably. For example, Kennedy addressed the graduating class at American University in June 1963 with the following words:

> Both the United States and its allies, and the Soviet Union and its allies, have a mutually deep interest in a just and genuine peace and in halting the arms race. Agreements to this end are in the interests of the Soviet Union as well as ours—and even the most hostile nations can be relied upon and accept those treaty obligations, and only those treaty obligations, which are in their own interest.[10]

Efforts at encouraging trade between the United States

and the Soviet Union were also begun within a year of the Cuban standoff. Despite dramatic changes in the leadership of both countries—Kennedy was assassinated in Dallas, Texas, in November 1963 and was replaced by his vice president, Lyndon Johnson, and a coup among the Soviet leadership in October 1964 replaced Khrushchev with the more hard-line government of Leonid Brezhnev and Alexei Kosygin—the next decade was marked by discussions of economic cooperation as opposed to military confrontation.

This post–Cuban missile crisis era was defined by the notion of détente, a French word signifying a marked improvement in (but not a complete reconciliation of) strained relations between rivals. The period of détente that emerged in the mid-1960s saw a decrease in the hostile and competitive official rhetoric that had marked the late 1950s and early 1960s. Despite their belligerent policies regarding proxy conflicts in Southeast Asia and Africa, Johnson and Brezhnev engaged less in the kind of inflammatory rhetoric that had been a staple of their respective predecessors. One of the great ironies of détente was that the interaction between the United States and Soviet Union was superficially more friendly than at any point since 1945, despite the fact that the global competition between client states of the two superpowers was at its most intense during these same years. Détente was an economically desirable policy for both superpowers in the mid-1960s. The Soviets ardently desired to expand their role in international trade and could not do so as long as the entire Western bloc, with its enormous consumer spending potential, was off-limits because of political rifts. On the other hand, Johnson's ambitious and idealistic plans for what he called "the Great Society," which he announced in a speech on May 22, 1964, demanded a sharp redirection of governmental spending away from defense toward social programs within the United States. Neither side could financially afford to continue the arms race at the pace both sides had maintained since the early 1950s, and détente seemed to offer a solution that allowed both sides to relax, but not retreat.

Simultaneously, though, a pair of developments complicated the relatively simple, if risky, order of the Cold War world. Relations between the Soviets and the Chinese had worsened dramatically during the early and mid-1960s, and by the time Brezhnev and Kosygin assumed power, almost no diplomatic ties remained between the two great Communist nations. The simple division of the world into the Communist East and the capitalist West was confounded by the Chinese antipathy toward the Soviets, in large measure because of the latter's apparent new willingness to coexist with capitalism. The Cultural Revolution that swept China during the late 1960s unambiguously reaffirmed the country's strict Communist principles under the leadership of Mao Zedong and helped widen the rift not only with the West but with the Soviet Union as well.

The intensification of what would become the Vietnam War also created new problems. American involvement in Vietnam dated back to the 1950s and the aftermath of the French Indo-China War, which had taken place roughly concurrently with the Korean War. Like Korea, Vietnam had been divided into two parts, a Communist north and a nominally democratic south, both of which declared themselves to be independent nations in 1955. Military and economic aid for both countries was readily available, from China and the Soviet Union for North Vietnam, and from the United States for South Vietnam. For the United States, this aid was justified by the domino theory, the thinking that had come to dominate President Johnson's Southeast Asian policy. Under this theory, the fall of one nation to communism would inevitably result in the eventual fall of all the others, and Johnson was fully committed to preventing this from happening. This policy led to another lengthy period of proxy warfare, even as trade cooperation and nuclear arms treaty negotiations between the United States and the Soviet Union accelerated.

In August 1964 Johnson asked Congress for increased power to use U.S. military force in Vietnam. His justification for doing so was an alleged attack by the North Vietnamese on a U.S. surveillance vessel in the Gulf of Tonkin (the truth of this attack has since been called into question). The subsequent resolution stopped short of a formal declaration of war—which allowed Johnson to continue cam-

paigning as an advocate for peace—but gave the president
the power to deploy massive numbers of troops to the region, and by 1967 half a million U.S. soldiers were engaged
in combat in Vietnam, fighting against the North Vietnamese troops, some of whom were backed by the Chinese
and others of whom were receiving Soviet aid. The proxy
war in Vietnam dragged on for nearly a decade and ended in
1975 with a partial justification of the domino theory. After
the pullout of U.S. troops and advisers, Communist governments were established in Vietnam as well as the neighboring states of Laos and Cambodia, both of which had been
drawn into the war during the early 1970s.

Unlike during the 1950s, though, when the Korean War
had seemed to aggravate the divisions of the Cold War, the
period of the Vietnam War was oddly one of the most outwardly peaceful between the Soviet Union and the United
States. The state of détente—a French word first used to describe international cooperation in the early twentieth century—that existed from the mid-1960s through the late 1970s
encouraged levels of trade and diplomacy that were unparalleled at any other time between 1945 and 1990. Not only did
the United States and the Soviet Union sign such groundbreaking agreements as the Nuclear Non-Proliferation
Treaty (1968), the Strategic Arms Limitation Talks (SALT,
1972), and SALT II (1979) during this time, but the relationship between the United States and China also improved. In
a related move, the two German states established formal
diplomatic relations with one another for the first time in
1972. What was perhaps even more surprising is that détente
was in large measure due to diplomatic efforts by individuals
whose ideological viewpoints tended toward division rather
than reconciliation. President Richard Nixon and his secretary of state, Henry Kissinger, had made their careers on the
strength of their anti-Communist positions, and both Brezhnev and China's Zhou Enlai were dedicated hard-liners in the
Stalinist and Maoist tradition, respectively.

The unlikely nature of détente also helps explain some of
the contradictions within this uneasy period of truce. The
economic strains of the nuclear arms race had become crip-

pling for the Soviet Union by the early 1960s (and to a lesser extent for the United States). Furthermore, the economic advances that had been made during the 1950s under Khrushchev's leadership had largely vanished by the 1960s, and the opportunities for international trade opened up by friendlier relations with the West were important for the survival of the Soviet Union. Correspondingly, U.S. farmers and manufacturers were eager to tap the gigantic, but previously closed, markets of the Communist bloc for their goods. Ideology gave considerable way to economics during détente, at least on the larger political stage.

On the other hand, competition for influence, both in Europe and in the Third World, was as high as ever during this period. The extent to which both sides would strive to maintain their position was demonstrated by the Soviet invasion of Czechoslovakia in 1968 and the United States's direct support for the overthrow and assassination of Chile's Marxist president Salvador Allende in 1973. Much as Khrushchev had done in Hungary in 1956, Brezhnev deployed Soviet-armed might to brutally put down an insurrection that threatened Communist rule in Czechoslovakia. Much as Kennedy had tried to do in Cuba, Nixon acted to keep any hint of Communist influence out of the Western Hemisphere by openly supporting the military coup of General Augusto Pinochet against the democratically elected Allende.

Even the reality of the arms race in the face of the numerous high-profile treaties helps make the case that détente was a relatively thin layer of cooperation that masked a more sinister status quo beneath. For example, the so-called doomsday clock on the cover of the *Bulletin of the Atomic Scientists*—which had symbolically measured the likelihood of nuclear war since 1947—was set closer to "midnight" (i.e., destruction) during all but twenty-seven months (June 1972–September 1974) of the détente era than it had been in 1963, the year immediatley following the Cuban Missile Crisis. In justification of his decision to set the clock ahead in 1974, editor Samuel H. Day wrote,

Despite the promise of the 1972 [SALT] accords, it is now

apparent that the two nuclear superpowers are nowhere near significant agreement on strategic arms limitations. . . . In anticipation of limitations agreements that have never come to pass or were of little consequence, more and more weapons have been built and tested, and more and more weapons systems have been developed and deployed. Far from restraining the forces which it was intended to curb, SALT has sustained and nourished them, providing acceptable channels for conducting business as usual.[11]

Coupled with the continuing buildup of nuclear arsenals (although at much lower levels than the United States and the Soviet Union) by China, France, and Great Britain during this period, Day's assertions make it clear that détente represented more of a symbolic retreat from the open hostility of the 1950s and early 1960s, rather than an actual move to end the ideological conflict between the two, possibly three (depending on one's view of China's role) sides.

A Renewal of Hostilities

The contradictions within détente ultimately proved to be too great to allow it to go on indefinitely. As the 1970s drew to a close, President Jimmy Carter came under increasing political pressure to take a harder stand with the Soviets regarding their continuing efforts at expansion, especially in the Middle East and Latin America. Anti-Communist groups like the Committee for Present Danger viewed détente as a dangerous policy of appeasement and self-deception and frequently invoked a growing "gap" between Soviet and U.S. nuclear arsenals, much as Kennedy had done in the 1960 presidential campaign, to undermine efforts at coexistence between the superpowers.

Increased Soviet activity in the Third World essentially forced Carter to abandon détente or risk the political suicide of being perceived as overly soft on communism. Crockatt points out that the threat of global Communist expansion seemed as extensive and imminent to worried U.S. observers during the late 1970s as it had during the late 1940s, when it was used as the central justification for the policy of containment:

What might be called the alarmists viewed Soviet support for radical regimes and left-wing insurgent movements as part of a coordinated strategy to undermine and displace Western influence in key strategic areas. . . . The intervention in Ethiopia in 1977 by Cuban troops, air-lifted by Soviet transports, . . . the Soviet acquisition of a naval base in South Yemen, coupled with increased naval activity in the Indian Ocean, and above all Soviet intervention in Afghanistan in 1979—these suggested, according to worst-case scenarios, a concerted Soviet push southwards with the ultimate goal of reaching the Persian Gulf and seizing control of Middle Eastern oil resources.[12]

Carter strenuously objected to the Soviet invasion of Afghanistan, which had deposed the U.S.-friendly prime minister Hafijullah Amin and replaced him with a socialist government led by Babrak Karmal. The Soviets would continue to occupy Afghanistan until 1989 and were opposed by bands of mujahideen guerrilla fighters who were supported by massive amounts of money and military training by the United States. Carter pulled the U.S. team out of the 1980 Summer Olympics in Moscow as a protest against the invasion, and a number of other Western nations followed suit (the Communist bloc returned the favor by boycotting the 1984 Olympics in Los Angeles). This symbolic action essentially announced the death of détente and the resumption of the sharply divided Cold War world order.

Ronald Reagan succeeded Carter as president in 1981, running on a platform of reduced taxation and unambiguous opposition to communism. Reagan left no doubt where he stood in the matter of the Soviet Union, referring to it as "the evil empire" in public and promising massive new spending on defense projects to protect the United States from the threat of the gigantic Soviet nuclear arsenal. In his first term, Reagan added fuel to the tensions between East and West with a number of strategic maneuvers that renewed fears of nuclear war on both sides. First, he placed U.S. nuclear missiles in Western Europe, often against the wishes of sizable portions of those countries' populations.

Next, he proposed the Strategic Defense Initiative, a space-based defense system against Soviet missiles that had been nicknamed "Star Wars." Its opponents feared that it would violate the Anti-Ballistic Missile (ABM) Treaty that had been signed at the height of détente in 1972 and set off an even more costly and dangerous arms buildup. Finally, he secretly funded anti-Communist troops in several Latin American nations, most notably the so-called contras in Nicaragua. The doomsday clock was moved farther toward midnight than at any point since 1953, and the editorial in the *Bulletin of the Atomic Scientists* summed up the diplomatic situation between the superpowers as follows:

> As the arms race—a sort of dialogue between weapons—has intensified, other forms of discourse between the superpowers have all but ceased. There has been a virtual suspension of meaningful contacts and serious discussions. Every channel of communications has been constricted or shut down; every form of contact has been attenuated or cut off. And arms control negotiations have been reduced to a species of propaganda.[13]

Although the tens of thousands of Soviet nuclear warheads were undoubtedly a very real threat, the Soviet Union was in a much weaker position in 1980 than it had been in 1950. As a result, many historians have viewed Reagan's version of the Cold War as more of a fight against a perception of an enemy than a reality. The expenditures over the previous decade that were required to support not only the growth of the Soviet nuclear arsenal but the widespread and substantial amounts of financial and military aid that the Soviets were bestowing on their global allies had crippled the nation economically. It was clearly a society in decline, with even the most basic staples often being unavailable in its cities. The lingering fiasco in Afghanistan not only eroded popular support for the regime but also diverted sorely needed money from the national economy.

The country was further hampered by the ill health and advanced age of nearly all of its leaders. Brezhnev died in November 1982 and was replaced by Yuri Andropov, who in turn died in February 1984. His replacement, Konstantin Chernenko, died in March 1985. The fearful image of Soviet leaders like Stalin and Khrushchev had been replaced in the West with an image of unhealthy old men being propped up to watch a May Day parade. The public perception of the Soviet Union had diminished considerably by the middle of the 1980s, making many of Reagan's claims about the grave danger represented by the Soviets ring somewhat hollow. By 1985 Reagan had toned down much of his belligerent rhetoric toward the Soviets, and the stage was set for the arrival of Mikhail Gorbachev, who took over as premier upon Chernenko's death.

The End of the Cold War

Gorbachev was a member of a much younger generation than the previous three Soviet premiers had been and brought a reformer's vision with him. A committed Communist and a lifelong party member, he nevertheless recognized that the Soviet Union could not continue for long on its current path and hope to maintain a position of global supremacy. He quickly proposed a pair of sweeping reforms to Soviet society that were intended to revive it from its deteriorated state. The policy of perestroika ("restructuring") made social and economic changes in the fabric of society that opened unparalleled opportunities for foreign, especially Western, investment in the Soviet Union. At the same time, his policy of glasnost ("openness") encouraged greater individual and social freedoms in the country. He also encouraged the Communist governments of Eastern Europe to follow similar practices within their countries.

Although his efforts marked a clear shift away from the neo-Stalinist tendencies of his predecessors, Gorbachev did not set out with the goal of ending the Soviet Union or even drawing the Cold War to a close. Several tense early summit meetings between Reagan and Gorbachev in 1986 and early 1987 illustrated that trust and goodwill had not necessarily been achieved simply by the announcement of enlightened policy changes by the Soviet leadership. By 1988, though, Gorbachev had demonstrated his sincerity through such actions as beginning the withdrawal of Soviet troops from Afghanistan and the Intermediate-Range Nuclear Forces (INF) Treaty—in which the Soviets dismantled more than fifteen hundred missiles deployed in Eastern Europe in exchange for slightly more than four hundred U.S. missiles deployed in Western Europe—and was arguably more popular in the United States than he was in the Soviet Union. The reforms he had introduced in Soviet society played well on the international stage, but the damage of the previous seven decades proved difficult, and ultimately impossible, for him to reverse.

In the summer of 1989, the Communist-led governments of the Eastern European satellite states began to fall in rapid succession. As they did, Gorbachev largely stood by and watched, as opposed to making forceful moves—as Khrushchev had done in Hungary in 1956 and Brezhnev had done in Czechoslovakia in 1968—to suppress the popular insurrections that were sweeping the old regimes out of power. For this inaction he was roundly criticized by the remaining hard-liners within the Soviet Union, but praised by the rest of the world. Within days of the demolition of the Berlin Wall in December 1989, Gorbachev and President George Bush met in Malta and declared the Cold War officially over.

Not everyone shared their optimism, and it would take another twenty months before the Soviet Union joined its former satellites in succumbing to the wave of reform. As individual republics began to break way from the Soviet Union in 1990 and early 1991, Gorbachev seemed momentarily to be relapsing to old Soviet habits. For example, he reasserted and even increased the power of the KGB in 1990 and distanced himself from several of his most trusted reform-minded advisers in an effort to appease the most reactionary Communists remaining in the government. This "old guard" attempted a short-lived coup in 1991 while Gorbachev was away on vacation. The coup failed after only three days, though, and the pro-democracy faction led by Boris Yeltsin became the popular choice to succeed Gorbachev. The Soviet Union was officially dissolved on December 31, 1991, and replaced with the similar-looking but non-Communist Commonwealth of Independent States (CIS). With the Communist nation that had dominated the popular imagination as the sworn enemy of the United States now officially gone—China was, of course, still alive and well as a Communist nation—the Cold War was undoubtedly over, replaced by what Bush called "the New World Order."

The Legacy of the Cold War

The shape of this New World Order and what lessons it would take away from the recently concluded conflict were the subject of debate from almost the moment the Cold War was declared over. Commentators could not necessarily agree on whether the West "won" the Cold War, but there was no shortage of speculation on what direction global politics would take now that the simple two-sided division of the world was at an end.

The CIS proved to be a relatively insubstantial political entity, and by 1995 all fifteen of the former Soviet republics had become fully independent nations, several of which possessed part of the old Soviet nuclear arsenal. This fact by itself complicated the New World Order considerably since it nearly doubled the number of individual countries that were members of the nuclear fraternity, even if it did not increase the actual number of weapons. Initial efforts at attracting Western investment to the new CIS met with a lukewarm response, and this stirred fear in a number of political analysts that the former Soviet republics would feel forced to trade with other nations either their actual nuclear weapons or the knowledge of how to construct them.

The end of the Cold War did not eliminate the anxiety surrounding nuclear weapons; rather, it changed it from a fear of massive nuclear combat that would result in total planetary annihilation to apprehension about the acquisition of nuclear bombs by terrorists or so-called rogue nations that would use them as tools of political blackmail. During the 1990s the United States sought aggressively to limit the spread of nuclear weapons to such countries as Iraq and North Korea, and it opposed the continued nuclear testing programs of nations such as India and Pakistan, which already possessed the bomb. Fear of potential nuclear terrorism increased after the attack on the World Trade Center and the Pentagon in September 2001. The stockpile of weapons that had been produced by the Soviets during the Cold War was singled out as one of the most likely potential sources from which potential terrorists could acquire nuclear bombs or the raw materials to make them. In this way, the military by-products of the Cold War have continued to affect the world more than a decade after its end.

Many of the visionary projections of a new era of economic internationalism and global cooperation seemed to be coming true during the first half of the 1990s, at least in the developed nations. The United States witnessed almost unparalleled economic growth, and Russia began a slow, often staggering climb toward reforming its society and economy along a more Western model. A number of European nations—mostly those that had been in the Western bloc during the Cold War—began moving toward closer economic and political ties through the European Union (EU) and even set plans into motion for creating a single European currency, the euro, to replace the separate currencies of the EU nations. The New World Order was deemed especially positive for the countries of the old First World, who could now focus more on the tasks of increasing trade and their own domestic affairs rather than fighting a constant battle against an intractable ideological enemy.

In other parts of the world, though, the aftereffects of the Cold War were more ambiguous. A number of nations that had relied heavily on foreign economic and military aid from the Soviet Union or the United States during the Cold War suddenly found themselves without a benefactor once their services were no longer needed in the defense of communism/capitalism. For example, after decades of massive aid to anti-Soviet rebels in Afghanistan, the United States largely disengaged itself from the country once the threat of Communist aggression was removed. The political structure of the country rapidly disintegrated from its already tenuous position and eventually was taken over in the mid-1990s by the fundamentalist Islamic Taliban movement, many of whose leaders were former members of the anti-Soviet mujahideen during the Cold War. Similarly, Cuba found itself increasingly isolated after the substantial aid that had flowed consistently from the Soviet Union since the late 1950s was cut off at the end of the Cold War.

Furthermore, the economic boom that was surging through Europe and North America was largely absent from or unstable at best in Asia, Africa, and Latin America. A massive economic crisis that originated in Asia in 1997 briefly threatened to undermine global trade and finance, and a number of large countries such as Argentina and Indonesia suffered near-collapse because of economic difficulties. Widespread ethnic violence flared up in places such as Somalia, Rwanda, East Timor, the former Yugoslavia (which, like the Soviet Union, had fragmented into a number of smaller independent nations after the end of Communist rule) and demanded the attention of the United Nations, which had been forecast by many to play a larger role in global affairs following the Cold War. Even as politicians and historians in the West refer to "the death of communism" that supposedly took place in 1989–1991, the Communist regime in China is still firmly in place (although China has adapted its economy to certain aspects of capitalism), and the divisive issue of Taiwan's sovereignty remains as a Cold War holdover dating back to the 1950s.

As is often the case, most of the predictions made in the heady days after the fall of the Soviet Union have turned out to be partly true and partly false. The legacy of the Cold War is still indeterminate as of 2002. Russia and the United States have become closer peacetime allies than at any point since before the Russian Revolution of 1917, and Russia was even accepted as a member of NATO in the spring of 2002. This move represents a full reversal of the Cold War order since NATO was created expressly to oppose the military might of the Soviet Union. However, the alliance of these two old rivals has not by itself produced a less dangerous or more predictable world than that which existed from 1945 to 1991. Issues and individuals related to the Cold War remain visible on the global stage more than a decade later, although often without the dangerous but effective simplicity of the us-versus-them context that the ideological division between communism and capitalism provided. For example, Russia and the United States differ in their views about a proposed U.S. missile defense system. Russian leaders claim it violates the ABM treaty, but the United States claims that that treaty is void since the country that signed it no longer exists. Just as this complex political question remains unanswered, the larger questions of how the hard lessons learned during the Cold War will be put to lasting use are still waiting to be resolved definitively.

Notes

1. Harry S. Truman, *Year of Decisions*. Garden City, NY: Doubleday, 1955, p. 416.

2. John Lewis Gaddis, *We Now Know: Rethinking Cold War History*. Oxford, UK: Clarendon, 1997, p. 56.

3. Quoted in Thomas Etzold and John Lewis Gaddis, *Containment: Documents on American Policy and Strategy, 1945–1950*. New York: Columbia University Press, 1978, p. 51.

4. Richard Crockatt, *The Fifty Years War: The United States and the Soviet Union in World Politics, 1941–1991*. London: Routledge, 1995, p. 60.

5. Harry S. Truman, address before a joint session of Congress, March 12, 1947, Avalon Project at Yale Law School. www.yale.edu.

6. Wilfried Loth, *The Division of the World, 1941–1955*. New York: St. Martin's, 1988, pp. 196–97.

7. Loth, *The Division of the World*, p. 203.

8. Crockatt, *The Fifty Years War*, p. 111.

9. John F. Kennedy, "Inaugural Address," *The Presidential Speech Archive of the Program in Presidential Rhetoric*. www.tamu.edu.

10. John F. Kennedy, "American University Speech," *The Presidential Speech Archive of the Program in Presidential Rhetoric*. www.tamu.edu.

11. Quoted in Mike Moore, "Midnight Never Came," *Bulletin of the Atomic Scientists*, November/December 1995, pp. 22–23.

12. Crockatt, *The Fifty Years War*, p. 258.

13. Quoted in Moore, "Midnight Never Came," p. 25.

Chapter 1

The Origins and Early Years of the Cold War

Turning | Points
IN WORLD HISTORY

The Origins of the Cold War: Dividing the World at Yalta

Caroline Kennedy-Pipe

With the defeat of Germany increasingly imminent, the three main Allied leaders—Joseph Stalin, Winston Churchill, and Franklin Roosevelt—met in the Black Sea port city of Yalta early in 1945 to discuss their vision for the postwar world. Caroline Kennedy-Pipe, professor of international relations at the University of Sheffield in England, examines the Yalta discussions and the resulting agreements and finds therein the basis for the Cold War in the ways the Allied leaders divided their influence over central Europe, especially Germany and Poland. Kennedy-Pipe disputes the widely held belief that the Soviets began the Cold War by violating their agreement, concluded at Yalta, to encourage democracy in the areas that they liberated from German control. She concludes that the Soviet postwar policy of setting up governments friendly to its own interests in Eastern Europe not only was consistent with its stated goals before Yalta, but was even encouraged by the Western Allies' willingness to grant the Soviets a greater measure of influence in the East in exchange for concessions on the postwar administration of Germany. Yalta represents the first step in the Cold War for Kennedy-Pipe because it sets in motion the division of Europe along ideological lines that would quickly solidify into the so-called iron curtain.

By the time the Allies met at Yalta [a city on the Soviet Black Sea coast], in February 1945, the Allied armies were converging on Germany from both east and west. The initial

Excerpted from *Stalin's Cold War: Soviet Strategies in Europe*, by Caroline Kennedy-Pipe (Manchester, England: Manchester University Press, 1995). Copyright © 1995 by Caroline Kennedy-Pipe. Reprinted with permission.

discussions at Yalta were concerned with the timing and the character of the final blow against Hitler. The German counteroffensive in the Ardennes had been successful, and [President Franklin] Roosevelt notified [Soviet premier Joseph] Stalin that, because of weather conditions, General [Dwight D.] Eisenhower did not intend to cross the Rhine until March. Therefore, the decisive assault on Germany from the west would have to be postponed until the spring. There seemed, however, to be no impediment to the progress of the Red Army. It had made spectacular gains throughout late 1944 and early 1945, covering 300 miles through central Poland, across the German frontier and to within forty miles of Berlin.

Despite the apparent strength of the Soviet onslaught upon Germany in early 1945, Moscow remained concerned by the tenacity of resistance. General [A.I.] Antonov predicted that the Germans would defend Berlin strongly and said that further fierce fighting was anticipated before the Red Army could move further west. Stalin concurred with this forecast saying that, although the Red Army had established five or six bridgeheads on the west bank of the Oder, he anticipated stubborn resistance before Germany fell. He was particularly concerned because the Germans were moving troops from the western battlefields to the eastern front. Stalin suspected that this was in preparation for a separate peace with the West—a peace that would deprive Moscow of its share in the victory. Reassurances were sought that Anglo-American forces would maintain pressure upon the Germans so that the removal of troops from the west would be impossible. Contrary to the Soviet anxieties, it was widely believed in the West that the Red Army would soon take Berlin.

It was not only the military advance of the Red Army that caused concern in the West over the future of Soviet power in Europe. The behaviour of Soviet forces in the liberated countries of East Europe caused anxiety. The United States was perturbed by the attitude of the USSR to the Western representatives on the Control Councils which governed the liberated territories. It was believed that Soviet actions in countries such as Romania and Bulgaria were curtailing the option of establishing 'democratic' representative governments. Western officials in those countries had complained that their views were being ignored. The Soviet chairman of the Control Council in Romania, for example, had been issuing orders without consulting the Anglo-American representatives. The Soviet Union counter charged that the Western officials were doing exactly the same in Italy.

The 'Declaration on Liberated Europe' and Its Effects

One of the primary aims of the American delegation at Yalta was to obtain agreement to a set of principles encompassed within the so-called 'Declaration on Liberated Europe' which aimed to create democratic institutions throughout Eastern Europe. To achieve this, the Allies would agree that

> The three governments will jointly assist the peoples in any European liberated state or former Axis satellite in Europe where in their judgement conditions require (a) to establish conditions of internal peace; (b) to carry out emergency measures for the relief of distressed peoples; (c) to form interim governmental authorities broadly representative of all democratic elements in the population and pledged to the earliest possible establishment through free elections of governments responsive to the will of the people; and (d) to facilitate where necessary the holding of such elections.

This was an attempt to claw back influence in those countries in which Moscow had established its interests. Despite the fact that [Soviet foreign minister Vyacheslav] Molotov viewed it as 'interference in the liberated territories', Stalin accepted the proposal but wanted support to be given to the political leaders who had taken an active part in the struggle against fascism. This suggestion was rejected by the Americans on the grounds that it would give Moscow the chance to promote its own followers at the expense of others.

The fact that Stalin agreed to the proposal has been dismissed as a mere negotiating ruse to ensure continuing Allied unity. It has been alleged that no attempt was made to abide by the principles of the declaration. Stalin, according to this line of reasoning, planned simply to install communist governments throughout East Europe. However, Soviet agreement to the declaration was not simply a matter of deception, and the apparent disingenuousness may be better construed in serveral ways.

The first explanation relates to the language of the declaration. It was recognised by American diplomats at Yalta that the declaration was open to varying interpretations. The use of words such as 'democratic' illustrates this. It is possible that although the West assumed, or found it easier to assume, that the Soviet Union understood 'democratic' in the Western sense, the Soviet Union did not. Immediately after the conference, a Soviet commentator, David Zaslavskii, wrote:

> England represents democracy in one of its historic types. The United States is another type and the USSR yet another. After the last traces of fascism and Nazism the people of liberated Europe will have the possibility of creating democratic institutions according to their own choice. They can take as an example any form of democracy that has been shaped by history.

The second explanation for the supposed Soviet volte-face [literally "turn-around" or "about face"] revolves around the question of expectations. It is possible that Stalin saw no reason at Yalta to oppose principles such as free elections in the liberated countries because he expected them to vote communist. It was widely believed that the Red Army would be welcomed by the peoples it had liberated and that this would be expressed in a vote for the indigenous Communist Party. In this spirit of confidence, elections took place in Hungary in November 1945. The communists, however, gained only seventeen per cent of the vote, undermining expectations of widespread popular support. Nevertheless, in February Stalin could not have been expected to foresee such a defeat.

A third explanation is that Moscow did not regard the Declaration on Liberated Europe as a matter of great importance. The agreements of the war years had proved that Stalin and the Soviet representatives believed in explicit agreements and achievements (e.g. a legally defined arrangement or a military presence) as the determining factors. Throughout the Great Power conferences the Soviet delegations had always tried to reach explicit agreements on matters they regarded as important—for example, the concern to reach agreement on Germany. Equally, it was Stalin who, in the hope of enlisting a US military presence in Austria, tried to persuade the Western Allies to arrive in Austria at the same time as the Red Army.

The declaration was neither an explicit agreement nor a troop presence. It was not inconsistent with Moscow's view of what was and was not binding for the Soviet government to ignore it. The problem was that respect for the proposals was crucial to the American view of a satisfactory post-war settlement. Many American diplomats believed that it was this declaration that would moderate Soviet behaviour in Europe. This, in many ways, was a reflection of the manner in which the United States liked to approach diplomacy—through the imposition of broad institutional structures. [U.S. diplomat] Charles Bohlen remarked that 'had it been implemented by the Soviet Union, it would have radically changed the face of Eastern Europe.'

The effort made at Yalta to moderate Soviet behaviour was disputed within American diplomatic circles, most notably by George Kennan. He believed that it would be much wiser if, instead of trying to interfere in countries dominated by the Red Army, the United States made a Churchillian deal with the Soviet Union:

> Why could we not make a decent and definitive compromise with it—divide Europe frankly into spheres of influence—keep ourselves out of the Russian sphere and keep the Russians out of ours?

In line with this proposal, Kennan suggested that the United Nations be disbanded and that Washington, unless it was prepared to go the whole way and militarily oppose Soviet domination of the area, 'write off' Eastern and South Eastern Europe.

Kennan's suggestions, however, ran counter to the prevailing American view. As Bohlen wrote:

As far as the partition of Germany, the domination of East Europe by the Soviet Union, and the general idea of dividing the continent into spheres of influence, I could not go along with Kennan. To me the acceptance of a Soviet sphere instead of relieving us of responsibility would compound the felony. Any formal or even informal attempt to give the Soviet Union a sphere of influence in East Europe would as soon as the agreement became known have brought a loud and effective outcry from our own Poles and Czechs.

Resolving Questions About Poland's Future

The clearest example of the Great Power debate over postwar planning arose with regard to Poland. The British and the Americans had accepted, unofficially, at Teheran [Stalin, Roosevelt, and Churchill had met there in November 1943], the Soviet view on the boundaries of the 'new' Poland. The Western concern was now to secure some influence in that country. This was the crux of the problem—how far would outside influence be permitted in an area regarded as a crucial security interest by the Soviet Union? The West, in particularly Britain, was determined to wrest some concessions from Moscow on the composition of any future government. The British objected to the Lublin government [after the Red Army moved into Poland, it helped establish an interim Polish government in the city of Lublin] as 'undemocratic' and sought the installation of a more representative regime. Stalin and Molotov were insistent, however, that the Allies should accept the Lublin government.

[British prime minister Winston] Churchill opened the discussions on Poland by pointing out that Britain had made concessions concerning the borders of Poland and now required concessions in return. He pointed out that, for Britain, the Polish question was a matter of honour. London had gone to war over the violation of Poland. Churchill said that Britain had conceded the Soviet view concerning borders but must insist on guarantees that a new 'national' government would be set up and that free elections would take place. Stalin responded that Poland might be a matter of honour for Britain but, to him, was a matter of security. Poland had twice been a corridor through which Russia's enemies had passed to attack. He too wanted a strong and independent Poland, but one that was 'friendly' to Moscow. The London Poles would be unacceptable, since not only had their agents, operating in Poland, attacked Red Army supplies, but they had also killed Russians. Stalin, furthermore, defended the Lublin government: it was as democratic as [French leader Charles] De Gaulle's regime.

An uneasy compromise was eventually achieved on the question of Poland. The Soviet Union agreed to a modification of the Lublin government. Additional representatives would be added in the form of emigres. Unfettered elections were guaranteed, and the Soviet Union agreed to the idea of a strong, free, independent and democratic state. It was this agreement, or rather the various interpretations of it, that became the primary cause of Western allegations of 'betrayal' after Yalta.

Both the British and the Americans knew that they were in a weak position during the negotiations on the Polish issue. Bohlen wrote: 'The Red Army gave Stalin the power he needed to carry out his wishes regardless of his promises at Yalta.' Not only did the Red Army occupy the country, but there was very little (short of military force—a strategy that was never seriously contemplated) that the West could do if the Soviet Union refused to concede any of the issues. Indeed, it was the movements of the Red Army that overshadowed the Yalta conference. In February 1945, the Red Army was within forty miles of Berlin. The Americans and the British were concerned to secure written assurances that the Red Army would respect 'Western' zones in Germany. On 1 February [U.S. secretary of state Edward] Stettinius and [British foreign secretary Anthony] Eden agreed that it was imperative to secure an agreement before the Red Army entered Berlin. The concern was that the Red Army would move into Western zones, and then refuse to negotiate the terms of occupation.

Soviet plans did indeed exist to take Berlin in February. On 4 February general operational instructions were issued to Marshal [G.K.] Zhukov to consolidate, regroup and resupply up to 10 February before taking Berlin, with a rapid thrust, on 15 and 16 February. However, on 6 February the orders were abruptly cancelled. Earlier on the same day, at Yalta, the three Allies had reached agreement on the zonal divisions and the machinery to be implemented for the future control of Germany. Following this agreement, the Red Army was redirected on a course of consolidation in Eastern Europe. Stalin had been willing to take Berlin in order to assert Soviet interests in Germany, but once he had obtained assurances that the Allies had agreed to the Soviet zone in Germany such action was no longer an immediate necessity. . . .

The Division of Germany

In 1948, Stalin remarked that 'the West will make Western Germany their own, and we shall turn Eastern Germany into our own state'. The roots of that philosophy are discernible in the Soviet attitude towards Germany in 1945. However, whilst Stalin wanted to maintain control of East Germany, he also wanted guarantees that a military stranglehold would operate upon the Western parts of Germany. This explains why Stalin had sought American management of West Germany at an early stage, and also why he had agreed to French help in maintaining an effective stranglehold on Germany.

It looked, at this point, as if the Soviet government was settling for the division and destruction of German power. This was apparent on the issue of reparations. Soviet proposals had a dual purpose. First, to ensure that Germany would never again be able to dominate Europe. Moscow wanted the destruction of German industries. Accordingly, it proposed that eighty per cent of all German industries should be dismantled, and Allied control established over the remaining industry. Second, it sought to rebuild its own devastated country with German industrial plant. In pursuit of this aim, Stalin and [Soviet diplomat I.M.] Maisky proposed that a system should be implemented whereby reparations would be allocated according to a country's contribution to the war effort and be based upon its direct material losses. They also suggested that reparations should be based upon a figure of $20 billion, with a Soviet share of $10 billion.

Before the Yalta conference, both Britain and the United

States had considered at great length the question of a German settlement. On the one hand, it was accepted that Germany should not be capable of posing a renewed threat to European security. On the other hand, it was understood that it should not be allowed to become an economic liability, literally dependent upon its Western conquerors. London and Washington wanted to find a formula whereby Germany would be restrained militarily but economically self-sustaining yet not capable of a standard of living higher than that of the Allies. However, they had not come up with any concrete plans. Whilst they were unwilling to implement Soviet suggestions, they lacked alternative proposals. The figure of $20 billion was agreed upon as the figure for the basis of reparations, which later gave rise to much ill feeling between the Allies, but the matter was referred to a reparations committee.

The Soviet aim, displayed at Yalta, was a patent desire to destroy German power. The Soviets sought affirmation of the Allied decision agreed at Teheran to the principle of dismemberment. The British and the Americans had reconsidered the matter; Churchill said that, although the British government was still inclined to favour partition, particularly any scheme that would isolate Prussia, it still had doubts over any really drastic measures. Similarly, although Roosevelt still favoured the idea of Germany being divided into five or seven states, he preferred to delay the decision.

The fact that Stalin sought Allied agreement to dismemberment has been explained as a ruse which would enable him later, in an attempt to communise the whole of Germany, to depict the West as the force that opposed German unity. However, this idea lacks credibility. It is more convincing, given Stalin's fear that the West might form a separate peace, that he simply sought assurances that Germany would be treated as harshly as it deserved, and that the future Soviet role in Germany would be secured. . . .

The Consequences of Yalta

From a Soviet perspective the Yalta conference produced mixed results. On the one hand, the USSR had failed to se-

cure definite Allied agreement on the question of reparations from Germany. On the other hand, the Allies had
agreed that it was appropriate to divide the responsibility for
Germany between them. It was an arrangement that made
the United States a long-term military fixture in Germany.
Attempts to undermine Soviet influence in Eastern Europe
had so far failed; the Declaration on Liberated Europe had
not registered as a threat.

Soviet actions in February and March 1945 seemed to
London and Washington deliberately to violate the Yalta
agreements. In particular, Soviet intervention in Romania,
which had resulted in the usurpation of the [Nicolae] Rade-
scu government and its replacement by the communist
[Petru] Groza government, was regarded with dismay. Soviet representatives in Hungary, Bulgaria and Romania also
continued to act without consulting with their Western colleagues. But the allegation that the Yalta agreements had
been 'betrayed' was based in particular on the Soviet attitude
towards Poland. The commission which had been appointed
at Yalta to 'compose' a new Polish government had failed to
reach agreement. Stalin insisted that the Yalta agreements
had intended the existing provisional government to form
the basis of any new government and that it, and only it, had
the power to 'approve' new members. A sense of grievance
in London and Washington was fuelled in March, when
Stalin refused to accede to demands for American service-
men in Poland to be returned and for observers to be allowed to supervise the process. On 13 March, Churchill
wrote to Roosevelt that the failure to resolve these problems
meant that they were confronted by a total breakdown of the
Yalta settlement.

The question for Western historians has been whether
Stalin did, in fact, cynically breach the Yalta agreements.
There are two ways of looking at it. Soviet behaviour was ac-
tually consistent with its character before Yalta. The primary
Soviet aim remained unchanged—the establishment and
maintenance of so-called 'friendly' governments in Eastern
Europe. Action such as dominating the Control Councils in
Romania and Hungary was, from a Soviet perspective, legit-

imate. Throughout the wartime alliance, the Western powers had sanctioned the pre-eminence of Soviet interests in Eastern Europe. Consequently, Soviet moves after Yalta did not necessarily contravene the Yalta agreements or indeed any other political agreements concluded with the West on the future political composition of Europe. This was in fact acknowledged by Churchill:

> We were hampered in our protests because Eden and I during our October visit to Moscow had recognised that Russia should have a largely predominant voice in Romania and Bulgaria, while we took the lead in Greece. Stalin had kept very strictly to this understanding.

The Western powers had, therefore, accepted, at least tacitly, Soviet domination in Eastern Europe; but there is little doubt that there was a problem of interpretation on the Western side. Churchill, for example, had hoped to influence the composition of the Polish government. The Soviet interpretation was that the existing government would continue to act. Stalin recognised that his views of Poland were in total opposition to those of Churchill. He remarked to Marshall Zhukov, with reference to the Yalta agreements, that 'Churchill wants the Soviet Union to share a border with bourgeois Poland alien to us, but we cannot allow this to happen.'

Churchill's "Iron Curtain" Divides the Cold War World

Lynn Boyd Hinds and Theodore Otto Windt Jr.

Lynn Boyd Hinds, professor of communication at Drury College in Springfield, Missouri, and Theodore Otto Windt Jr., professor emeritus of communication at the University of Pittsburgh, examine the context and content of a speech that provided one of the most memorable phrases of the Cold War. In 1946, Winston Churchill, who only recently had been voted out of power as prime minister of Great Britain, gave a speech at a small Missouri college in which he likened growing Soviet control in Poland, Czechoslovakia, Hungary, Romania, and the eastern portion of Germany to the lowering of an "iron curtain." Churchill claimed that this "curtain" separated Eastern and Western Europe, and he used this metaphor to call for a stronger alliance between the United States and Britain than had existed in the year that had passed since the end of World War II. Although Churchill's speech did not accomplish many of its explicit goals, Hinds and Windt point out that Churchill's vivid image nevertheless contributed significantly to the popular and political conception of the relationship between the Communist East and the capitalist West for the next forty-five years.

Although it seems virtually impossible to speak about the origins of the cold war without discussing the significance of Winston Churchill's "Iron Curtain" speech at Fulton, Missouri in early 1946, there is anything but consensus about the role it played. Did it merely reflect the actual state of relations between the United States and the Soviet Union or was it instrumental in defining a new set of relations? John Spanier stated plainly that "Churchill, in short, said bluntly that the cold war had begun." It is that perspective that we share. But the question remains, how did Churchill's great speech contribute to the cold war reality?

There has been widespread recognition that the speech came at a crucial time in the development of the strained relations among the wartime allies. There is a weight of evidence to support John Blum's conclusion that "at least until the time of Fulton, the possibility existed of a practical accommodation between the United States and the Soviet Union." But Churchill proclaimed an international crisis, ideological in character, global in scope. He declared that the one world the allies hoped to build after World War II had been divided by an "iron curtain" into two antagonistic camps. By giving popular currency to this vivid metaphor of division, Churchill set in motion the dynamic of a public rhetorical process that was to give Americans a new interpretation of the world and their place in it. Churchill supplied basic elements for a vocabulary that would be picked up and widely spread by opinion leaders, so that these linguistic elements eventually became *the* way to perceive and to talk about disputes between the Soviet Union and the West, to the exclusion of other interpretations. Louis Halle observed that "in a matter of months this term [iron curtain] would be an accepted part of everyone's vocabulary. . . . Those who responded with initial disapproval would shortly be using it themselves." Churchill's call for an Anglo-American alliance was rejected, for the most part, by the general public; his "iron curtain" metaphor, however, was accepted as an accurate description of the world. This striking metaphor became more than a convenient designation for one interpretation of world tensions; it became the shorthand way of stating the political context within which issues were perceived and interpreted, the way they were discussed and debated, and the ideological context within which subsequent decisions were made.

The background of Churchill's invitation to speak at Westminster College in Fulton, Missouri is straightforward and hints of no political intrigue. Churchill had been voted out of office during the meeting of the Big Three at Potsdam [The leaders of the three major Allied nations met in this eastern German city to discuss postwar strategy. Churchill represented Britain, Truman represented the United States, and Stalin represented the Soviet Union] in July 1945. His unexpected defeat struck him like "a physical blow" and he returned home to become a private citizen. Lord Moran, his personal physician, reported the former prime minister's view of what his defeat meant to negotiations with Stalin: "After I left Potsdam, Joe [i.e., Joseph Stalin] did what he liked. The Russian's western frontier was allowed to advance, displacing another eight million poor devils. I'd not have agreed and the Americans would have backed me." When he was invited to speak at a college in Missouri in 1946, Churchill emerged from his "black dog" depression because he saw a new opportunity to persuade Americans to his view of international affairs. . . .

The prospect of being introduced by the president of the United States promised extensive attention for what Churchill might say. He quickly accepted the invitation.

If there was political intrigue between [President Harry] Truman and Churchill, it occurred as the date for the speech approached. Any postwar ambiguities that Churchill had expressed regarding the Soviet Union were gone by the time he arrived in the United States in January 1946. He had reverted to his earlier antibolshevism with a vengeance. He was already using the term "iron curtain," a metaphor originally coined by [Nazi minister of propaganda] Joseph Goebbels in the last days of the war, in both private letters and public speech. Now, he would make it famous worldwide. By the time of Fulton, Churchill had excised ambiguity from his thinking in favor of an alliance between the United States and Great Britain that he believed was necessary for dealing with the Soviet expansionism in Europe. . . .

The interpretation of Soviet intentions expressed in [American diplomat George] Kennan's "long telegram" was fast catching hold within the Truman administration. [In early 1946 Kennan had sent a telegram to Truman from

Moscow in which he indicated his strong belief that the Soviet Union was becoming increasingly hostile toward the United States.] The coincidence of Churchill's speech provided the first public statement of this analysis. That is not to say that Churchill spoke from Kennan's work, but rather that he and Kennan had come to similar conclusions about the nature of the Soviet Union. In a real sense Churchill, an Englishman, gave the public its first inkling of what those inside U.S. government circles were now discussing. The most likely explanation for Truman's appearance with Churchill and his subsequent reluctance to embrace Churchill's ideas publicly is that the president was waiting to see what kind of political reception the speech received. Fulton provided a convenient trial balloon. A shift from one political reality to another is not easily or quickly accomplished. Without first preparing the groundwork for public receptivity, the announcement of a new policy based on a new reality is politically dangerous. Churchill happened along at a time that was propitious for the administration to test public and congressional reaction.

Churchill met Truman in Washington, and the two traveled by private train to Jefferson City, Missouri. When the subsequent motorcade arrived in Fulton on Tuesday, March 5, the community of some 7,000 swelled to nearly 40,000, including some 300 members of the press. About 2,500 people crowded into the Westminster College gymnasium to see Churchill receive an honorary degree and to hear him speak. Truman gave Churchill the promised introduction, saying that he understood that Mr. Churchill would have something useful to say. Of course the man who had rallied his countrymen to their finest hour needed no introduction as an orator. His reputation as the man who had "mobilized the English language and sent it into battle," as John F. Kennedy was to characterize him, was world-famous. Also, in the months before Fulton, the American conservative press had kept Churchill in the public eye. *Reader's Digest* lionized him as "a personality unsurpassed in history," who "will be quoted as long as Shakespeare." In its January 7, 1946 issue, *Life* reproduced some of Churchill's paintings and described him as a "superb orator" and "talented historian." Who better then than an orator-historian-statesman to survey the broad stretches of the postwar world, its confusions and fears, and to give clear meaning to it? . . .

Churchill's Message to America

Churchill defined a new political reality for the postwar world. He brought clarity to confusion. The new world was not one world, as the war-weary allies had hoped, but two worlds: "From Stettin in the Baltic to Trieste in the Adriatic, an iron curtain has descended across the continent. Behind that line lie all the capitals of the ancient states of Central and Eastern Europe." With a few short sentences the former prime minister captured a new vision of the world. "Warsaw, Berlin, Prague, Vienna, Budapest, Bucharest and Sofia," all, proclaimed Churchill, now lay behind the iron curtain. It was an ominous litany.

In the iron curtain worldview, a bipolar view, there was no longer a multilateral political reality, consisting of Great Britain, the United States, the Soviet Union, and every other nation, each with its own national interests. Nor was there a group of victorious allies striving for peace. Now there were but two sides. On the one side lay the repository of "the joint inheritance of the English-speaking world and through which Magna Carta, the Bill of Rights, the Habeas Corpus, trial by jury, and the English common law find their most famous expression in the Declaration of Independence." On the other side lay a tyrannical communism controlled by the Soviet Union and desiring "the fruits of war," a growing challenge and peril to "Christian civilisation." In this ideological dichotomy there was no middle ground. The sharp division was a paradigm in which European nations were already either on one side of an iron curtain or the other, and the other nations of the world had become the battlegrounds to determine on which side they would eventually fall.

The speech was based on two pillars: the Soviet Union posed a massive threat to world peace, and only an alliance of Great Britain and the United States could respond effectively to this threat. Churchill planted the ideological seeds for what would later blossom into a tiresome rhetorical litany about the Soviet menace. In fact, his speech foreshadowed the primary themes of Truman's declaration of American policy a year later, even as it struck additional themes that Truman chose to omit because they received negative responses.

The sections of the speech describing the communist menace struck many of the major chords of anticommunism. The Soviets were tyrannical and totalitarian. He drew upon comparisons to Nazi Germany to magnify the threat. Communism, Churchill asserted, was expansive seeking to extend its control over other nations in the Middle East and Far East. One method they used to achieve this

Winston Churchill

goal was through subversive "fifth columns" in other nations, although he carefully noted that domestic communism was only "in its infancy" in England and America. In all, he painted, as befits an amateur painter, a dark and foreboding picture of the Soviet Union (where "control is enforced upon common people by various kinds of all-embracing police government, to a degree which is overwhelming and contrary to every principle of democracy") and her intentions in the world ("Nobody knows what the Soviet Union and its Communist international organization intends to do in the immediate future, or what are the limits, if any, to their expansive and proselytizing tendencies."). Although he denied knowing Soviet intentions, Churchill described the Soviet Union as expansionist and international. Thus, in a single sentence he had both denied knowing intentions and attributed intentions to the Soviet Union. It was the latter that left a lasting impression.

The second pillar of his speech concerned an Anglo-American alliance to meet the threat communism posed in the world. [Historian Fraser] Harbutt pointed out that this alliance was not presented as an effect caused by the first. Rather Churchill used it as a theme running parallel to the theme of Soviet expansionism within the address so that no one could miss his meaning, but so that he also could deny that he actually stated it. Only the United States, Churchill said, could provide the leadership necessary to prevent catastrophe at this "breathless" moment in history. He assured Americans that Great Britain was ready to join in that great effort. The two nations were bound together through common language and law, and therefore fit to repulse the new "danger" to the world. He contended that the alliance should not seek a balance of power in Europe because the two nations could not "afford to work on narrow margins." Instead he said an alliance must be established that enforced the principles of the United Nations, even to the point of creating an international armed force for the U.N. Churchill avowed his loyalty to the nascent United Nations Organization, but declared that an association between Britain and America would be not only beneficial to the success of the world organization but indispensable, lest the U.N. become nothing more than a "Tower of Babel." Nonetheless he returned again and again to his primary theme: the need for the United States, now at the pinnacle of its power, to take the lead in recognizing the new threat to world peace and the forceful means needed to confront that threat.

Although Churchill divided the world into two camps on either side of an iron curtain, he hedged his bets. He paid lip service to establishing "lasting friendships" with the Soviets. He claimed to understand the Soviets "need to be secure on her western frontiers from renewal of German aggression," but this brief mention was overwhelmed by the hostile argument of the speech. Like other Western speakers before him, Churchill avoided saying what measures nations on his side of the iron curtain could take to reassure the Soviet Union that its frontiers were secure. That omission stood in stark contrast to the specific action he urged upon Americans to meet the growing danger directed from the other side of the iron curtain. In sum, Churchill's great speech exploded the belief that the world could be made whole after the devastation of World War II. Instead, the whole point of Churchill's address was that the world was already divided even more dangerously after the war than it had been before the war. His transcendental metaphor for that division dominated all other concerns he voiced, and it was on that metaphor that all his subsequent arguments rested. . . .

The Aftermath of Churchill's Speech

Although the Fulton speech met with mixed immediate reactions, in the following months, Churchill succeeded beyond his wildest dreams. His address sowed the seeds for a rhetorical process that was to blossom into a new world order, a new political reality. These effects lay not in his arguments, but in his language, especially his dominant metaphor, the iron curtain. As his terms for describing the meaning of international disputes were spread by the news media, they were adopted by opinion leaders in speeches and editorials so that Churchill's way of talking about the world became the prevailing coin for discourse. Lewis Broad correctly concluded, just five years after Fulton, that "today the terms of this address are the commonplace of the weekend speaker." While the policies that Churchill advocated were discussed and debated, the language of Churchill's rhetoric became the dominant language for those discussions and debates. Gradually, over a period of time, the language of Fulton, expanded and reinforced by Truman and others, became accepted as the commonsense perception of the "real" meaning of the actual events and disputes that caused the original confusion. For example, Senator Burneat Maybank of South Carolina declined to endorse a military alliance because he doubted that it would curb what seemed to be the "indefinite expansion" of the Soviet Union's "power and doctrine." Still, he accepted that Soviet expansionism and communist ideology posed the central problem, using almost the exact words the prime minister had used to state the problem. Senator Edward Robertson of Wyoming went further. He said that he believed the cooperation with Britain and other nations of the United Nations was important until the USSR "rolls up the iron curtain." In other words, the discussion proceeded within the division Churchill had drawn, especially by adopting the dominant metaphor, iron curtain, to symbolize that division. . . .

As people assimilated the terms of the speech as part of their everyday talk about Soviet-American relations, especially their use of the iron curtain metaphor, they also adopted the definitions and meanings subsumed in these terms. Once a definition of a situation is accepted as "the nature of things," that is, once it gives meaning to events, it creates the reality of those events. From that point on, particular policies and responses to events seem preordained, leading from a rhetorical meaning to specific policies consistent with those meanings as naturally as day follows night. The success of Churchill's speech lay in the future, in the day-by-day use of the division he had memorialized.

A single speech cannot accomplish a major change in political reality overnight. Such a change requires a rhetorical process of some sophistication. Churchill initiated that process at Fulton. As the process proceeded, was expanded, maintained, and legitimated by the rhetoric of the Truman Doctrine and other rhetorical efforts, it altered the prevailing reality. Ordinary Americans eventually responded, not in terms of realpolitik, [a political philosophy based on acting flexibly to meet immediate concerns rather than by primarily addressing long-term considerations] but in terms of a moralistic crusade. Churchill drew a picture of the Soviet Union as a massive threat to Americans in order to argue for a political alliance. In this sense, he relieved the confusion of the present through the clarity of his interpretation of the current state of the world.

Containing Communism: The Truman Doctrine

Richard Crockatt

Richard Crockatt, Reader in American History at the University of East Anglia in Norwich, England, has written extensively on the Cold War, including *The Fifty Years War,* a lengthy study of U.S.-Soviet relations between 1941 and 1991. In this excerpt, Crockatt discusses the Truman Doctrine, instrumental in defining America's adversarial stance toward the Soviet Union during the first decade of the Cold War. Crockatt examines the concept of containment, a compromise between open hostility and cooperation that was central to the Truman Doctrine. He first traces the political origins of containment, notably diplomat George Kennan's assessment of the threat of Soviet expansion in his so-called Long Telegram of 1946. Next, Crockatt analyzes President Harry S. Truman's development of the concept into a broader (and more rhetorically charged) doctrine, or guiding national principle. Crockatt concludes that the Truman Doctrine proved significant in establishing two basic, but overly simplistic, Cold War premises: All global conflict was viewed in terms of its relation to the struggle between two superpower adversaries, and both the Soviet Union and United States were seen as, and saw themselves as, having the power and ability to control the destiny of other countries.

[President Franklin] Roosevelt had returned from [the meeting of Allied leaders at] Yalta in February 1945 declaring in his message to Congress (in words borrowed from [Secretary of State] Cordell Hull) that the agreements

Excerpted from *The Fifty Years War: The United States and the Soviet Union in World Politics, 1941–1991,* by Richard Crockatt (London: Routledge, 1995). Copyright © 1995 by Richard Crockatt. Reprinted by permission of the publisher.

'ought to spell the end of unilateral action, the exclusive alliances, the spheres of influence, the balances of power, and all the other expedients that have been tried for centuries—and have always failed'. Roosevelt's hopes for a clean slate were, quickly undermined in the events of 1945–46, but some fluidity still remained in US-Soviet relations. In 1946 and into 1947 they were still talking to each other, trying to give tangible form to their aspirations for cooperation. In the event, the outcome of these efforts was precisely those despised talismans of the bad old politics—spheres of influence, exclusive alliances, and the rest. By 1950 they had become firmly institutionalized, and management of cooperation had given way to management of conflict.

'Containment' supplied the philosophical rationale for the Truman administration's new orientation and was classically expounded by [American diplomat] George Kennan in his anonymously published article 'The Sources of Soviet Conduct' ('X', *Foreign Affairs*, July 1947). In effect it was a public version of his 1946 'Long Telegram' [which had been sent privately to Truman]. Both in turn presented views of the Soviet Union which, in broad outline, he had held for a number of years. The key to the influence of the 'Long Telegram' and subsequently the 'X' article, as Kennan pointed out in his memoirs, was timing. The first reached government circles at a critical moment, as policy-makers sought an explanation for the breakdown in communication with the Soviet Union over Eastern Europe. The second offered a public rationale for the containment policies already embarked upon in the form of the Truman Doctrine.

Kennan did not view the Soviet Union as bent upon immediate fulfilment of its ideological goals. While Soviet ideology assumed the inevitable downfall of capitalism, no timetable was laid down by the Kremlin. The Soviets were prepared for the long haul. Given the doctrine of the infallibility of the Kremlin and the iron discipline of the Party, the Soviet leadership was 'at liberty to put forward for tactical purposes any particular thesis which it finds useful to the cause at any particular moment and require the faithful and unquestioning acceptance of that thesis by the members of the movement as a whole'. Caution and persistence characterized Soviet policy, and America must respond with 'policies no less steady in their purpose, and no less variegated and resourceful in their application, than those of the Soviet Union itself'. In these circumstances the United States must seek to contain Soviet power by the 'adroit and vigilant application of counterforce at a series of constantly shifting geographical and political points'.

Kennan's prescriptions for American policy appear to be unmistakably global in scope and to carry strong military implications. In fact Kennan, the supposed architect of containment, dissociated himself from many aspects of its implementation, emerging as a critic of both the Truman Doctrine and NATO. Since Kennan played such an important and ambiguous role in policy-making during these years, we can usefully employ his writings as a vantage point from which to view the institutionalization of the cold war.

The Origins of Containment

Containment had already been enacted in the form of the Truman Doctrine before Kennan supplied the policy with a label. In March 1947 Britain announced that it could no longer afford to sustain its support for the Greek government in the civil war which had raged intermittently after the liberation of Greece from the Germans in 1944. Greece had been conceded by [Soviet premier Joseph] Stalin as a Western sphere of influence in the percentages agreement with [British prime minister Winston] Churchill in October 1944. It is now clear that Stalin held to this agreement and not only withheld support from the Greek communists but was disturbed by the prospect of a communist revolution with indigenous roots. Such distinctions, however, meant little to American leaders who could only see in the flow of arms from Yugoslavia and Albania to the Greek rebels the hand of the Soviet Union. In Turkey too, although not at risk domestically to the same degree as Greece, Soviet pressure for control of the Black Sea straits was perceived as a bid not merely for influence in Turkey but as a stepping-stone to gains in the Middle East.

The striking feature of the American response to the announcement of British withdrawal is not so much the actual decision to send military and economic aid to Greece and Turkey as the manner in which [President Harry S.] Truman strove to create a consensus for a fundamental reorientation of American policy. Presenting a stark contrast between two alternative ways of life, 'one based upon the will of the majority and one based upon the will of a minority forcibly imposed upon the majority', he declared in his speech to Congress on 12 March 1947 that 'it must be the policy of the United States to support free peoples who are resisting subjugation by armed minorities or by outside pressures'.

Harry S. Truman

There seems little doubt, as historians have shown, that one of Truman's motives for pitching the rhetoric of his message so high was the need to convince a cost-conscious Congress and an American public opinion, not yet fully cognizant of the extended role the United States was about to assume, that the stakes in Greece and Turkey were indeed as high as he claimed. But it is equally clear that Truman and his advisers sincerely believed that the crisis was much wider than the situation in Greece and Turkey. To that extent, as [historian] Daniel Yergin has pointed out, while the message to Congress was conceived as a 'sales job', it was not a cynical manoeuvre. A second consideration lay behind the presentation of the Truman Doctrine—the need to 'avoid the appearance of standing in for London in the Middle East, of simply taking over traditional British responsibilities'. Aid to Greece and Turkey must be promoted as an American policy, based upon consideration of its own interests, and not as a matter of 'pulling British chestnuts out of the fire once again'. The occasion thus demanded a comprehensive statement of a distinctively American purpose.

In the congressional hearings on the Greece and Turkey Aid Bill the administration was pressed on the extent of the commitment the United States was undertaking. Under-Secretary Dean Acheson sought to calm fears that the Truman Doctrine was a blank cheque to be drawn on at will in other comparable situations, but he barely succeeded. Each case, he said, would be considered according to the specific circumstances, but he could not disguise the fact that the Truman Doctrine speech had established the framework within which such cases would be judged. This is clear in an exchange with Senator [Arthur] Vandenberg, a leading Republican Senator whose influence in this and other crucial policy initiatives laid the basis for bipartisan support for Truman:

> Vandenberg: . . . In other words, I think what you are saying is that wherever we find free peoples having difficulty in the maintenance of free institutions, and difficulty in defending against aggressive movements that seek to impose upon them totalitarian regimes, we do not necessarily react in the same way each time, but we propose to react. Acheson: That, I think, is correct.

George Kennan objected strongly to the universalist character of the message but also to the specifics of the aid to Greece and Turkey. He opposed any aid to Turkey and felt that the emphasis in the proposals for Greece was excessively military. These distinctions appear puzzling in the light of his 'X' article with its apparent globalism and military terminology ('adroit and vigilant application of counterforce . . .'). In his memoirs Kennan admits to serious deficiencies in his exposition of containment: the failure to make clear that he considered containment as primarily political and economic, and 'the failure to distinguish between various geographic areas and to make it clear that the "containment" of which I was speaking was not something I thought we could, necessarily, do everywhere successfully'. Much debate has revolved around whether Kennan's after-the-fact 'correction' of his 'X' article statement can be accepted at face value, an issue which need not be resolved here. Suffice it to say that his overriding intention was evidently to underline the seriousness of the Soviet threat which he felt was insufficiently appreciated. Certainly his other writings at the time, in his new capacity from 1947 as head of the State Department's Policy Planning Staff (PPS), show a much more nuanced and pragmatic grasp of the Soviet challenge and of options open to the United States. In the July [1947] article, perhaps anxious to promote his salient point, he overplayed his hand. Attention was thus deflected from arguably his most important suggestion, that 'the issue of Soviet—American relations is in essence a test of the overall worth of the United States as a nation among nations'. By extension the West's strongest card in its conflict with communism was the health and vigour of its own democratic traditions and values. This view became central to the Marshall Plan. Kennan himself has noted the irony that his name should be associated with the Truman Doctrine, about which he had serious reservations and in which he was scarcely involved, rather than the Marshall Plan, in which he was a prime, if largely unseen mover.

The Significance of the Truman Doctrine

The Truman Doctrine was of profound significance for a number of reasons. Firstly, it set a precedent for the tendency of superpower policy-makers to view all global conflict within the framework of the cold war. Bipolarity [seeing things from a strictly "us-versus-them" perspective] was not merely a matter of the structure of international relations but a state of mind. Thinking and acting in terms of simple dichotomies became second nature, even when actual conflicts, such as those in the Middle East, fitted awkwardly within this mould. In part this was a question of rhetoric, a necessary simplification of complex realities for the purpose of explaining unfamiliar commitments to domestic audiences. Rhetoric was not the whole story, however, since in the aftermath of the war the United States and the Soviet Union did in fact possess a disproportionately large power to affect the destinies of other nations. Less-favoured nations indeed looked to the superpowers, but above all to the United States, to authenticate their own aspirations, whether it be Ho Chi Minh seeking endorsement in 1945 of his goal of an independent Vietnam or the Western European nations seeking aid for economic recovery. There was an element of illusion in this, only fully exposed when the unusual conditions of the immediate post-war years had passed: the illusion that the United States could or would supply precisely what other nations wanted. So long as basic interests coincided, as was broadly the case between the United States and Western Europe, reality sustained the illusion, though even here as time went on interests diverged. In the case of Vietnam and many other former colonial territories of European powers, however, the gap between illusion and reality quickly appeared. Despite the possession of enormous power, the United States was not always able to dictate the direction of events in the Third World and elsewhere, but because it possessed enormous power the United States continued to believe that this was possible.

The second significant feature of the Truman Doctrine lies in its connection with the United Nations. Why, asked many Congressmen and commentators, had the United States government not sought to resolve the crisis in Greece and Turkey through the United Nations? Truman had stated in his message to Congress that 'in helping free and independent nations to maintain their freedom, the United States will be giving effect to the principles of the United Nations'. Truman did not, however, risk actually relying on the United Nations to achieve these goals. The pragmatic reason for acting unilaterally is clear: the certainty that the Soviet Union would use its veto. The end result, though, was the devaluation of the original aspiration for collective security as the basis for the new international order.

Finally, it is noteworthy that the occasion for this major departure in American policy concerned not the heartland of Europe but its south-eastern rim. Taken in conjunction with the Iranian crisis of 1946 [The United States and the Soviet Union exchanged angry words over the slow withdrawal of Soviet troops from oil-rich northern Iran after the end of World War II], it shows the susceptibility of what has been called the 'Northern Tier' of the Middle East to superpower conflict. The reason is not far to seek: Turkey and Iran bordered the Soviet Union directly while Greece bordered Soviet bloc territory (i.e.: Bulgaria, Yugoslavia, and Albania). The possibility of the extension of Soviet power to the Middle East proper was an added reason for American concern, though, as it turned out, there was a delay of several years before this materialized. American fears that the Soviet Union would take the Arab side in the conflict, over the establishment of the state of Israel in 1948 were unfounded. The Soviet Union promptly recognized the new state and gave it substantial military aid at a critical time during the first Arab-Israeli war of 1948–49. It was the early 1950s before the increasingly close relations between the United States and Israel led to the Sovient Union's shift towards firm support of the cause of Arab nationalism. Meanwhile, in 1947 both the United States and the Soviet Union were more preoccupied with events in Europe. The Truman Doctrine was only the opening gambit in the development of containment.

The Beginnings of "Nuclear Diplomacy"

Jonathan M. Weisgall

The July 1946 atomic bomb tests (code-named Operation Crossroads) conducted near the Bikini Atoll in the Pacific Ocean symbolize the era of "nuclear diplomacy" that marked the postwar portion of Harry Truman's presidency (1944–1950). Jonathan M. Weisgall, an attorney who has represented the inhabitants of the Bikini Atoll since 1975, examines the tumultuous year leading up to the Bikini tests in the context of the U.S. government's increasing willingness to use its monopoly on atomic power as a bargaining chip against the Soviets in international affairs. Weisgall chronicles the disintegration of the wartime alliance between the United States and Soviet Union in the context of international atomic policy. He claims that a combination of Western leaders' distrust of Stalin and ominous signs of Communist expansion early in 1946 helped to undo plans for cooperation between the Americans and Soviets on atomic bomb technology. As a result, the Operation Crossroads tests became not only an opportunity to conduct further testing of a new and potent weapon in the U.S. arsenal, but a chance to send an indirect message to the Soviets about the potential consequences of continued expansion. The long-term effect of this decision, though, was to begin the nuclear arms race that would last for the remainder of the Cold War.

In the first few months of his presidency, [Harry] Truman relied heavily on his new secretary of state, James F. Byrnes, a familiar and friendly figure from his early Senate days, for

Excerpted from *Operation Crossroads: The Atomic Tests at Bikini Atoll*, by Jonathan M. Weisgall (Annapolis, MD: Naval Institute Press, 1994). Copyright © 1994 by Jonathan M. Weisgall. Reprinted with permission.

leadership on foreign policy issues. A former senator from South Carolina and Supreme Court justice, Byrnes had twice just missed the vice-presidential nomination, losing to Henry Wallace in 1940 and to Truman in 1944. He had served in all three branches of the federal government—the only American ever to serve as governor, secretary of state, Supreme Court justice, congressman, and senator—and he believed himself much more qualified to serve as president than Truman.

Eager to assert his new power, Byrnes was convinced that America's atomic monopoly would help him win concessions from the Soviet Union at the upcoming London Conference of Foreign Ministers. He was determined not to brandish the bomb, he told [Secretary of War Henry L.] Stimson, but to rely instead simply on its existence as an "implied threat" to strengthen his negotiating position. The Russians, though, made light of the bomb. At a reception in the House of Lords shortly after the start of the conference in September 1945, Byrnes approached Russia's Foreign Minister [Viacheslav] Molotov and asked him when the sightseeing would end so the conferees could "get down to business." Molotov, sounding like Stimson in Washington, asked Byrnes in turn if he had an "atomic bomb in his side pocket."

"You don't know Southerners," Byrnes replied. "We carry our artillery in our hip pocket. If you don't cut out all this stalling and let us get down to work, I am going to pull an atomic bomb out of my hip pocket and let you have it."

If Byrnes really believed that the atomic bomb would make the Soviet Union more manageable, he was mistaken. If anything, Molotov proved to be more stubborn than ever, and atomic diplomacy failed to achieve American objectives. The three-week conference was a failure and ended without even a final communiqué. Determined to try a new approach after London, Byrnes abruptly decided to adopt Stimson's proposal for U.S.-Soviet cooperation on the bomb. In November, he proposed a second meeting of the Council of Foreign Ministers in Moscow in late December, hoping to use the conference to reach an agreement on the control of atomic weapons as a means of resolving other East-West issues. This time he would use the atomic bomb as a carrot, not as a stick, and he would go right to Stalin. George F. Kennan, the State Department's top Soviet expert and future ambassador to Russia, questioned Byrnes's motives. His weakness in dealing with the Russians, thought Kennan, was that his purpose was "to achieve some sort of an agreement, he doesn't much care what."

Divisions in Policy Toward the Soviets

Truman remained of two minds. Publicly he took a tough stance. At a Navy Day speech in New York on October 27, 1945, with forty-seven U.S. warships displayed along the Hudson River and 1,200 Navy planes flying overhead, Truman spoke of America's military strength. Clearly directing his remarks toward Moscow, he declared that the United States would not "recognize any government imposed upon any nation by the force of any foreign power," and he emphasized that America would hold the atomic bomb as a "sacred trust" for humanity. Privately, though, he told aides it was "inevitable that we should have real difficulties but we should not take them too seriously." These differences could be resolved "amicably if we gave ourselves time." Truman thought the Russians were having "very real problems at home," and he viewed [Soviet premier Joseph] Stalin as a "moderating influence" on more conservative Kremlin leaders, such as Molotov. "It would be a real catastrophe if Stalin should die at the present time," he said. Given this assessment, the strategy of approaching Stalin directly made sense. Byrnes and Truman thought that a generous American offer on the control of atomic weapons would create a give-and-take atmosphere in which Stalin would make concessions as well.

Byrnes held two meetings with Stalin during the Moscow conference and achieved some small agreements, all the while keeping Washington largely uninformed. Much to Byrnes's surprise, Stalin even agreed to the American plan for the creation of a United Nations Atomic Energy Commission under the jurisdiction of the Security Council. Byrnes, acting pleased with the results of the conference, spoke to the country on the major radio networks upon his return to the United States on December 30. "The meeting in Moscow did serve to bring about better understanding," he said. Peace required both justice and wisdom, he declared, and there was "ample scope for the achievement of these essential results" at Moscow.

[Chief of Staff William D.] Leahy and other hardliners saw Byrnes as too eager to accommodate the Russians. Truman, buffeted about by his advisors and more concerned with domestic issues such as mounting labor strife and inflation, seemed to agree with all sides. He certainly wanted to get along with the Russians, and he felt that he could negotiate with Stalin. "I like Stalin. He is straightforward," he wrote his wife from Potsdam [an eastern German city in which Churchill, Stalin and Truman met in July 1945] after their first meeting. He noted in his diary that the Russian leader was frank, honest, and willing to compromise, and he told [Secretary of Commerce] Henry Wallace that Stalin was a "fine man" who simply wanted to do the right thing. His trust in the Russians, though, had waned considerably by the end of 1945. "There is no evidence as yet that the Russians intend to change their habits as far as honoring contracts is concerned," he told Forrestal in early December.

Shortly after Byrnes's radio talk, Truman summoned him to the White House and told him the Moscow agreements were just a general promise from the Russians. The president, reading from the text of a handwritten letter, told Byrnes that the "Russians have been a headache to us" since Potsdam, and he proceeded to tick off his grievances. Truman no longer doubted Soviet intentions. "Unless Russia is faced with an iron fist and strong language another war is in the making." The continued presence of Soviet troops in Iran was an "outrage if I ever saw one," and he was convinced that Russia intended to invade Turkey and seize the Black Sea Straits. "I'm tired of babying the Soviets," he exclaimed, and on January 8 he announced that he did not consider himself bound by the Moscow agreement.

Truman undoubtedly hoped for international control of atomic weapons, but he also recognized that America was not ready for international control of a new technology monopolized by the United States. "Maybe we could get world government in a thousand years or something like that," he told a friend in October 1945, but it was nothing more than a theory. He was not alone. His proposal to Congress in October to consider a program of international cooperation on atomic energy met with a chilly response. "We have the jump on the rest of the world in [the bomb's] development and use," declared Senator Edwin C. Johnson of Colorado. "We should not . . . fritter away that significant and tremendous advantage by surrendering its know-how and its formulas to anyone." Ninety percent of those Congressmen polled opposed sharing information on the bomb with any country at all, and a nationwide poll showed that nearly the same percentage of Americans shared these views.

Bad News from All Sides

The new year brought on the formal end of the World War II Grand Alliance and the emergence of the Cold War. As the historian Melvyn Leffler has noted, "It is hard to overstate how portentous the international situation appeared to U.S. officials in early 1946." Truman and his top advisors had spent the previous eight months vacillating in their views toward the Russians and trying to develop a cohesive policy. The Cabinet was split between confrontation and cooperation, but neither approach seemed to make a difference. Truman, however, was unable to focus much of his attention on foreign affairs because of the increasingly serious domestic problems of wages, prices, and strikes. On January 19, 800,000 steel workers walked off their jobs in the biggest strike in U.S. history. At one point in the first part of the year, more than 1 million workers were on strike. [American labor leader] John L. Lewis called a nationwide coal strike, General Motors workers struck, and a nationwide rail strike virtually brought the country to a standstill.

Every day in the new year seemed to bring more ominous news. On February 3, Drew Pearson stunned listeners to his evening radio program with the disclosure that a Russian spy ring was operating in Canada. When Canadian authorities arrested twenty-two government scientists and technicians on February 15, Moscow did not even deny the allegations. Stalin left no doubts about Soviet intentions in a February 9 speech at the Bolshoi Theater. His blunt tone marked the return of ideological rhetoric. World War II was a victory for the "Soviet system," and gone were the usual references to Russia's wartime allies. The "hostile" international environment facing Russia and the "capitalist encirclement" of his country, he said, could lead to another war. He declared that international peace was "impossible under the present capitalist development of world economy," and he announced a five-year plan to more than double Russia's output of iron, steel, coal, and oil "to guarantee our country against any eventuality." [American ambassador to the Soviet Union] Averell Harriman was now convinced that Stalin was intent on exporting communism to the rest of the world, and

Truman Suggests International Controls

On September 23, 1949, only slightly more than three years after the Bikini tests, President Harry Truman addressed the United States with the shocking news that the Soviets had successfully detonated an atomic bomb of their own. In doing so, they exceeded predictions by many of Truman's advisers that it would possibly take decades for Soviet scientists to achieve what the Manhattan Project had done in 1945. With his nuclear trump card now taken away from him, Truman's tone shifted somewhat from using the bomb as a possible threat to establishing international controls on atomic energy.

I believe the American people to the fullest extent consistent with the national security are entitled to be informed of all developments in the field of atomic energy. That is my reason for making public the following information.

We have evidence that within recent weeks an atomic explosion occurred in the U.S.S.R.

Ever since atomic energy was first released by man, the eventual development of this new force by other nations was to be expected.

even Supreme Court Justice William O. Douglas, a leading liberal, called it "the declaration of World War III."

Three days later, on February 12, the Soviets announced that a new Communist government had been formed in North Korea, and there were reports of large Soviet troop movements in the area. A February 21 report from the Joint Chiefs of Staff to President Truman reflected the military's hardening position toward the Soviets. "The consolidation and development of the power of Russia is the greatest threat to the United States in the foreseeable future," it stated, adding that the proliferation of the atomic bomb would wipe out the military advantage America enjoyed during the war. Atomic warfare would mean that "our long term potential . . . owing to the length of time required for mobilization . . . might not be sufficient to avert disaster."

The very next day, George F. Kennan, the chief of mission

This probability has always been taken into account by us.

Nearly four years ago I pointed out that "scientific opinion appears to be practically unanimous that the essential theoretical knowledge upon which the discovery is based is already widely known. There is also substantial agreement that foreign research can come abreast of our present theoretical knowledge in time." And, in the three-nation declaration of the President of the United States and the Prime Ministers of the United Kingdom and of Canada, dated November 15, 1945. It was emphasized that no single nation could, in fact, have a monopoly of atomic weapons.

This recent development emphasizes once again, if indeed such emphasis were needed, the necessity for that truly effective and enforceable international control of atomic energy which this Government and the large majority of the members of the United Nations support.

A Decade of American Foreign Policy: Basic Documents, 1941–49, Prepared at the request of the Senate Committee on Foreign Relations by the Staff of the Committee and the Department of State. Washington, DC: Government Printing Office, 1950. Also available from: www.yale.edu/lawweb/avalon/decade/decad244.htm.

at the U.S. embassy in Moscow, sent his famous "Long Telegram" to Washington. Taking his cue from Stalin's February 9 speech, Kennan asserted that Russian leaders were motivated by a "political force committed fanatically to the belief that . . . there can be no permanent *modus vivendi* [a way of peacefully co-existing]" with America. Marxism, he reasoned, was merely a "fig leaf" for the "neurotic" Kremlin leaders, who couched themselves in a new ideology, but, like the czars before them, were obsessed with the "instinctive Russian sense of insecurity." As a response, he recommended military preparedness. "Soviet power," he wrote, is "impervious to the logic of reason, and it is highly sensitive to the logic of force." This policy, later dubbed containment, was dependent upon the West drawing a line against further Soviet expansion.

As Kennan later wrote, the effect of his Long Telegram was "nothing less than sensational." It was "one of those moments when official Washington . . . was ready to receive a given message," and it galvanized American thinking. Truman read it, [Secretary of the Navy James V.] Forrestal circulated it throughout the government, and it was soon released to the press. Hardliners such as Harriman and Forrestal shared Kennan's frustrations in dealing with Russian intransigence, but Kennan proposed a solution no one else had offered: concede Eastern Europe to the Soviets but draw the line there and forge an alliance with other Western nations to counter this Russian sphere of influence.

The Onset of Atomic Diplomacy

The crucial event of those months was the crisis in Iran. Moscow refused to honor a March 2 deadline to remove troops from parts of Iran it had occupied during the war, and it supported a Communist-led separatist movement in a northern province bordering on the Soviet Union. This was not Eastern Europe, where the Soviet Union could make out a claim for legitimate security concerns and a sphere of influence, but an area of vital strategic and economic importance to the West. It was appearing more and more clear that Russia's search for security had ended and its quest for expansion had begun. In response to new cables from Kennan warning that the Soviets' goal was the "virtual subjugation, penetration and domination of the entire country" and Bahrain, Kuwait, and Turkey as well, Truman sent the battleship *Missouri* to the eastern Mediterranean and began to supply aid to the Tehran government.

If there was a single moment during these first postwar years that was seen as the breaking point between East and West, it was Winston Churchill's speech in Fulton, Missouri, on March 5. With Truman's presence on the podium seen as a U.S. endorsement, Churchill declared that an "iron curtain" had descended from "Stettin in the Baltic to Trieste in the Adriatic," and he called for a revival of the Anglo-American wartime alliance against a new enemy—the Soviet Union. The key to this association was the atomic bomb, asserted Churchill. It would be "wrong and imprudent to entrust the secret knowledge or experience of the atomic bomb" to the new United Nations, and it would constitute "criminal madness to cast it adrift in this still agitated and un-united world."

Operation Crossroads's critics would charge that the 1946 tests were designed to send a clear signal to Moscow that the United States, with its atomic monopoly, was prepared to perfect the bomb and use it on the Soviet Union. Their views were similar to those of others who argued that the atomic bombs were dropped on Japan with a real eye toward the Soviet Union. The atomic bomb was superfluous, these critics argued, because Japan was already on the verge of collapse and ready to surrender. Rather, this show of force was intended to impress the Soviets and warn them not to overrun Eastern Europe. As P.M.S. Blackett, the Nobel Prize-winning British physicist, suggested, "The dropping of the atomic bombs was not so much the last military act of the second world war, as the first major operation of the cold diplomatic war with Russia." Truman's comment at Potsdam about the bomb's effect—"I'll have a hammer on these boys"—lent credence to this theory, but few historians have accepted it.

The timing of Operation Crossroads led many critics to

view the tests as yet another saber-rattling gesture toward the Soviet Union, and President Truman took no measures to change that view. The tests were first conceived in August 1945, however, well before U.S.-Soviet relations deteriorated, and they grew directly out of the decades-old Army-Navy rivalry that resurfaced with the advent of the atomic bomb and the end of World War II. The AAF [Army Air Force] emerged from the war challenging the Navy's traditional role as the nation's first line of defense, and both services sought to stake out their roles in a postwar nuclear age that would see new strategic doctrines, unification of the services and, inevitably, fewer defense dollars.

In just one year, though, Truman had radically changed his perception of U.S.-Soviet relations. By the spring of 1946, he no longer trusted Russia and no longer viewed disputes with the Soviets as the inevitable results of competing national interests that could be resolved through quiet diplomacy. Like Kennan, he viewed the Russians as trying to extend their power and their sphere of influence. He still believed in coexistence, but it could only be achieved from a position of U.S. military strength, and the atomic bomb epitomized that strength. Harvard University president James B. Conant, Roosevelt's science advisor and administrator of the Manhattan Project, shared Truman's views and thought the Bikini tests would intimidate the Russians. Asked at an off-the-record talk sponsored by the Council on Foreign Relations in April whether Operation Crossroads would help or hurt the goal of international control of atomic weapons, he replied that "the Russians are more rather than less likely to come to an effective agreement for the control of atomic energy if we keep our strength and continue to produce bombs." As the Joint Chiefs of Staff remarked just before Operation Crossroads, the fact remained that the atomic bomb was the "one military weapon which may for the period until Russia obtains it exert a deterrent effect upon her will to expand." Operation Crossroads, like Hiroshima and Nagasaki, was not designed to intimidate the Kremlin, but Washington certainly saw the bomb as a strong diplomatic tool and was anxious to reap its anticipated benefits.

American Attitudes Toward the Bomb During the Early Cold War Years

Paul Boyer

In the decade following the use of the atomic bomb by the United States on the Japanese cities of Hiroshima and Nagasaki, the attitude of both the general public and the government of the United States toward this new weapon was ambivalent. Paul Boyer, professor of history at the University of Wisconsin at Madison, has written two books about the atomic bomb and Cold War culture. Using sources ranging from the popular press to congressional hearings on atomic energy, Boyer examines American perceptions of nuclear weapons and their role in the ideological conflict of the Cold War in its initial stages. Boyer argues that a significant number of atomic physicists, journalists, and government figures opposed the use of the bomb, as either a deterrent threat or an actual weapon. He claims that support for the use of atomic weapons in the effort to contain the spread of communism, however, rebounded from a momentary decline immediately after World War II to become both the majority opinion among Americans and a theoretical element of military strategy during the early years of the Korean War.

Of the many American magazines galvanized into activism by the atomic bomb, one of the most outspoken had been *Business Week*. Repeatedly in 1945–1946 it warned of the bomb's menace, publicized the scientists' movement, and campaigned for international control. Within a few short years, however, all this had changed. In April 1949, *Business*

Excerpted from *By the Bomb's Early Light: American Thought and Culture at the Dawn of the Atomic Age*, by Paul Boyer (New York: Pantheon Books, 1985). Copyright © 1985 by Paul Boyer. Reprinted by permission of Random House, Inc.

Week reported that the "technical problems" of atomic-bomb production had been solved, leaving only "such normal managerial problems as how to reduce costs [and] . . . speed lagging operations." Bomb output was "now rolling very smoothly," it said, and "by 1950 or 1951 . . . could be practically doubled."

And so we have come full circle. For a fleeting moment after Hiroshima, American culture had been profoundly affected by atomic fear, by a dizzying plethora of atomic panaceas and proposals, and by endless speculation on the social and ethical implications of the new reality. By the end of the 1940s, the cultural discourse had largely stopped. Americans now seemed not only ready to accept the bomb, but to support any measures necessary to maintain atomic supremacy.

From the earliest post-Hiroshima days, demands for stockpiling atomic bombs and even using them against the new postwar enemy, Russia, emerged as a minority (but far from negligible) position in public-opinion polls and letters to the editor. [In 1946, John Hersey published *Hiroshima*, an acclaimed journalistic account of the atomic blast.] "I read Hersey's report," a subscriber wrote the *New Yorker* in 1946. "It was marvelous. Now let us drop a handful on Moscow." As we have seen, the nation's atomic-weapons program had continued after the war, and while official secrecy blurred details, this fact was public knowledge. The Bikini tests made clear, commented I.F. Stone in 1946, that "the atom bomb is part of our active war equipment and an integral part of our future military strategy."

At first, this program either received little public attention or, if noted at all, was cited to underscore the urgency of international control. By 1948, however, it was being much more openly and even boastfully reported. *Newsweek* described the AEC's [Atomic Energy Commission] success in transforming "a frenzied wartime patchwork . . . into an orderly permanent enterprise" that had put bomb production on "a firm and secure basis." Under the headline "HOW MANY ATOM BOMBS? ENOUGH ON HAND FOR U.S. TO FIGHT MAJOR WAR," *U.S. News and World Report* extrapolated from known figures on plutonium production to estimate the nation's atomic-bomb arsenal at 200 to 250, with a possible increase to 1,000 by 1950. (These numbers were apparently something of an overestimate at the time, if recently released figures are accurate, but the 1,000 total was, of course, soon reached and far surpassed). "What was for the most part a bluff in 1945," wrote Harry Davis in his 1948 popularization *Energy Unlimited*, "has now been replaced by a hand well backed with atomic aces."

At about the same time, in public speeches and articles in *Life* and other magazines, top military leaders like Gen. George C. Kenney of the Strategic Air Command began to discuss openly the Pentagon's strategic plans for a massive atomic attack on Soviet cities and industrial centers in the event of war. Writing in September 1948, [nuclear physicist] Eugene Rabinowitch expressed dismay over this "callous public discussion of plans for atomic warfare." Though part of the war of nerves with the Soviets, he said, it could also have important domestic consequences: "We do not suggest that" such speeches and articles

> arise from a deliberate desire of the military to "condition" American public opinion to the indiscriminate killing and maiming of millions of civilians; but is not their actual effect to soothe in advance all moral revulsion, and to make American people accept the possibility of atomic slaughter as something, perhaps deplorable, but natural in this imperfect world?

In short, Rabinowitch wondered, were such previews of atomic holocaust a way of "asking the American people to acquiesce in advance to the final conversion of war into genocide?" If so, he warned, "the American conscience must refuse to be pacified."

But pacified it was. These same years saw an increase in Americans' expectations of war. The percentage anticipating another war "within the next twenty years or so" grew from 59 percent in October 1945 to 77 percent by late 1947. In 1948, the Gallup poll found 57 percent of Americans expecting war within ten years, and 43 percent within three or four years. "The world has virtually accepted the inevitability of another war," concluded Norman Cousins gloomily that December. But rather than generating support for a redoubled diplomatic effort to reduce the atomic threat, these rising war fears had the reverse effect, leading to an increased reliance on the bomb as the best source of security in a threatening world. The postwar belief that fear would promote the cause of peace, wrote University of Chicago law professor Malcolm Sharp in 1948, had given way to the feeling that "if atomic energy is to be used to destroy people and their works, it had better be the Russians and their works." In a summer 1949 Gallup poll, an overwhelming 70 percent of Americans opposed any U.S. pledge not to be the first to use atomic weapons in a future war. Such, then, was the national mood on the eve of the most unsettling news since August 1945.

The Effect of the "Russian Bomb"

On September 24, 1949, a terse announcement from Washington struck a largely unprepared nation: the Soviet Union had tested an atomic bomb! Leading atomic scientists had predicted a Russian bomb within three to five years of Hiroshima, but influential figures like [former head of the wartime Office of Scientific Research and Development] Vannevar Bush and General [Leslie R.] Groves had dismissed the possibility. "Few atomic people are inclined to think the Russians have made much progress," *Business Week* had said in April 1949. Editorialists and opinion-molders treated the Soviet test as a momentous event. "The prospect of a two-sided atomic war," said Raymond Moley in *Newsweek*, meant a "towering change in the world outlook." "An historic bridge has been crossed," observed a chastened *Business Week*. "From here on, all the rivers run the other way." A Herblock cartoon pictured Uncle Sam as Robinson Crusoe discovering a footprint in the sand.

Given the surprise and the portentous editorializing, public reaction was surprisingly muted. Raymond Moley remarked on "the apparent lack of serious concern"; a Washington journalist found nothing comparable to the "agitation and ferment" the Hiroshima news had caused. "It didn't take long for the shock to wear off," observed *Newsweek* laconically.

ructive memory; the captive nations were not
vivid reality, and Soviet hostility and duplici
r granted. . . . "Who lost China?" was the que
our. Alger Hiss was convicted in early Januar
ish atomic spy] Klaus Fuchs confessed just fo
Truman's final decision.

luential periodicals trumpeted the Rus
ftpedaled the threat of the hydrogen bom
made little sense in the "pure economi
id *Business Week* but its "psychological anc
. would be tremendous." In a special issu
menace two weeks after the hydrogen-b
it a mushroom cloud on its cover; warned
re "preparing for war" and would use
ent" as a pretext to promote "the victor
hroughout the world"; and printed alarr
a supposed "Red Military Advantage."
omb remained, but in the context of the (
an bomb, and repeated assertions of So
nd perfidy, bigger American bombs see
ly hope. The process that had begun gr
7, in which the image of the bomb as a r
ated was effaced by its image as a vital
ng struggle with the Soviet Union, vastl
eptember 1949. Political efforts to dimi
it were now seen as a snare and a delu
in keeping ahead. In this competition, /
reassuringly in July 1950, the Russians
eting with professionals." They had
crash basis, and "you don't get a broad
ique that way." *Look* reported in Nover
tion's "long-hairs" (that is, scientists)
ntinental ballistic missiles that would (
of mass death and destruction." But ra
rightening prospect as an argument fo
ional negotiations, as it surely would
ook concluded: "What we must do ne
oduction facilities to the ideas of our 'l

In part, this muted response reflected government media manipulation. ("I warn you, don't overplay this," Defense Secretary Louis Johnson had told reporters.) It also reflected the fact that for four years Americans had been imagining vivid scenarios of atomic attack—scenarios that simply assumed that the U.S. atomic monopoly would be brief. Above all, this response reflected the changed political climate of the late 1940s and the shift from the goal of control to the goal of superiority. To be sure, some voices were raised in a familiar refrain, insisting that international control and Big Power agreements on atomic energy were now more urgent than ever. [Noted chemist] Harold C. Urey called for a "bold political program" to combat the worsening atomic threat. *Christian Century* urged "a new beginning" in disarmament efforts.

The dominant reaction, however, was a grim determination to increase America's lead in nuclear weaponry. The Russian bomb accelerated the shift toward viewing the atomic bomb not as a terrible scourge to be eliminated as quickly as possible, but a winning weapon to be stockpiled with utmost urgency. The United States must "establish unquestioned and unmistakable leadership" in atomic weapons, [AEC head] David Lilienthal declared late in 1949, to "buy time for reason to prevail." The tabloid *New York Daily News* made the point succinctly in a punning headline: "U.S. HAS SUPREMACY, WILL HOLD IT: A-MEN." Rejecting "wishful thoughts . . . about atomic disarmament and control," *Newsweek* columnist Ernest K. Lindley said the Russian bomb meant U.S. nuclear weapons production must remain "as high as is necessary to maintain a great superiority in quantity for a long time to come." If Americans wanted security, said *Time*, they "would have to buy the full, costly package." The Hearst press urged the stockpiling of four atomic bombs for every Soviet one. With the bomb now in the hands of "totalitarians . . . remorselessly driven toward war," said *Life*, America must maintain a "clear, unchallenged, demonstrable" nuclear supremacy and secure its defenses. Russian atomic bombs, warned *Life*, could be delivered by many means, including even commercial freighters that could unload concealed bomb components for ground transport to secret interior sites for assembly. (The latter threat was illustrated with photographs of a Russian freighter unloading and a truck rolling along a highway.)

Senator Brien McMahon, stalwart supporter of the postwar scientists' movement, was driven almost to distraction by the Russian bomb. Only a preemptive atomic attack on Russia, he insisted to David Lilienthal, could prevent an ultimate, world-destroying holocaust. Late in 1949, McMahon's Joint Committee on Atomic Energy lifted all limits on AEC spending and told it to exercise "boldness, initiative, and effort" to "maintain our preeminence in this field." As one journalist who attended the committee's hearings put it, the message boiled down to: "We don't care how or where you spend it; just keep us out in front."

The Prospect of the Hydrogen Bomb

Behind these generalizations lay a very specific objective. Almost from the moment of Hiroshima, there had been hints of a vastly more terrible "superbomb." Edward Condon warned early in 1946 of bombs a thousand times more powerful "in the near future"; diplomat John J. McCloy made the same prediction in a December 1946 speech, specifically mentioning a hydrogen bomb. After September 24, 1949, theoretical speculation became a matter of urgent policy discussion, and on January 31, 1950, President [Harry] Truman made it official: the AEC would proceed with work "on all forms of atomic weapons, including the so-called hydrogen or superbomb."

The inner history of the hydrogen-bomb decision has been told in the memoirs of participants and in such books as Herbert York's *The Advisors: Oppenheimer, Teller, and the Superbomb* (1976). The conflict between scientists like Edward Teller, Ernest Lawrence, and Luis Alvarez, who favored the hydrogen bomb (who indeed were "drooling" at the prospect, according to Lilienthal), and others who opposed it—including Lilienthal and the eight scientists on the AEC's general advisory committee chaired by Oppenheimer—is by now familiar. As for the larger cultural context of the decision, discussion has focused mainly on the fact that it was made with

no involvement by th
debate with only a fe
tional security advise
has written; "no sern
from defenders of se
phe—no public discu
consulted, some ha
been different. This
of far-reaching natic
scrutiny of pertinen
Bacher, a former A
critic. "The superb
American people,"
must be given the
to embark on this

Would public p
sion? Probably no
percent favored bu
pressed "reluctant
proved. Indeed, 1
sponse of any so
ready to think abc
from around the
thing else but."

Fear of the So

In reflecting on
the hydrogen-bo
political climate
"for internationa
said Robert Bach
and aggravated
is easily convinc
from all of this
of the hydroge
stressed the bro

By the end of
ace was seen

cent and ins
slogan but a
were taken f
tion of the h
and [the Brit
days before

Indeed, inf
menace and so
self. The bom
destruction," s
litical effects .
the communist
decision, *Life* p
the Soviets we
atomic agreem
Communism t
charts showing

Fear of the b
War, the Russi
aggressiveness
to many the on
ally around 194
ace to be elimir
in the intensifyi
celerated after
the atomic thre
the best hope la
ness Week wrote
"amateurs comp
their bomb on a
phisticated techr
1950 that the n
designing interc
"awesome vistas
than using this f
tensified interna
in 1945–1947, l
apply our vast pr

In part, this muted response reflected government media manipulation. ("I warn you, don't overplay this," Defense Secretary Louis Johnson had told reporters.) It also reflected the fact that for four years Americans had been imagining vivid scenarios of atomic attack—scenarios that simply assumed that the U.S. atomic monopoly would be brief. Above all, this response reflected the changed political climate of the late 1940s and the shift from the goal of control to the goal of superiority. To be sure, some voices were raised in a familiar refrain, insisting that international control and Big Power agreements on atomic energy were now more urgent than ever. [Noted chemist] Harold C. Urey called for a "bold political program" to combat the worsening atomic threat. *Christian Century* urged "a new beginning" in disarmament efforts.

The dominant reaction, however, was a grim determination to increase America's lead in nuclear weaponry. The Russian bomb accelerated the shift toward viewing the atomic bomb not as a terrible scourge to be eliminated as quickly as possible, but a winning weapon to be stockpiled with utmost urgency. The United States must "establish unquestioned and unmistakable leadership" in atomic weapons, [AEC head] David Lilienthal declared late in 1949, to "buy time for reason to prevail." The tabloid *New York Daily News* made the point succinctly in a punning headline: "U.S. HAS SUPREMACY, WILL HOLD IT: A-MEN." Rejecting "wishful thoughts . . . about atomic disarmament and control," *Newsweek* columnist Ernest K. Lindley said the Russian bomb meant U.S. nuclear weapons production must remain "as high as is necessary to maintain a great superiority in quantity for a long time to come." If Americans wanted security, said *Time*, they "would have to buy the full, costly package." The Hearst press urged the stockpiling of four atomic bombs for every Soviet one. With the bomb now in the hands of "totalitarians . . . remorselessly driven toward war," said *Life*, America must maintain a "clear, unchallenged, demonstrable" nuclear supremacy and secure its defenses. Russian atomic bombs, warned *Life*, could be delivered by many means, including even commercial freighters that could unload concealed bomb components for ground transport to secret interior sites for assembly. (The latter threat was illustrated with photographs of a Russian freighter unloading and a truck rolling along a highway.)

Senator Brien McMahon, stalwart supporter of the post-war scientists' movement, was driven almost to distraction by the Russian bomb. Only a preemptive atomic attack on Russia, he insisted to David Lilienthal, could prevent an ultimate, world-destroying holocaust. Late in 1949, McMahon's Joint Committee on Atomic Energy lifted all limits on AEC spending and told it to exercise "boldness, initiative, and effort" to "maintain our preeminence in this field." As one journalist who attended the committee's hearings put it, the message boiled down to: "We don't care how or where you spend it; just keep us out in front."

The Prospect of the Hydrogen Bomb

Behind these generalizations lay a very specific objective. Almost from the moment of Hiroshima, there had been hints of a vastly more terrible "superbomb." Edward Condon warned early in 1946 of bombs a thousand times more powerful "in the near future"; diplomat John J. McCloy made the same prediction in a December 1946 speech, specifically mentioning a hydrogen bomb. After September 24, 1949, theoretical speculation became a matter of urgent policy discussion, and on January 31, 1950, President [Harry] Truman made it official: the AEC would proceed with work "on all forms of atomic weapons, including the so-called hydrogen or superbomb."

The inner history of the hydrogen-bomb decision has been told in the memoirs of participants and in such books as Herbert York's *The Advisors: Oppenheimer, Teller, and the Superbomb* (1976). The conflict between scientists like Edward Teller, Ernest Lawrence, and Luis Alvarez, who favored the hydrogen bomb (who indeed were "drooling" at the prospect, according to Lilienthal), and others who opposed it—including Lilienthal and the eight scientists on the AEC's general advisory committee chaired by Oppenheimer—is by now familiar. As for the larger cultural context of the decision, discussion has focused mainly on the fact that it was made with no involvement by the American people. "This was a secret debate with only a few participants," McGeorge Bundy [national security adviser to presidents Johnson and Kennedy] has written; "no sermons pro or con, no dire public warnings from defenders of security or Cassandras of nuclear catastrophe—no public discussion at all." If only the public had been consulted, some have suggested, the outcome might have been different. This was what could happen "when decisions of far-reaching national significance are made without public scrutiny of pertinent information," wrote physicist Robert F. Bacher, a former AEC commissioner and hydrogen-bomb critic. "The superbomb issue needed to be put before the American people," agreed Eugene Rabinowitch; "Americans must be given the opportunity to decide whether they want to embark on this course."

Would public participation have led to a different decision? Probably not. In a Gallup poll of early February, 69 percent favored building the hydrogen bomb, 9 percent expressed "reluctant approval," while only 14 percent disapproved. Indeed, Truman's announcement aroused little response of any sort. "Many Americans were by no means ready to think about it," observed *Life*, summing up reports from around the nation; "People wanted to talk about anything else but."

Fear of the Soviet Bomb Sped Up the Arms Race

In reflecting on this acquiescent public response, critics of the hydrogen-bomb decision invariably linked it to the larger political climate of 1949–1950. Americans had lost all hope "for international agreements which will have any meaning," said Robert Bacher. "Pumped full of hysteria from Red scares and aggravated by political mudslinging, the average citizen is easily convinced that he can find some security and relief from all of this in the hydrogen bomb." In his 1982 analysis of the hydrogen-bomb decision, McGeorge Bundy, too, stressed the broader political context:

By the end of 1949 the cold war was raging, the Soviet menace was seen everywhere; . . . the Berlin blockade was a recent and instructive memory; the captive nations were not a slogan but a vivid reality, and Soviet hostility and duplicity were taken for granted. . . . "Who lost China?" was the question of the hour. Alger Hiss was convicted in early January, and [the British atomic spy] Klaus Fuchs confessed just four days before Truman's final decision.

Indeed, influential periodicals trumpeted the Russian menace and softpedaled the threat of the hydrogen bomb itself. The bomb made little sense in the "pure economics of destruction," said *Business Week* but its "psychological and political effects . . . would be tremendous." In a special issue on the communist menace two weeks after the hydrogen-bomb decision, *Life* put a mushroom cloud on its cover; warned that the Soviets were "preparing for war" and would use "any atomic agreement" as a pretext to promote "the victory of Communism throughout the world"; and printed alarming charts showing a supposed "Red Military Advantage."

Fear of the bomb remained, but in the context of the Cold War, the Russian bomb, and repeated assertions of Soviet aggressiveness and perfidy, bigger American bombs seemed to many the only hope. The process that had begun gradually around 1947, in which the image of the bomb as a menace to be eliminated was effaced by its image as a vital asset in the intensifying struggle with the Soviet Union, vastly accelerated after September 1949. Political efforts to diminish the atomic threat were now seen as a snare and a delusion; the best hope lay in keeping ahead. In this competition, *Business Week* wrote reassuringly in July 1950, the Russians were "amateurs competing with professionals." They had built their bomb on a crash basis, and "you don't get a broad, sophisticated technique that way." *Look* reported in November 1950 that the nation's "long-hairs" (that is, scientists) were designing intercontinental ballistic missiles that would open "awesome vistas of mass death and destruction." But rather than using this frightening prospect as an argument for intensified international negotiations, as it surely would have in 1945–1947, *Look* concluded: "What we must do next is apply our vast production facilities to the ideas of our 'long-hairs.' Then we will be ready for the war of tomorrow." In a January 1951 report on the nation's atomic arsenal, *U.S. News* noted that while "city busting" bombs remained the "mainstay," an array of smaller tactical bombs and even atomic artillery had been added as well. America's "headstart in atomic development is being maintained and even extended. If Russia wants an atomic war, she'll get it in more ways than she expects."

Fear of the Russians had driven fear of the bomb into the deeper recesses of consciousness. That the public did not participate in the hydrogen-bomb decision "hardly mattered," said *Business Week*, since Truman's directive so clearly reflected the general will. "In the frightened months right after the Soviet atomic explosion," it said, "the mere public intimation that a [hydrogen bomb] might be possible guaranteed the attempt." In a 1950 poll of 2,700 Cornell University students, 40 percent said "an all-out war to stop communism, would be either "Very Worthwhile" (26 percent) or "Fairly Worthwhile" (14 percent). In a July 1950 Gallup poll, 77 percent of Americans said the United States should use the atomic bomb in any future world war. The following January, 66 percent said the U.S. should drop the bomb first in any full-scale war with Russia.

In November 1950, President Truman asked Congress for a billion dollars for nuclear-weapons production. The Du Pont Corporation undertook to build a giant hydrogen-bomb facility for the same "dollar-a-year" fee it had received during the Manhattan Project. Research on the "Super" under Edward Teller again turned Los Alamos into a bustling center where the mood, according to *Business Week*, was "adventurous" and "exuberant." The AEC's contract with General Electric to build a prototype atomic-power plant was terminated to free more scientists and technicians for bomb production. These developments attracted little public attention. The terrible simplifications of the Cold War had seized the American mind, and all issues, even the atomic threat, realigned themselves along the new ideological lines of force. As MIT mathematician Norbert Wiener wrote in July 1950, the probability of atomic annihilation would remain high "so long as we are dominated by a rigid propaganda which makes the destruction of Russia appear more important than our own survival."

Should the Bomb Be Used in Korea?

The extent to which Cold War obsessions overrode earlier atomic fears is evident in the discussions surrounding the possible use of atomic bombs in the Korean War. Some periodicals advised against it. "The best hope now of preventing the 'police action' from ballooning into a superwar," said the *Saturday Evening Post*, "may lie in a conservative attitude toward the A-bomb." Others, however, discussed the matter quite coolly, as a viable option to be carefully weighed. *Science News Letter* concluded that North Korea's few urban-industrial centers probably did not "warrant" atomic bombing. After an assessment of the tactical pros and cons that ignored any larger considerations, *U.S. News and World Report* concluded that American use of atomic weapons in Korea would probably be "sparing."

"The first flash of the Communist guns," in Korea, wrote William L. Laurence, had unmasked "the Kremlin's ultimate intentions to enslave mankind" and "illuminated for us more clearly than ever before the path we must follow in our policy on atomic weapons": full speed ahead, especially on the hydrogen bomb. On a different cultural front, composer Fred Kirby's 1950 country song "When the Hell Bomb Falls" mingled images of nuclear destruction with the wish that God would "lend a helping hand" in Korea. In Roy Acuff's "Advice to Joe" (1951), the wish became explicit with the warning to the Russians that when Moscow has been obliterated, they will regret their aggressive ambitions. "When atomic bombs start falling," the song asks Stalin, "do you have a place to hide?"

And what of the man in the street? In August 1950, the Gallup poll found 28 percent of Americans in favor of using the atomic bomb in Korea. When Chinese troops entered the war in November, *U.S. News* noted a "wave of demand" for atomic bombing them. By November 1951, with the war in a costly, frustrating stalemate, 51 percent supported dropping the bomb on "military targets."

In this instance, mass culture and popular attitudes mirrored thinking at the highest level of government. In 1952, in two memos evidently drafted for his eyes only, President Truman contemplated a nuclear ultimatum to the Soviets and the Chinese as a way of ending the war. In 1953, President Eisenhower and the National Security Council seriously considered the direct use of atomic weapons against the Chinese and North Koreans.

Chapter 2

Cold War Hot Spots: Confrontation in the Nuclear Age

Turning|Points
IN WORLD HISTORY

The Korean War and the Limits of the Cold War Balance of Power

David Rees

Historian David Rees enjoyed a lengthy and diverse schol-
arly career, which included authoring one of the first and
most respected histories of the Korean War. Here Rees
discusses the conflict in Korea in terms of two separate
showdowns: first, the military struggle between the North
Koreans (and their Chinese allies) and the South Koreans
(and their U.S. allies); second, the political struggle between proponents of limited American involvement, such
as Harry S. Truman, and those who favored all-out en-
gagement to counteract communism, such as Douglas
MacArthur. Rees claims that the battle in Korea tested
Truman's resolve in containing the advance of communism (a strategy he had adopted in 1947) as well as his
ability to prevent the escalation of a regional conflict into
nuclear world war. Rees notes that the difficulty of the latter was compounded by MacArthur, who used his public
standing as a hero of World War II to criticize Truman's
military policies, which MacArthur considered too hesi-
tant in answering communist aggression. The outcome of
the Korean War, Rees maintains, reaffirmed the status
quo: Communism was prevented from advancing into
South Korea but was allowed to retain a foothold in
North Korea, and the United States deemed the Soviet
Union, not Red China, its primary Cold War enemy.

When the massed armies of Communist China crossed the
Yalu in October 1950 to enter the Korean War, fighting had

Excerpted from *The Age of Containment: The Cold War, 1945–1965*, by David Rees
(London: Macmillan, 1968). Copyright © 1967 by David Rees. Reprinted by permission of the publisher.

already been going on for four months in what had been known for centuries as the 'Land of the Morning Calm'. The development of the war in Korea has a special importance in the history of the cold war, for it is the only instance—at the time of writing [1968]—in which the Communists have resorted to direct conventional military aggression. And the manœuvres of the great powers involved to limit the savage fighting to Korea are relevant in answering the question: how does the West best defend its interests in an age when general war will result in the atomic holocaust?

But in any case, no one foresaw in 1947 that it would be in Korea that [Soviet premier Joseph] Stalin's great offensive against the West would come to its climax. The country was partitioned between the Russians and the Americans in 1945 as a military arrangement to facilitate the Japanese surrender, and the demarcation line of the 38th Parallel soon became the iron curtain in the Far East. By 1948 two rival régimes, each claiming sovereignty over the whole country, had been established, the Republic of Korea in the south, and in the north the Democratic People's Republic of Korea. The southern regime was established after UN-supervised elections; but that in the Soviet zone was a creation of the Russian occupation authorities. In June 1949 US occupation troops were withdrawn from South Korea, and both General Douglas MacArthur, who had ruled Japan in vice-regal style as the Supreme Commander for the Allies since 1945, and the Administration in Washington had decided that South Korea lay outside the US Pacific defence-perimeter, a fact which [President Harry S. Truman's secretary of state Dean] Acheson publicly acknowledged in January 1950. Budgetary economies also contributed to the US withdrawal.

American Withdrawal Creates an Opportunity for Communist Expansion

With Soviet expansionist adventures blocked in Europe by NATO, the withdrawal from South Korea unfortunately created a certain ambiguity in American policy; it seems likely that Moscow calculated that the United States *might* tolerate a take-over in South Korea, a country in a remoter sector of the cold war. Ample evidence exists of a North Korean Army build-up during the winter of 1949–50; and on 25 June 1950 seven North Korean infantry divisions and an armoured division struck across the 38th Parallel. The invaders were equipped with Soviet arms, including T-34 tanks and Yak fighters; Soviet instructors advised the higher echelons of the North Korean Army; that the invasion could have been launched without Moscow's sanction is inconceivable. Truman's historic response to this brazen aggression is described in his *Memoirs* as 'the toughest decision' of his presidency. Air and naval assistance was immediately given to the Republic of Korea (ROK); and following this action the UN Security Council, free to act for once owing to the absence of the Soviet delegate and his veto which had paralysed the Council ever since 1945, recommended to UN members that they furnish aid to South Korea 'to repel the armed attack'. Eventually, fifteen UN members sent forces to Korea to serve in the UN Command, although of course the basis of the resistance to the Communist armies was American power.

Within a week of the invasion Truman had ordered MacArthur to send in US ground troops from Japan. As the UN forces were pushed back to the Pusan perimeter in south-east Korea—many prophesied an evacuation—MacArthur (designated the first UN Commander) planned and executed the Napoleonic manœuvre of the Inchon landing on 15 September 1950; the old soldier placed a Marine division two hundred miles behind the enemy's lines. The North Korean Army disintegrated, and the UN General Assembly voted for a 'united, independent and democratic Korea'— which could only come about by a US advance to the Manchurian border. Yet the drive to Yalu, which got under way in October 1950, was an abandonment of containment [the established policy of limiting, rather than reversing, Communist expansion]—it aimed at the 'liberation' of a Communist satellite. Direct Soviet intervention to save the North Korean régime might well have precipitated general war; it was left to Communist China to salvage the Pyongyang government. In mid-October the first of 350,000 men of the Chinese Communist Forces (CCF) crossed the

Yalu; in late November MacArthur's final 'Home by Christmas' offensive to the Yalu was smashed on the Chongchon River by the Chinese, who then moved south to the 38th Parallel. When Truman and [British prime minister Clement] Attlee, meeting in Washington in December 1950, decided to abandon the aim of uniting Korea, but to defend the 38th Parallel, MacArthur protested that the conflict should be carried to the 'privileged sanctuary' of Manchuria to win the war.

Disagreement Between Truman and MacArthur

The next few months were crucial as the battlefront seesawed up and down the peninsula. In early 1951, reinforced US divisions, with a strong British contingent, held the CCF (Chinese Communist Forces) south of the 38th Parallel while inflicting huge casualties. When MacArthur continued his public protests ('There is no substitute for victory. . . .') Truman, on 11 April 1951, dismissed his overmighty subject and outlined his policy as one of fighting a limited war in Korea, so as to avoid a third world war. Yet on his return to the United States, MacArthur was given a Roman triumph in New York. But first he had outlined his views on the Korean War to a joint session of Congress on 19 April [1951], after receiving a welcome in the nation's capital almost unsurpassed in its history:

> Mr. President [of the Senate], Mr. Speaker, distinguished members of Congress. . . . I do not stand here for any partisan cause, for the issues are fundamental and reach quite beyond the realm of partisan consideration. They must be resolved on the highest plane of national interest if our course is to prove sound and our future protected. . . . I address you with neither rancour nor bitterness in the fading twilight of my life but with one purpose, to serve my country. . . .
>
> Our victory [in Korea] was complete and our objectives within reach when Red China intervened with numerically superior ground forces. . . . While no man in his right mind would advocate sending our ground forces into continental China, and such was never given thought, the new situation did urgently demand a drastic revision of strategic planning

if our political aim was to defeat this enemy as we had defeated the old. . . .

(1) The intensification of the economic blockade of China.

(2) The imposition of a naval blockade against the China coast.

(3) Removal of restrictions on air reconnaissance of China's coastal areas and of Manchuria.

(4) Removal of restrictions on the forces of the Republic of China on Formosa with logistical support to contribute to their effective operations against the Chinese mainland. . . .

It has been said [MacArthur went on] in effect that I was a war-monger. Nothing could be further from the truth. I know war as few other men living know it, and nothing, to me, is more revolting. I have long advocated its complete abolition, as its very destructiveness on both friend and foe has rendered it useless as a means of settling international disputes. . . . But once war is forced upon us, there is no other alternative than to apply every available means to bring it to a swift end. . . . War's very object is victory, not prolonged indecision. In war there is no substitute for victory. There are some who, for varying reasons, would appease Red China. They are blind to history's clear lesson, for history teaches, with unmistakable emphasis, that appeasement but begets new and bloodier war. It points to no single instance where this end has justified that means. . . . Like blackmail, it lays the basis for new and successively greater demands until, as in blackmail, violence becomes the only other alternative. Why, my soldiers asked of me, surrender military advantage to an enemy in the field? I could not answer. . . .

MacArthur's attack on the Truman administration's concept of limited war in Korea was followed by a historic Congressional investigation, by the Senate Foreign Relations and Armed Services committees, into the General's dismissal, the Korean War, and indeed the whole basis of American foreign policy. To MacArthur's charge that the Truman administration had 'no policy . . . nothing . . . no plan or anything,' General George Marshall, the Defence

Secretary, outlined the essence of the containment policy in words that are as apposite today as they were in 1951:

> There can be, I think, no quick and decisive solution to the global struggle short of resorting to another world war. The cost of such a conflict is beyond calculation. It is therefore our policy to contain Communist aggression in different fashions in different areas without resorting to total war. . . . The application of this policy has not always been easy or popular. . . .

Marshall was followed by General [Omar] Bradley, Chairman of the Joint Chiefs of Staff, who deflated MacArthur's strategy of total victory in Korea by reminding his listeners of the classical approach that the most dangerous enemy was the strongest enemy:

> The Joint Chiefs of Staff, in view of their global responsibilities and their perspective with respect to the world-wide strategic situation, are in a better position than is any single theatre commander to assess the risks of general war. Moreover the Joint Chiefs of Staff are best able to judge our own military resources with which to meet that risk. . . . From a global viewpoint . . . our military mission is to support a policy preventing Communism from gaining the manpower, the resources, the raw material and in the industrial capacity essential to world domination. If Soviet Russia ever controls the Eurasian land mass, then the Soviet-satellite imperialism may have the broad base upon which to build the military power to rule the world. . . . Korea, in spite of the importance of the engagement, must be looked upon with proper perspective. It is just one engagement, just one phase of the battle. . . . As long as we keep the conflict within its present scope, we are holding to a minimum the force we must commit and tie down. . . . We have recommended against enlarging the war. . . . Red China is not the powerful nation seeking to dominate the world. Frankly, in the opinion of the Joint Chiefs of Staff the [MacArthur] strategy would involve us in the wrong war, at the wrong place, at the wrong time, and with the wrong enemy. . . .

Yet the drama was not ended with the uproar surrounding

MacArthur's recall. Two further mass CCF offensives, aimed at the conquest of South Korea, in April and May 1951, were smashed by US firepower in a spectacular trial of strength around the Parallel, a victory which we see in retrospect marked the beginning of the end for Stalin's great offensive against the West. Defeated on the battlefield, the Communists sued for peace on the basis of the *status quo*, and in July armistice negotiations began at Kaesong, being later transferred to Panmunjom. Bitter fighting still went on at the main line of resistance slightly north of the Parallel, as at Panmunjom the delegations argued interminably over the armistice terms, and over north-west Korea, where massed formations of Russian-built MIG jet-fighters based in Manchuria attacked UN air formations, 'some of the greatest air battles of history were fought at this time', according to the USAF Korean War historian, Robert Futrell—evidence of the achievements of Soviet technology which had also developed the hydrogen bomb during the war.

The armistice agreement, signed at Panmunjom on 27 July 1953, after [Eisenhower administration secretary of state John Foster] Dulles had threatened Peking through Indian diplomatic channels that atomic war might soon be carried to mainland China, confirmed the partition of Korea based essentially on the battlefront of July 1951. Communist China had fought the United States to a standstill. As far as the United Nations and the United States were concerned, aggression had been repelled and collective security upheld though at the sacrifice of 140,000 US casualties. The total casualties of this great war without victory totalled four million. Fittingly enough, Stalin's war was not ended until after Stalin's death [Stalin died in March 1953]. But by the time of the Panmunjom armistice new leaders were implementing new strategies on both sides of the iron curtain.

Anticommunism and the "Red Scare" of the 1950s

Stephen J. Whitfield

The "red scare" of the early 1950s was the direct result of demonizing the Soviets but being unable or unwilling to engage them militarily, argues Stephen J. Whitfield, professor of American Studies at Brandeis University in Waltham, Massachusetts. Whitfield claims that growing frustration among Americans at the resilience of the Soviets led to the punishment of supposed Communist sympathizers in the United States because striking out against the Soviets directly involved too great a risk of nuclear war. Whitfield argues that as anticommunism became the ideological norm not only in American politics but in the society in general, anti-Communist zealots like Senator Joseph McCarthy adopted behaviors that were, ironically, a milder form of the authoritarianism they found so objectionable in the Soviet Union. Whitfield stresses that the repression of dissent in the Soviet Union was generally more consistent and severe than in the United States (even at the height of "McCarthyism"), but also argues that the "red scare" represents the inherent potential for abuse when extreme patriotism and a single-minded ideology are combined.

Since a preventive nuclear war to roll back the Soviets was excluded as a policy option, anti-Communism seemed to redouble its energies at home. The invulnerability of so resolute an enemy as the Soviet Union was novel to American statecraft, and this fact helps render intelligible the punitive and malicious excesses of the Red Scare. Forbearance was

Excerpted from *The Culture of the Cold War*, 2nd ed., by Stephen J. Whitfield (Baltimore, MD: Johns Hopkins University Press, 1996). Copyright © 1996 by Johns Hopkins University Press. Reprinted with permission.

too ambiguous. Unable to strike directly at the Russians, the most vigilant patriots went after the scalps of their country-men instead. Since [Soviet premier Joseph] Stalin and his successors were out of reach, making life difficult for Americans who admired them was more practicable. Since NATO [the North Atlantic Treaty Organization] would not come to the rescue of Eastern Europe, at least some politically sus-pect writers could be kept from traveling to Western Eu-rope. Since breath could not be restored to all the victims whom the N.K.V.D. [the precursor to the KGB and the group that carried out the Stalinist "terrors" of the 1930s] murdered, at least some Hollywood screenwriters could be sent to prison. Since the Korean War was a stalemate, per-haps the Cold War could be won at home. And also because few citizens could sustain a lively interest in foreign policy, anti-Communism was intensified on American soil.

With the source of the evil so elusive and so immune to risk-free retaliation, American culture was politicized. The values and perceptions, the forms of expression, the sym-bolic patterns, the beliefs and myths that enabled Americans to make sense of reality—these constituents of culture were contaminated by an unseemly political interest in their roots and consequences. The struggle against domestic Commu-nism encouraged an interpenetration of the two enterprises of politics and culture, resulting in a philistine inspection of artistic works not for their content but for the *politique des auteurs* [politics of their authors]. Censors endorsed the boy-cott of films that they had not seen; vigilantes favored the re-moval from library shelves of books that they had not read.

The Arts Under Suspicion

The confusion of the public and private realms was also characteristic of the era. Thus, the Federal Bureau of Inves-tigation compiled dossiers on novelists who seemed unduly critical of their native land, and the bureau got into the movie business by secretly filming the patrons of a left-wing bookstore, Four Continents, in New York. At the same time, some representatives of Hollywood presented themselves to Congress as authorities on the theory and tactics of

Marxism-Leninism. An awed member of the House Committee on Un-American Activities (HUAC) hailed even the mother of musical star Ginger Rogers as "one of the outstanding experts on communism in the United State," for example. While legislators were interrogating musicians and actors about their beliefs, university administrators were using political instead of academic criteria to evaluate the fitness of teachers. Even as some clergymen were advocating ferocious military measures to defeat an enemy that was constantly described as "atheistic," government officials were themselves asserting that the fundamental problem presented by Communism was not political but spiritual.

Citizens were expected to enlist in the Cold War. Neutrality was suspect, and so was a lack of enthusiasm for defining American society as beleaguered. Near the end of playwright Arthur Miller's testimony before HUAC, a congressman asked him to help make literature *engagé* [involved in the ideological fight against communism]. "Why do you not direct some of that magnificent ability you have to fighting against well-known Communist subversive conspiracies in our country and in the world?" Representative Clyde Doyle (D-Cal.) asked. "Why do you not direct your magnificent talents to that, in part? I mean more positively?" The right of officialdom to interfere in cultural affairs was so taken for granted that occasional skepticism stood out. On one occasion a senator, his young aides, and a right-wing newspaper columnist were discussing with Martin Merson, the assistant director of the International Information Agency, whether to blacklist the music of Aaron Copland, the nation's most distinguished composer. Sitting in on "the Copland colloquy," Merson "was suddenly struck by the ludicrousness of the whole evening's performance. [Roy M.] Cohn, [G. David] Schine, [Senator Joseph R.] McCarthy, [George] Sokolsky, and for that matter the rest of us, meeting to discuss the manners and morals of our times. By whose appointment? By what right? What qualification did any of us have?" No more, certainly, than did Congressman Donald L. Jackson (R-Cal.), who objected to the participation of the Soviet Union's most honored composer at the "Cultural and Scientific Conference for

World Peace," held in New York in 1949: "[Dmitri] Shostakovich has the same right to attend a cultural conference as a rattlesnake has to be at the altar of a church.". . .

Citizens Under Suspicion

In the United States the application of political tests was not systematic, though it was not entirely haphazard either. Sometimes the tests were imposed by agencies of the federal government and were designed to intimidate other branches or the private sector. Sometimes the demands of hyperpatriotism reflected the efforts of private employers, sometimes of self-appointed monitors of political morality who acted with official complicity. Sometimes the private sphere was ahead of the government in such efforts at regulation and purification. But the effect was the same: the suffocation of liberty and the debasement of culture itself. Even by the narrowest chauvinistic criteria of the Cold War, the United States thus diminished its ability in the global struggle to be seen as an attractive and just society. The politicization of culture might win the allegiance of those who cherished authority, but not of those who valued autonomy. The politicization of culture might appeal to reactionaries abroad, but not to foreigners who appreciated creativity or critical thought.

And though the state was intimately involved in restricting liberty, it acted with popular approval and acquiescence; the will of the majority was not thwarted. In effect, Americans imposed a starchy repression upon themselves, and without denying rights to minorities—certain political factions on the right, for example. Indeed, American Legionnaires and the Catholic War Veterans were exercising their First Amendment rights in seeking to prevent other Americans from attending particular films and plays. The opportunity to dissuade other citizens from patronizing an institution or an individual has long been included in the definition of a democracy, and the marketplace—including the marketplace of ideas—has accepted the notion that unpopularity is decisive. No company, including a movie studio or a television network, is obligated to keep on its payroll those from whom the public has explicitly withdrawn its favor. Nor did principled foes of the right to boycott condemn such tactics; differences arose only over the choice of targets.

Government agencies acted improperly because they barged into areas where they did not belong and thus cor-

---

A Satirical Take on Nuclear Anxiety

Tom Lehrer led an unusual double life, working for much of his life as a mathematics scholar—including a stint at the Los Alamos National Laboratory, where the original atomic bomb was built—but also enjoying a lengthy career as a writer of satirical songs. A frequent topic of his dark sense of humor was nuclear war, as is the case with his 1959 song "We Will All Go Together When We Go." In this song, he comically expresses the growing nuclear anxiety of the 1950s by explaining how nuclear war would eliminate the need for grieving since everyone would "go" at the same time.

> When you attend a funeral,
> It is sad to think that sooner or
> Later those you love will do the same for you.
> And you may have thought it tragic,
> Not to mention other adjec-
> Tives, to think of all the weeping they will do.
> But don't you worry.
> No more ashes, no more sackcloth.
> And an armband made of black cloth
> Will some day never more adorn a sleeve.
> For if the bomb that drops on you
> Gets your friends and neighbors too,
> There'll be nobody left behind to grieve.
> And we will all go together when we go.
> What a comforting fact that is to know.
> Universal bereavement,
> An inspiring achievement,
> Yes, we all will go together when we go.
> We will all go together when we go.
> All suffuse with an incandescent glow.
> No one will have the endurance
> To collect on his insurance,
> Lloyd's of London will be loaded when they go.

rupted the sphere of expression that the First Amendment was designed to protect. In denying to the assorted talents who contributed to the nation's culture a level playing field, the House Committee on Un-American Activities, the Sub-

---

Oh we will all fry together when we fry.
We'll be french fried potatoes by and by.
There will be no more misery
When the world is our rotisserie,
Yes, we will all fry together when we fry.
Down by the old maelstrom,
There'll be a storm before the calm.
And we will all bake together when we bake.
There'll be nobody present at the wake.
With complete participation
In that grand incineration,
Nearly three billion hunks of well-done steak.
Oh we will all char together when we char.
And let there be no moaning of the bar.
Just sing out a *Te Deum*
When you see that I.C.B.M. [intercontinental ballistic missile],
And the party will be "come as you are."
Oh we will all burn together when we burn.
There'll be no need to stand and wait your turn.
When it's time for the fallout
And Saint Peter calls us all out,
We'll just drop our agendas and adjourn.
You will all go directly to your respective Valhallas.
Go directly, do not pass Go, do not collect two hundred dolla's.
And we will all go together when we go.
Ev'ry Hottenhot and ev'ry Eskimo.
When the air becomes uranious,
And we will all go simultaneous.
Yes we all will go together
When we all go together,
Yes we all will go together when we go.

Tom Lehrer, "We Will All Go Together When We Go," from *More of Tom Lehrer*, Lehrer Records #TL 102, 1959. Rereleased Rhino Records, *Songs and More Songs by Tom Lehrer*, R2 72776, 1997.

committee on Investigations of the Senate Committee on Government Operations, the Senate Internal Security Sub-committee, and the Federal Bureau of Investigation were the most conspicuous offenders. To acknowledge that their efforts were often clumsy, spasmodic, and feckless, or that some citizens were plucky enough to defend themselves, is proof that a genuinely totalitarian impulse could gain little traction on American soil. But to minimize the danger that such interference posed is like saying that fear of rape is unfounded because its attempt was bungled or resisted. . . .

Anti-Communism Begins to Resemble Communism . . . Sort Of

Central to totalitarianism, for example, was the denial of what the political philosopher Hannah Arendt had called "the right to have rights." For both the Third Reich and the Soviet Union had turned certain groups into pariahs, whose exclusion from the political community was so complete that they could make no claims upon it. Nothing so absolute happened in the 1950s to American Communists, or those believed to be Communists, or those who might be sympathetic to Communists. But their "right to have rights" was imperiled. Their opportunities for political association and utterance, their freedom of movement, their chances of employment (even when the risk to national security was irrelevant), were all withdrawn or seriously curtailed. [President Dwight D.] Eisenhower's 1954 State of the Union address had even proposed depriving Communists of their citizenship. According to a national poll that Harvard's Samuel A. Stouffer administered, 80 percent of the populace agreed with the president's suggestion; 52 percent wanted all Communists jailed; 77 percent wanted them banned from the radio. For good measure, 42 percent of those polled thought that *no* member of the press should be permitted to criticize the "American form of government."

For Stalinism was considered so dangerous and so sinister that democratic procedures could be suspended in the effort to combat it, and so urgent and pervasive was this crisis that anti-Communism assumed some of the same guises as its target. The most ardent variety of anti-Communism became, in the phrase of the political scientist Michael Paul Rogin, a species of "political demonology," in which the threat was exaggerated, intensified, and finally dehumanized. "The counter-subversive needs monsters to give shape to his anxieties and to permit him to indulge his forbidden desires," Rogin argued. "Demonization allows the counter-subversive, in the name of battling the subversive, to imitate his enemy."

Consider that the Committee on Socialism and Communism of the Chamber of Commerce proposed in 1946 and 1948 to remove liberals, socialists, and Communists from opinion-forming agencies. Communists, fellow-travelers, and "dupes" would not be permitted to teach in schools, or work in libraries, or write for newspapers, or participate in the entertainment industries. By 1952, this advocacy of thought control had become the official position of the Chamber of Commerce. Those of dubious political reliability would also be prohibited from employment in "any plant large enough to have a labor union"—thus foreclosing for radical workers as well as left intellectuals opportunities to earn a living. The implementation of such purges could not be entrusted to authorities but was to be a civic responsibility. Local members of the Chamber of Commerce were advised to "be on the alert for Communist sympathizers in your community," to "find out from reputable sources such as *Counterattack, Alert* or the American Legion about Communist sympathizers in the entertainment field," to be on the lookout for Communists "promoting appeasement in the name of peace," to "support patriotic ex-Communists who cooperate with the FBI," and to "identify public officials . . . displaying softness toward Communism." The systematic scope of the political mobilization that the Chamber of Commerce recommended was a facsimile of totalitarianism.

Another example of this mimetic [imitative; taking on the characteristics of something else] effect was the attitude toward historical knowledge. About three months after Stalin's death, his successors on the Presidium of the Soviet Central Committee decided to shoot Lavrentii P. Beria, the secret police chief. Soon thereafter the owners of the *Great Soviet Encyclopedia* received so important an article on the Bering Straits that readers were instructed to cut out with a razor blade the published biography and photo of Beria and insert the new geographic information instead. The late head of the M.V.D. [the Soviet Ministry for State Security] thus sank into a black hole of oblivion. The next year the American poet Langston Hughes published a set of biographical essays, *Famous American Negroes,* and acceded to the wishes of his publisher [Dodd, Mead] by dropping the entry on W.E.B. Du Bois, who was the most distinguished Afro-American intellectual who ever lived. But by 1954 Du Bois had also become a reliable fellow traveler, and thus he risked transformation into a nonperson. He was not even mentioned in Hughes's chapter on Booker T. Washington, who had been Du Bois's chief antagonist in the black community at the turn of the century. Such Orwellian airbrushing of history was more arbitrary, ephemeral, and inefficient than in the Soviet Union, and in the United States such efforts at inducing amnesia could also backfire. Less than a decade later, several publishers yielded to right-wing intimidation and dropped from their own history textbooks the name of—among others—Langston Hughes.

The difference between Stalinist Russia and America—even when the superpatriots could play out their most vindictive fantasies—was still extreme, however. In the Soviet Union, the penalties for dissidence were lethal; countless innocent citizens were tortured, suffering ostracism and penury even if they managed to survive. For other Soviet citizens, the right to privacy, as well as the option to be nonpolitical, was also denied. During a 1934 writers' conference in Moscow, Isaac Babel had puckishly championed a right to silence. Three years later the self-proclaimed "master of the genre of silence" was arrested; he died—perhaps shot to death—in the Gulag Archipelago in 1939 or 1940. A phrase like "the great fear," coined just before the French Revolution and applied by historian David Caute to American society during the Cold War, fits Stalinist Russia best of all.

In the United States, the penalties for political dissidence were capricious. The sanctions were generally economic and social rather than legal. The victims of this Red Scare were usually deprived of their livelihood, not of their lives. For the "natural" tendency of Bolshevism was domination and subjugation, the denial of legitimacy to any political opposition. "We are all Chekists," Lenin had once asserted to Party comrades, affirming their complicity with the secret police. The "natural" tendency of the American political system, however, has been the give-and-take of partisan bargaining, the compromises negotiated according to the accepted rules of a rambunctious democracy. Jefferson's first inaugural address had proclaimed that "every difference of opinion is not a difference of principle. . . . We are all Republicans, we are all Federalists." And the few Americans who were not might well have meditated on the virtues of such comity [civility, tolerance].

Berlin and Cuba: Cold War Confrontation at Its Peak

Norman Friedman

The Cuban Missile Crisis of October 1962 is perhaps the single most identifiable historical moment of the Cold War, but it has largely overshadowed another equally perilous showdown that took place a year earlier in the occupied German city of Berlin. Naval historian and military strategist Norman Friedman compares the nature and relevance of these two confrontations between the United States and Soviet Union, examining them both in relation to President John F. Kennedy's political philosophy. Friedman argues that Kennedy's frequent practice of overstating the military capabilities of the Soviet Union was in part responsible for escalating conflicts over Berlin in 1961 and over the placement of Soviet missiles in Cuba in 1962. Friedman claims that Kennedy's campaign rhetoric about a dangerous "missile gap" developing between the United States and the Soviet Union, combined with Soviet premier Nikita Khrushchev's confrontational and inconsistent foreign policy, created a series of misunderstandings, deceptions, and bluffs that greatly exaggerated the willingness of either nation to enter into actual combat with the other. According to Friedman, this artificially inflated atmosphere of hostility resulted in the military and political maneuvers in Germany and Cuba that seemed to bring the two superpowers to the brink of direct combat.

The wars of national liberation [a series of regional conflicts in Africa, Latin America, and Southeast Asia during the early 1960s in which the United States and Soviet Union finan-

Excerpted from *The Fifty Year War: Conflict and Strategy in the Cold War*, by Norman Friedman (Annapolis, MD: Naval Institute Press, 2000). Copyright © 2000 by Norman Friedman. Reprinted with permission.

cially, and occasionally militarily, supported rival factions] were not [President John F.] Kennedy's only Communist problems. His habit of overdramatization and his ignorance of nuclear reality caused near-disaster, first in Berlin and then in Cuba. By 1961 Walter Ulbricht of East Germany really was facing a crisis. Due to its four-power status, [Berlin had been divided into four zones of control after WWII, with Britain, France, the United States, and the Soviet Union each controlling a part] a relic of the 1945 peace settlement, Berlin was the one gap in the wall that contained the East Germans. About four million East Germans left between 1948 and 1961, including the best engineers and technicians. By 1961 so many workers had left that the ratio of workers to children was only four to three, and only 45 percent of the East German population was male. For example, an attempt to gain prestige by developing an East German airliner failed when too many of the engineers involved went West. In the spring of 1961 it seemed to [Soviet premier Nikita] Khrushchev that East Germany might collapse. A wag on Khrushchev's staff told him that soon the only one left in East Germany would be its unpopular ruler, Walter Ulbricht.

The situation was aggravated by efforts to prop up the East German economy: Westerners were buying goods the Soviets were subsidizing, taking advantage of the low prices and the low exchange rate. Ulbricht demanded foodstuffs, such as butter, which was in short supply within the Soviet Union. Khrushchev refused to provide replacements for the fleeing East Germans: "We won the war; our workers will not clean your toilets." However, Ulbricht knew that an East German collapse would be a disaster for Khrushchev, who badly wanted to announce some sort of victory at the Twenty-second Party Congress in October 1961.

The Vienna Meeting

Khrushchev tried once more to obtain a peace treaty, which would cut off West Berlin by ending its four-power status. In February 1961 he told the West Germans that a peace treaty must be concluded before their fall elections. As the crisis deepened, Kennedy met Khrushchev in Vienna on 4 June. Khrushchev demanded a settlement by December. After that the United States would have to fight for access to the city. That would mean nuclear war. Unlike Eisenhower, Kennedy would not bet that Khrushchev did not consider Berlin worth that price.

Kennedy spoke to Khrushchev as though the two countries were at rough strategic parity. His words probably echoed his missile gap campaign rhetoric. [Kennedy had won the 1960 presidential election in part thanks to stirring fears about a growing gap between U.S. and U.S.S.R. nuclear arsenals] Khrushchev was astounded. He knew Kennedy enjoyed crushing superiority. If Kennedy behaved so weakly when he held most of the cards, he would really become cooperative as Khrushchev's forces grew. It did not help when Kennedy spoke of Sino-Soviet forces to a man under attack for alienating the Chinese. Kennedy had completely forgotten his recent briefings on the developing schism. To his advisors, Khrushchev stressed Kennedy's ignorance and narrowness; he could not match Eisenhower.

Khrushchev seems to have been little affected by what Westerners considered Kennedy's disastrously weak demeanor in the face of Khrushchev's threats and his self-confidence. Kennedy said that Khrushchev had "treated him like a little boy." He told *New York Times* reporter James Reston that the meeting with Khrushchev was the "worst thing in my life. He savaged me." Khrushchev knew that Kennedy was sensitive about wars of national liberation: he called them holy wars. He clearly felt he had won the summit; he was in very high spirits when he returned to Moscow.

Thus Kennedy was partly defeated by a combination of poor U.S. intelligence (the JCS [Joint Chiefs of Staff] figures he got grossly overestimated Soviet forces) and by his continuing belief in a nonexistent missile gap. Khrushchev managed to conceal his gross weakness from a very uncomfortable Kennedy. His bluff paid off; Kennedy emerged badly frightened. In much the same way he later justified his decision to fight in Vietnam, he told Fred Dutton, secretary of the cabinet, that he had to fight for Berlin; he could not tolerate a third defeat after the Bay of Pigs and Laos. Dutton translated: "It's more than the Cold War. It's saving Kennedy's presidency." However, he must already have been nervous. Dean Acheson, a key advisor, argued that in the past Berlin had been protected by U.S. nuclear threats, but that in the wake of the summit they were no longer credible. He concluded that Kennedy ought to prepare for nuclear war. Kennedy probably doubted that Berlin was worth that much.

Confrontation in Berlin

A Berlin Task Force developed a contingency plan to send a force down the autobahn to the city. It would fight if necessary, even though it would be destroyed. Larger forces would then be drawn in. The Soviets had at least one spy on the task force; Khrushchev knew about the plan, and about its likely consequences.

Khrushchev was more realistic than Kennedy was. He wanted a tactical victory, not nuclear chaos. If he signed the threatened separate treaty with the East Germans, Ulbricht was just foolish enough to try to throw the Westerners out of the city. Late in July Khrushchev decided to solve the problem by closing the border, despite physical and political problems raised by his German experts and by his ambassador to East Germany. This should not have been a total surprise. As early as March, in a Top Secret eyes-only cable for the president and the secretary of state, Ambassador Llewellyn Thompson had predicted from Moscow that sooner or later the Soviets would seal off East Berlin to stop the flow of refugees. Thompson asked what the U.S. would do if the Soviets acted without disturbing Allied access.

What happened next is puzzling. Probably Khrushchev managed to let Kennedy know what he intended to do. On 25 July Kennedy made a belligerent speech, almost threatening nuclear war—but he referred to West Berlin, rather than to Berlin itself. He seemed to imply that there would be no reaction as long as West Berlin was left undisturbed. The speech can, therefore, be read as posturing, cloaking Kennedy's retreat. On a 30 July television show, moreover, Sen. William Fulbright, chairman of the Senate Foreign Relations Committee, in effect suggested that Khrushchev close off East Berlin. Kennedy remarked simply that the U.S. neither encouraged nor discouraged refugees, which was hardly the usual anti-Communist stance.

Khrushchev had probably already made his decision. On 13 August the East Germans began to wall off East Berlin. Kennedy later admitted his relief; with the wall up, it was no longer nearly so urgent for Khrushchev to threaten West Berlin. His weak response probably encouraged Khrushchev to keep the threat of a separate peace treaty alive.

Probably in September, Kennedy learned that he might have a real window of opportu-

Nikita Khrushchev

nity. New studies confirmed that the Soviet early warning system had little chance of detecting low-flying bombers. A small force of twenty-one such aircraft might virtually disarm the Soviet Union by destroying forty-two key targets. Few civilians would be killed. The first bombs to go off would tell the Soviets they were under attack, but their ICBMs [intercontinental ballistic missiles] at standby status, would take one to three hours (according to the JCS) to get to launch status—more than enough time for SAC [Strategic Air Command] bombers to destroy them. A surprise attack plan was prepared as a response to possible Soviet action over Berlin.

In fact, after August, the crisis was an illusion. Khrushchev took until November to withdraw his December deadline for a settlement, but from his point of view the crisis had ended with his decision to build the wall and thus end Ulbricht's own problem. Berlin had never been worth dying for.

Meanwhile [Secretary of Defense Robert] McNamara learned that NATO already had much of the nonnuclear capability Kennedy wanted, particularly since the Soviets were moving troops to the Chinese frontier in view of the continuing schism. He was surprised at the cool reception he received. The Europeans feared that if the wild Americans realized that the NATO army could stand off a Soviet attack, they might be encouraged to precipitate a war out of some random crisis like Berlin. There was no sign that the Kennedy administration understood the problem.

Khrushchev Restarts Atomic Tests

With the Berlin crisis still in bloom, Americans were surprised late in August 1961 when Khrushchev announced that he would resume atmospheric nuclear testing. He had agreed to a moratorium after discussions with Eisenhower in 1958. The 1961–62 series was unusually intense. Some Americans took it as a particularly nasty way for Khrushchev to apply pressure, comparable to the ICBM and Sputnik. However, the new series seems more explicable in terms of the ongoing weapons program. To be producible and deployable, his new ICBMs had to be much lighter than the original missile, R-7 (SS-6). They could not throw heavy warheads, and initially that meant less powerful warheads. To develop a new lightweight warhead as powerful as the older, heavier one required a new series of tests. The Soviets also needed new warheads for a host of tactical weapons (developed for Khrushchev's military revolution) and for new antiballistic missile (ABM) weapons. Without testing, none could be fielded. Probably Khrushchev had not realized just how important testing would be when he negotiated the 1958 agreement.

There was certainly an element of propaganda. The 1958 moratorium had precluded tests of a new one-hundred-megaton bomb, by far the largest ever designed. Now Khrushchev ordered it exploded at reduced yield, fifty-eight megatons, which is still the most powerful in history. Khrushchev saw the bomb mainly as a propaganda device, to cow the West; American analysts suggested that it might destroy a target leaving minimal fallout (a high altitude blast would flatten an area without raising much dust). Very high yield bombs might create subtle nuclear effects and secondary thermal radiation. Multiple high-yield explosions might do disproportionate damage to a hardened target. Because the United States had never built as powerful a weapon, no hard data were available. An ICBM was designed to deliver it. Another new ICBM warhead (twenty-five megatons) also was tested.

Meanwhile, Khrushchev was getting some very depressing news. At a conference at Gagra in February 1962, he learned that the U.S. edge was likely to last a long time. The new Soviet missile industry was finding it very difficult to produce key components like inertial guidance mechanisms. All of the ICBMs under production were affected. Because the Soviets were fielding large numbers of MRBMs, [medium-range ballistic missiles] the CIA missed the production problem with ICBMs, which required better subsystems. Khrushchev had said that he needed hundreds of ICBMs; surely his command economy would soon provide them. Not understanding just how deep Soviet industrial poverty was, U.S. analysts tended to see apparent cuts as reflections of policies of restraint rather than as symptoms of brutal reality.

Khrushchev ordered a new generation of ICBMs in April. As a backup, he ordered a new submarine-launched missile, to be carried on board a submarine the West nicknamed "Yankee" because of its superficial resemblance to American Polaris submarines. This missile, an IRBM [intermediate-range ballistic missile] could hit American targets because its submarine could take it into range. Unlike earlier Soviet submarine-borne weapons, it did not have to get so close that it risked detection by the increasingly effective U.S. underwater surveillance systems.

Through the spring of 1962, Kennedy seemed increasingly assertive. He rebuffed Khrushchev's offer of a nuclear test ban treaty despite a major concession, a limited number of on-site inspections (many fewer than Kennedy wanted). More likely Kennedy feared that signing a treaty would have political consequences at home; he could not seem soft with the fall 1962 congressional elections coming. In addition, Kennedy continued to threaten [Fidel] Castro's regime in Cuba. A defeat for Castro would be the first rollback of a Soviet-backed regime, and thus a very serious defeat for Khrushchev, and disastrous in the ongoing struggle with China. Khrushchev seems to have guessed that Kennedy had finally awakened to his impotence. He did not realize just how obsessed Kennedy was with Castro.

Soviet Missiles in Cuba

Khrushchev badly needed an equalizer. His MRBMs and IRBMs worked, and his factories were turning them out at a satisfactory pace. Cuba offered him what Italy, Turkey, and the United Kingdom offered the United States; IRBM bases within range of the main enemy. Moreover, if the missiles were sold as a deterrent to U.S. invasion, they would bind Castro to Khrushchev. Khrushchev would later flit between the two explanations of his deployment, and would give different versions of its timing. Sometimes he said that he got the idea while walking on a Black Sea beach bear Sofia [in Bulgaria]. An aide pointed across the sea to Turkey, where U.S.-supplied Jupiters were emplaced. Khrushchev apparently broached the idea to his foreign minister, [Andrey] Gromyko, on the flight back to Moscow. At about this time Khrushchev was told that the Soviets lagged so far behind the Americans in ICBMs that it might well take at least a decade to catch up. The idea was ratified unanimously at a 24 May 1962 Presidium meeting. The Cubans were told soon afterwards.

Because Khrushchev feared that U.S. forces might abort the missile installation, Operation Anadyr (after a Polar air base) was conducted in secret. Ships carried missiles and other equipment below decks, with agricultural machinery visible topside. Their captains knew nothing until they opened their sealed orders at sea. Because Khrushchev feared that the Americans would find out and board the ships at sea, he ordered them fitted with antiaircraft guns. Captains were ordered to flood their holds (where the missiles were) if their ships were boarded.

Veterans of the Kennedy administration have said that they would have found it difficult to oppose open Soviet deployment, given U.S. missile deployments in Britain, Italy, and Turkey. Castro wanted open deployment, on the ground that Cuba had nothing to be ashamed of in accepting Soviet weapons. Khrushchev seems to have thought that the missiles would not be an effective deterrent unless they were kept secret until ready. His view was satirized in the movie *Doctor Strangelove*, in which the world is destroyed because the Soviets have built and started up—but not announced—a "doomsday machine" which will explode in the event of a U.S. attack.

[In October 1961,] as the missiles were being set up in Cuba, the Twenty-second Party Congress opened in Moscow, with Chinese Premier Chou En-lai in attendance. Chou obliquely criticized Soviet policy. He left before the end of the Congress, telling his Chinese colleagues that it had been "revisionist." The Chinese demonstrated their anger by refusing to accept delivery of Soviet and East European equipment already on order.

Word of the Soviet deployment began to leak. During the run-up to the November 1962 congressional elections, the Republicans adopted Kennedy's 1960 strategy. They charged that he was doing nothing about Soviet missiles going into Cuba. Kennedy vigorously denied the charge. He may have felt personally embarrassed—and endangered at the polls—when denial became impossible. He reacted violently. When the Soviets continued to deny that missiles were being deployed, he displayed U-2 photographs. Kennedy justified his angry reaction on the rather quaint basis that it was unacceptable to be lied to in the Oval Office. In fact the crisis presented him with an opportunity. He could now justify an invasion of Cuba, to wipe out the shame of the Bay of Pigs. Plans were drawn, but virtually at the last minute Kennedy drew back. He substituted a blockade. The situation recalled that in Berlin: Kennedy built up the crisis, then backed away as he was forced to confront the danger in which he had placed himself.

Resolution and Lessons Learned

The solution seems to have come out of a chance conversation. Kennedy remarked that Khrushchev's deployment was as outrageous as if the United States had deployed missiles to Turkey. He was surprised to find that the United States already had missiles—the Jupiters—in that country. The previous year he had asked that they be withdrawn—and then had forgotten about the whole subject. He offered Khrushchev a deal: he would withdraw the missiles from Turkey in return for withdrawal of the Soviet missiles and a pledge not to invade Cuba. To avoid the appearance of a sellout, Khrushchev agreed to allow Kennedy to delay the Turkish withdrawal for a few months. The agreement remained secret for many years because it was privately agreed between Kennedy and Khrushchev rather than between their governments.

Gen. Lauris Norstad pointed out that Kennedy was as much as admitting that his position on the Cuban missiles was weak. Moreover, it was a clear sell-out of the Turks. To camouflage the deal, the administration pulled the analogous missiles out of Italy. In his [Fiscal Year 1963 Dept. of Defense] Annual Report, McNamara falsely claimed that Britain, Italy, and Turkey had decided on their own to phase out the missiles. The Turks did manage to extract a quid pro quo: nuclear-capable F-104G fighter bombers as well as other military aid. Polaris submarine patrols in the Mediterranean were no substitute for seminational control of the Jupiters. The British had already agreed to give up their missiles, on the ground that they were obsolete; they could never be fired quickly enough in the event of an attack.

Castro had been sold out. Soviet missiles supplied, in theory, to protect him from invasion had been quickly withdrawn in the face of U.S. threats, without any attempt to consult him. He was furious that virtually nothing had been extracted from the Americans: not recognition, not withdrawal from [the American military base in the Cuban town of] Guantánamo. The Soviets also had withdrawn the bombers they had offered, so Castro could not threaten the bases in Central America from which another attempt to unseat him could be mounted. For the moment, Castro's instinctive reaction was to befriend the Chinese, at the least to show how angry he was. However, the Chinese could not supply the fuel and other goods on which he depended.

Castro was not the only one shocked by the Missile Crisis sellout. At the opening of the UN session in the fall of 1963, Romanian Foreign Minister [Corneliu] Manescu privately told U.S. Secretary of State Dean Rusk that his country had not been a party to Khrushchev's decision. His country would remain neutral in any future conflict so ignited, and he wanted U.S. assurances that it would not be struck due to any mistaken U.S. assumptions. He offered assurances, including an inspection, that there were no Soviet nuclear warheads on his soil. Romania had begun the withdrawal from the Warsaw Pact, which it announced in April 1964.

Khrushchev seems to have been shocked to discover that Kennedy seemed willing to risk nuclear war to deal with the sort of threat he had been living with for years. In retrospect, it is difficult to understand why Soviet weapons in Cuba were worth a global war. Quite soon, Soviet submarine-launched missiles would impose much the same sort of threat. Kennedy seems not to have understood what was happening.

Both leaders spoke darkly of the imminence of global nuclear war; of how close the world had come to catastrophe. Probably it was in everyone's interest to laud the statesmanship shown at the time. To make communication easier, a special "hot line" was installed between the Kremlin and the White House. To avoid ambiguities and translation errors, the line was a teleprinter, not a telephone. By all accounts it was almost never used.

Kennedy did not want to seem weak; his retreat (from a fairly absurd position) could be seen as strength only if the alternative were utter destruction. Later, when participants met to discuss the crisis, the Soviet Union was collapsing, and Mikhail Gorbachev badly wanted Western support. To ensure that support, he emphasized the danger of nuclear miscalculation. He alone could make sure that no subordinate got the wrong ideas. It should not have been a surprise, then, that a senior Soviet officer said that those on the spot had had the authority to use the tactical nuclear weapons brought in to cover the Soviet missile installation. Later it became clear that the opposite had been the case, as many at the time had suspected. Khrushchev was daring, but he was hardly insane.

Bringing the Cold War to Africa

Carol R. Saivetz and Sylvia Woodby

With the notable exception of the Cuban Missile Crisis, the major confrontations of the first two decades of the Cold War took place in Europe (the Berlin crisis) or Southeast Asia (the Korean War). With the rapid end of European colonial domination at the end of the 1950s, however, the continent of Africa became an important new ground of ideological—and sometimes military—conflict between communism and capitalism. Carol R. Saivetz, a research associate at the Davis Center for Russian Studies at Harvard University in Cambridge, Massachusetts, and Sylvia Woodby, a former associate professor and chair of the international relations program at Goucher College in Baltimore, Maryland, examine developments in Soviet policy toward many of the newly independent African states in the early 1960s. Saivetz and Woodby chronicle various aspects of the competition between the superpowers for influence in Africa, including the military, economic, and political assistance that both the United States and Soviet Union provided in large quantities during the 1960s and 1970s. They note that the Soviets initially used a very direct approach in wooing potential new political partners on the continent, but moderated this strategy after setbacks such as those in the Congo, where a heavily American-backed faction prevailed over a more pro-Soviet one.

Decolonization in Africa proceeded steadily in the late fifties and early sixties. Yet at the time, the gradual sequence of steps leading to self-government appears to have obscured an appreciation of the magnitude of the political changes

Excerpted from *Soviet–Third World Relations*, by Carol R. Saivetz and Sylvia Woodby (Boulder, CO: Westview Press, 1985). Copyright © 1985 by Westview Press. Reprinted with permission.

taking place. Soviet relations with African states, in the pattern of the Khrushchev-Bulganin tour of South Asia [the two Soviet leaders Nikita Khrushchev and Nikolai Bulganin had visited several Asian nations in 1955 in an effort to stimulate closer ties between those nations and the USSR], began with friendly approaches (in 1956) to the oldest independent African state, Ethiopia. Diplomatic relations (broken during World War II) were reestablished at the ambassadorial level in 1959, and Emperor Haile Selassie was invited to the Soviet Union for a state visit. Moreover, the Soviets offered Ethiopia a generous credit (about half the size of initial offers made to Afghanistan and India [in 1955], but about the same as that offered to Indonesia).

The Soviet Union Becomes Involved in West Africa

The most extensive and dramatic Soviet involvement in Africa, however, centered on certain key radical states that were cultivated and welcomed as "comradely" allies. Guinea, an anomaly in the gradual decolonization process, proved an attractive and logical target of Soviet interest. Ahmed Sékou Touré was the only leader of a French colony to reject association with [French leader Charles] de Gaulle's French Community [an association of former French colonies] in the 1958 referendum. By voting "no," Guinea chose full independence. The French then withdrew completely, leaving the new state to fend for itself. Touré quickly established diplomatic relations with both the USSR and China and adopted a militant anti-imperialist foreign policy. He concluded trade agreements with a number of socialist states. In September 1959, a Communist Party of the Soviet Union (CPSU) delegation attended a meeting of the vaguely Marxist Democratic Party of Guinea (PDG). The Soviets subsequently identified this party as a "revolutionary democratic" one, entitled to maintain regular ties with the CPSU. Touré visited the Soviet Union in 1959 and again in 1960. Soviet press and leadership were enthusiastic about Guinea's militant anti-imperialism, as expressed in nationalization of foreign property, involvement in the Afro-Asian Peoples Solidarity Organization, and encouragement to liberation movements elsewhere in Africa. In

1961 during [Leonid] Brezhnev's visit to Guinea, Touré was awarded a Lenin Peace Prize.

Relations did not proceed completely smoothly, however. Guinea also developed ties with the United States and France, and when Touré's plans for socialist development fell into difficulty in the early sixties, he chose to encourage foreign and private investment. In December 1961, Touré angrily accused the Soviets of involvement with opponents of his regime and ordered the Soviet ambassador expelled. Despite this incident, new Soviet credits were extended the following year, and government and party relations continued to develop. Soviet analysts recognized Guinea as a progressive state, and the up-to-date vocabulary of acceptable Marxist categories was applied to this country.

Ghana (formerly the Gold Coast), which gained independence under an increasingly radical leadership, proved to be another favored client. Diplomatic relations were established and a trade agreement concluded in 1959. In 1960 and 1961 the Soviets offered credits amounting to about half the sum offered to Ethiopia. Soviet assistance programs included training for Kwame Nkrumah's security force. Many Ghanaians traveled to the USSR and the Eastern bloc for programs of study. Nkrumah adopted favored Soviet foreign policy positions as his own. Soviet-Ghanaian foreign policy cooperation in the Congo crisis, at the United Nations, and other international organizations was extensive enough to provoke Western charges that Ghana had become a "satellite." In 1963 Nkrumah stated his belief in "scientific socialism," which was then duly incorporated into the program of his Convention People's Party (CPP). The development of party relations between the CPSU and the CPP encouraged public Soviet enthusiasm about Ghana's political prospects.

Mali (formerly the French Sudan) attracted Soviet attention soon after independence when it chose a radical path in close contact with Guinea and Ghana. Mali's leader Modibo Keita proclaimed himself in favor of a truly neutral foreign policy and pledged himself to socialist economic planning. At the same time, he requested that the French withdraw their military bases, and Mali left the franc zone [the region of Africa still economically tied to France]. Diplomatic relations were quickly established with China and the USSR. Soviet credits were promised in 1961 and 1962, and visits were exchanged by government and military delegations. Keita's ruling party, the Sudanese Union-African Democratic Rally, announced the adoption of scientific socialism in 1962. Subsequently, the Sudanese Union was invited to attend Soviet party functions, while its youth group attended Komsomol [a Soviet youth organization] conferences. Along with Ghana and Guinea, Mali was regularly listed with pride in Soviet reviews of the progressive changes in Africa, which pointed to the inevitable triumph of socialism.

A Cold War Showdown in the Congo

In the Belgian Congo, independence was granted with very little preparation. As the announced date for independence (June 1960) approached, aspiring Congolese political leaders maneuvered frantically for places in the new government. Joseph Kasavubu, who became the first president, represented a federalist and pro-Western approach to Congo's future. Patrice Lumumba, who became prime minister, urged a strongly centralized government structure. A leftist friend of Nkrumah, Lumumba became the Soviet favorite. Within a few weeks of independence, the fragile Congolese government was beset with mutinies and public disorder. Most serious, the mineral-rich province of Katanga seceded. When Belgian forces intervened in apparent sympathy with the secessionists, the new government appealed to the United Nations for help.

Although the USSR followed the lead of the majority of African states in endorsing the dispatch of a UN peacekeeping force, the Soviets remained skeptical about the motives of the Western powers in the Congo. Prime Minister Lumumba shared these apprehensions. He concluded that the UN forces were too cautious about removing the Belgians, and appealed to the USSR directly for help. In August, the Soviet government issued a warning that it would "not hesitate to take decisive measures aimed at repelling the aggressors." On request from Premier Lumumba, the Soviets actually airlifted some supplies, delivered trucks, and ferried Ghanaian troops to the combat zone. UN commanders considered the actions to be unilateral interference, in violation of UN directives, and closed Congolese airports to Soviet supply missions. The Soviets angrily charged partisanship, and proceeded to denounce the UN's activities and officials. Ultimately, United Nations forces did restore order in the Congo and helped to subdue two rebellious provinces.

At the same time, internal political conflict intensified within the Congo. At one point in 1960, Kasavubu and Lumumba attempted to dismiss each other. They sent rival delegations to the United Nations, each claiming to represent the legitimate government of the Congo. U.S. pressure helped ensure victory of the Kasavubu group in the credentials fight at the United Nations, and Western support helped him remain in control in the Congo. When Lumumba was assassinated early in 1961, the Soviets blamed the West for his death and withdrew their ambassador from the Congo temporarily. The pro-Western character of the Congo operations and their political results brought continued Soviet complaints and demands that the office of the UN secretary general be redesigned. Khrushchev himself went to the United Nations session in 1961 to argue in favor of a "troika" [Russian, literally a carriage pulled by a team of three] proposal, to replace the secretary general with a threesome of Western, Eastern, and "neutral" representatives. Soviet refusal to pay for military operations in the Congo produced a serious crisis at the United Nations in 1964, once arrears had reached the point where the USSR should have lost its General Assembly vote.

Thus what began as participation in multinational assistance to a new African regime degenerated into a frustrating battle for control over the political future and alignment of the Congo. Lumumba's death left the USSR without an ally. At the end of 1961 diplomatic relations were reestablished with the central government, but they were not particularly friendly ones. In 1963, two Soviet diplomats were charged with helping to prepare an aborted coup and expelled. The Soviets were also apparently involved in 1964 in a regional rebellion, which was put down with U.S. and Belgian assistance. The ensuing government was not only pro-Western, but was headed by Moise Tshombe, the secessionist leader of Katanga province who had invited in the Belgians and had fought against his countrymen with South African mercenaries. The regime that emerged in the Congo (renamed Zaire) from this tumultuous beginning was to remain firmly anti-Soviet.

As the decolonization process continued, other states were courted by the Soviets. The Kremlin appeared to be very pleased with the "positive neutrality" aspirations of the new Sudanese government. During his 1962 trip to Africa and the Middle East, Brezhnev, then chairman of the Presidium of the Supreme Soviet, stopped in Sudan, where he offered Soviet credits and a trade pact. After a number of changes of leadership, a 1964 coup left communists included in the government, and Soviet reaction was appropriately approving. When Somalia gained its independence in 1960, the Soviets established diplomatic ties almost immediately and apparently offered military aid in 1963. In 1964 the USSR, with warnings against British naval interference, moved naval vessels into the vicinity of the newly independent leftist regime in Zanzibar. At the same time, a limited amount of Soviet assistance seems to have reached African liberation movements, particularly through aid to Nkrumah and Touré, whose territories were host to a number of training camps for rebel groups. . . .

Soviet Involvement Becomes More Cautious

Soviet relations with Africa [from 1965 to 1973] were shaped by military coups, which were becoming a regular feature of Third World politics. The Soviets lost several carefully cultivated nationalist leaders (Nkrumah in Ghana, Keita in Mali), and the replacement military regimes were not always so interested in close relations with the USSR, or in socialism. But the USSR also gained through military regimes that did profess an interest in Soviet assistance, in Somalia, the Sudan, and Uganda.

In Mali, although the new regime maintained a fairly close relationship, and military and economic aid continued, sources of aid were diversified, and the ruling party the Soviets had praised was dissolved. At intervals the Malian government became critical of Soviet policies in Africa, and even expelled some Soviet diplomats. The new Ghanaian government that ousted Nkrumah claimed that the Soviet role in their country was harmful. Soviet advisors were sent home and the number of diplomatic personnel permitted was cut. The deposed Nkrumah took up residence in Guinea, and there the Soviets allegedly provided aid to his supporters, who hoped to regain power. In October 1968, a nasty incident developed when the Ghanaian government protested Soviet activities in Guinea by seizing two Soviet fishing vessels. The ships and their crews were held for five months and charged with subversive activity. In March 1969, four Soviet warships sailed into the area, and the sailors were eventually released. Subsequently, Soviet journalists and diplomats were expelled, and it was many years before relations could be described as cordial.

African regimes in general, both military and civilian, increasingly were single-party or highly personalistic governments. Almost all were troubled by separatist movements or were plagued by serious internal tribal divisions. In a few cases, the Soviets became associated with unsuccessful leftist dissenters. In Kenya, for example, they apparently extended some aid to Oginga Odinga, a Luo [a minority ethnic group within Kenya] rival to Jomo Kenyatta's ruling group. In the Congo (Zaire), the Kinshasa government expelled several Soviet diplomats for affiliation with leftist rebels. It should be noted that attempts by the USSR to supply or associate with these groups were in part stimulated by the competing presence of the Chinese, who were less inhibited about arming rebel groups. Through their bases in Guinea, the Soviets became involved in aiding liberation movements in Guinea-Bissau and in Cape Verde.

In 1970 the Soviets made much of their role in helping to repel a Portuguese attack on Guinea. The Portuguese were annoyed over the refuge Guinea provided for colonial rebels. Guinean leader Sékou Touré appealed for aid to both the United States and the USSR, but it was the Soviets who provided small arms to the Guinean armed forces and sent naval vessels to Guinean ports. In exchange, the Soviets were permitted to use Guinea's airport facilities for reconnaissance flights over the Atlantic and arranged to buy Guinean bauxite at favorable prices. However, although Soviet ships were allowed to refuel and make use of Guinea's shore facilities, Touré refused Soviet requests for permission to construct a naval base. An important reason for Soviet protection of Guinea was an interest in securing a sanctuary for the national liberation forces operating against the Portuguese in Guinea-Bissau. The African Party for the Independence of Guinea-Bissau and Cape Verde (PAIGC) was a principal target of Portuguese military raids. In January 1973, the PAIGC leader Amilcar Cabral was assassinated in the Guinean capital, and a number of his supporters were seized for return to Portuguese Guinea. Although the Soviets did not claim public credit for it, these PAIGC members were rescued by nearby Soviet ships.

Shifts in Soviet Policies

By the late sixties, it appeared the Soviets had shifted to a more cautious orientation that would associate Moscow with the position of the Organization of African Unity (OAU) in favor of strict observance of existing borders. This approach proved increasingly necessary in order to cultivate new allies among the independent African states. When civil war broke out in Nigeria in 1967, the Soviets decided to support the central government in its battle with separatists, who declared their independence as the state of Biafra. The Soviet shipments of military assistance helped the government's campaign to restore its authority. Moreover, Soviet policy was in harmony with the position of the OAU and the majority of Third World states. Soviet willingness to come to the assistance of the Nigerians in this emergency contrasted with U.S. equivocation. The British were supplying the central Nigerian government with some military aid, but they had been reluctant to supply aircraft. Soviet willingness to step in with both fighters and bombers did much to improve the Soviet image in West Africa at the time. The Soviets were also approving when the Nigerian government took steps to control the oil industry, and in the years following the civil war offered generous credits (designed in particular to help with development of Nigeria's oil resources) and an active program of educational and cultural exchange. Soviet attention to the Nigerian Marxist party (the Nigerian Socialist Workers and Farmers Party) was not appreciated however, and a delegate who attended the international communist meeting in Moscow in 1969 was arrested on his return home.

In Sudan, the leftist government that came to power in October 1964 was replaced in 1965 by a new regime, which banned the communist party. Soviet relations with this new government improved by 1968 so that trade, military, and technical assistance agreements were concluded. Then, in 1969 a military coup produced a government that was much more pro-Soviet. The new leader, Colonel Gafar Numayri, was a nationalist who was prepared to conduct an anti-imperialist foreign policy and eager to receive Soviet military aid. Soviet efforts to cultivate Numayri's regime were fruitful until trouble occurred between the Khartoum government and the Sudanese Communist Party. After severe disagreements, military groups with communist backing staged an unsuccessful coup attempt in 1971. Both Egypt and Libya helped President Numayri recover his post, and were not sympathetic when the Soviets apparently asked them to intercede on behalf of the arrested conspirators. Despite a personal appeal by [Soviet premier Alexsey] Kosygin, Sudan's leading communists were executed. Moreover, the Sudanese president accused the Soviets of involvement in this coup, and Soviet-Sudanese relations remained frosty for some time.

Developments in Somalia offered another prospective client. The regime of General Siyad Barre, which took power in a 1969 coup, proclaimed a devotion to socialism that attracted favorable Soviet commentary. Aid and trade agreements were forthcoming, and party relations were successfully cultivated. Soviet military aid, including tanks and aircraft, was increased. In 1972 construction started on extensive port facilities at Berbera. Soviet naval visits began on a regular basis, leading to speculation that the Soviets would eventually have a secure naval base in this important country at the Horn of Africa.

In East Africa, the Soviet record in this period was uneven. Idi Amin Dada, who replaced Milton Obote as head of state in Uganda in 1971, carried out a shift of policy that eventually included pro-Arab positions. Amin also displayed an interest in Soviet military assistance, and a number of trade agreements and assistance pacts were concluded in 1972 and 1973. Elsewhere in East Africa, Soviet efforts to extend their presence were not notably successful. Tanzania did accept a very small Soviet credit in 1966, as did Zambia in 1967. The pro-Soviet record of the Kenyan president's political opposition restricted possibilities of improved relations with that government.

To Use or Not to Use: Implications of Nuclear Weapons

Tom Engelhardt

As early as 1950, the United States had formulated plans under which it would launch a preemptive nuclear first strike against the Soviet Union. Tom Engelhardt, historian and consulting editor at Henry Holt/Metropolitan Books, discusses the reasons why such a first strike (or any other nonretaliatory use of nuclear weapons) was never a realistic option during the early years of the Cold War, before the acceleration of the arms race made deterrence the only seemingly viable nuclear strategy. Engelhardt examines both sociological and strategic limitations to the use of the atomic bomb, including the way in which a first strike would invalidate Americans' sense of living in what he calls a "victory culture." Engelhardt identifies this as an American national self-image based on the belief that violence should only be used as a final means of righteous self-defense, such as was the case in World War II, which the United States entered only after the Japanese attack on Pearl Harbor. Engelhardt claims that growing concern among the American populace of the side effects of nuclear weapons, such as radioactive fallout, coupled with strategic difficulties—use of nuclear weapons against any target less than cities was realized as hugely disproportionate—caused U.S. military and political leaders to shun the use of the bomb in conflicts such as the Korean War. Engelhardt argues that this hesitation caused the Eisenhower administration to adopt a more hostile, self-protective rhetoric regarding the bomb in order to justify the existence of what had become a "shameful" technological innovation.

Excerpted from *The End of Victory Culture: Cold War America and the Disillusioning of a Generation*, by Tom Engelhardt (New York: BasicBooks, 1995). Copyright © 1995 by Tom Engelhardt. Reprinted with permission.

By 1953, the United States had close to 1,000 A-bombs [atomic bombs], H-bombs [hydrogen bombs], and tactical nuclear weapons. In 1962, during the Cuban missile crisis, President John F. Kennedy commanded 112 sea-launched ballistic missiles, 284 land-based intercontinental ballistic missiles (ICBMs), 105 intermediate range ballistic missles, and 659 nuclear-armed B-52s; while Soviet Premier Nikita Khrushchev, as historian Geoffrey Perret has noted, had only "150 long-range bombers of dubious worth and 35 ICBMs of proven unreliability." As it turned out, this was just the beginning. The Kennedy administration funded a 60 percent buildup of strategic nuclear forces as well as "battle-field" nuclear weapons, like a miniaturized atomic bomb two GIs could fire from a rocket launcher.

Certain military men had long considered a nuclear first strike against the Soviet Union. As early as 1950, the Strate-gic Air Command [SAC]'s Curtis E. LeMay urged the im-plementation of SAC Emergency War Plan 1-49, which in-volved delivering "the entire stockpile of atomic bombs . . . in a single massive attack," 133 A-bombs on 70 Soviet cities in 30 days. Such plans only grew more awesome. SAC's aim later that decade became the destruction of "more than 100 Soviet cities and towns, plus 645 military installations, in a single crushing strike . . . [in] less than a day."

The Russians were as incapable of warding off such an at-tack as they were of delivering their minimalist arsenal to American shores. In fact, when *Life* magazine first tried to imagine such a scenario in 1949, the best it could come up with was the smuggling of a bomb into the country. Undra-matic photos of a merchant ship and trucks on a highway were captioned, "Russian freighter unloads her cargo unmo-lested in U.S. port. Atomic bombs could be exploded at dockside or transferred to trucks to be driven to target." In the mid-1950s, the Pentagon was still seriously considering defenses against similar scenarios.

Although the Soviet Union test-fired the world's first ICBM in August 1957 (two months before it sent aloft the first satellite), and John F. Kennedy slipped into the presi-dency in part by decrying a "missile gap," Soviet delivery systems were hardly in better shape in January 1961 than they had been twelve years earlier. Given the Soviet decision not to build a first generation of ICBMs, the ship-and-truck option was still probably their best bet—and President Kennedy soon knew it. Photographs from the new *Discoverer* satellite proved definitive. The Soviets had only 4 operational missiles, not the 50–500 of various intelligence estimates.

As Robert McNamara was to learn just before becoming secretary of defense, the military's secret plan for blowing away the Communist world—2,500 targets in Eastern Europe, Russia, China, and North Korea—would have resulted in an estimated 360 million casualties without response, a one-way massacre so chilling that McNamara was stunned. While President Kennedy, in an interview in 1962, indicated that there were circumstances under which the United States might launch a first strike, these were idle words. No president proved willing to loose the massive one-way attack that seemed the logic of U.S. strategy, just as the many plans and threats, public and private, to use atomic weaponry in more "minor" ways in Iran, Korea, China, Indochina, and elsewhere "on the periphery" were never carried out.

Social and Strategic Constraints on Using the Bomb

Constraints already existed to the implementation of this finale to the spectacle of slaughter. To deliver such a sneak attack would have made a mockery of victory culture. Although any plan—from a convulsive first strike to the use of nuclear weapons on Third World battlefields—always had its high-level proponents, and a number seemed to come within a hairsbreadth of happening, none ever did.

U.S. officials expressed this unexpected sense of constraint on their ability to make war to the fullest in two ways. First, they translated their hesitations into fears of how "our allies" or "the world" would react to the use of such weaponry. British Prime Minister Clement Atlee's cross-Atlantic rush to dissuade President [Harry S.] Truman from using A-bombs in Korea attested to allied fears of U.S. nuclear intentions (and of the outbreak of World War III in Europe). However, as French requests for nuclear support in

Many Americans built backyard bomb shelters to prevent exposure to radioactive elements in the event of a nuclear attack.

Indochina indicated, desires for the weaponry to be used also existed. Whatever other countries' fears and desires, a deeper restraining impulse was at work.

The second way these constraints were expressed was as a form of hardheaded cost analysis and pragmatic puzzlement. This came into play whenever the possibility arose of bringing atomic weaponry to bear in the Third World. Once a first strike against the Soviet Union had been ruled out, upon what or whom could the bomb be dropped to offer a reasonable return on investment? Russian forces occupying northern Iran? A set of bridges over the Yalu River? The jungle around the besieged French outpost of Dienbienphu? ("You could take all day to drop a bomb. . . . No opposition. And clean those Commies out of there and the band could play the Marseillaise and the French would come marching out . . . in fine shape," recalled Air Force Chief Nathan Twining, who supported the use of three A-bombs there in 1954. "And those Commies would say, 'Well, those guys may do this again to us. We'd better be careful.'") But each place chosen that was not the Soviet Union seemed ludicrously disproportionate for weapons systems geared to wipe out large cities.

That "deterrence" existed before any deterrent force came into being was the determining fact of the Cold War. Although critics of government policy making have been struck by revelations of how many times the United States considered using atomic weapons, the post-Nagasaki inability to use them, even when they resembled more ordinary weapons like artillery shells or land mines, was far more significant. The atomic stalemate preceded by well over a decade the Soviet nuclear strike force that was its explanation (and even briefly the development of "deterrence theory"), reflecting the limits of what the American story, American national identity, could withstand.

By the late 1950s, much of the public was aware that an atomic attack could not be restricted to its target. Strontium 90 and other radioactive elements released in aboveground bomb tests had traveled invisibly thousands of miles to land on the grass American cows ate and so entered the milk American children drank. Imagine, then, the effects on the United States of a massive first strike on enemy territory. In the long run, there was no way Americans could be protected from their country's greatest weapons except by an unpalatable program of disarmament (as a few peace organizations urged).

The Bomb Gets a Bad Reputation

America's proudest technological achievement, its victory weapon, was driven into invisibility. Atomic secrecy was guaranteed through the Atomic Energy Act of 1946. Later, bomb tests went underground, as did nuclear missiles, while carefully crafted "friendly atom" propaganda covered over much evidence of the bomb's baleful effects on human health. Presidents spoke circumspectly, at best, of atomic policy, and the military's first-strike plans were so secret that even a secretary of defense might be kept partially in the dark about them.

The weapons that should have been a boon to Americans and a terror to any enemy proved instead an embarrassment that had to be buried. To display them proudly in one's own country, no less brandish them abroad, was to shatter an image of "national security" crucial for domestic audiences. Yet if not openly tested for use and used, atomic arms radiated a sense of weakness, not strength.

From the long rifle to the B-26 [bomber], American arms had been a source of pride. The lopsided statistics of victory were always seen as due, in part, to the technological inventiveness of Americans. When fused with the character of the frontiersman or the jungle fighter, advanced weaponry made a one-against-many story possible, and there was nothing faintly shameful in that. Now, the uselessness of the nuclear arsenal became the unbearable and shameful torment around which global policy had to be built. Somehow, the enemy had to be convinced that tough-minded leaders would not hesitate to bring into play the very weapons they hesitated to use in conflicts from Berlin to Korea.

As the [Dwight D.] Eisenhower White House struggled in the post-Korean War years to keep military expenditures under control, policy makers fell back on the threat of the bomb. As Secretary of State John Foster Dulles spelled it out in 1954, the United States was not to respond to each thrust and jab of "the mighty landpower of the Communist world," but react "vigorously at places and with means of its own choosing"; with, in the euphemistic language of the time, "the further deterrent of massive retaliatory power." In other words, the United States was officially committing itself to turn conflicts with the enemy, large or small, anywhere in the world, into one-sided nuclear wars.

Formulating the Strategy of Deterrence

Spencer R. Weart

By the mid-1950s, the nuclear stockpiles of the United States and Soviet Union were both rapidly becoming so large as to render traditional military strategy—that is, striking first and decisively destroying an enemy—obsolete. Instead, both sides adopted a policy of deterrence, by which each side would maintain a nuclear arsenal large enough to guarantee a complete retaliatory strike even in the case of a successful surprise attack. Spencer R. Weart, director of the Center for History of Physics at the American Institute of Physics in College Park, Maryland, examines the history of deterrence strategy in the late 1950s and early 1960s. Weart discusses the paradox of a strategy based on possessing enough weapons to guarantee never having to use those weapons. He also discusses some of the offshoots of this risky policy, such as the notion of escalation, which theorized that even nuclear conflict could be contained at levels, or "rungs" on a ladder of violence, below complete destruction. Weart focuses especially on physicist Herman Kahn, one of the leading proponents of deterrence theory, whose advice helped shape American nuclear policy from the Kennedy administration onward.

The keystone concept in the debate [over nuclear strategy in the 1950s] was deterrence. The first national leader to explain the idea clearly to the public was [British prime minister] Winston Churchill, speaking to the House of Commons in 1955. He said that by the end of the decade both the United States and the Soviet Union would be able to guarantee total destruction of an enemy, and he called that a stable and even a welcome situation. In one of his last unforgettable aphorisms, Churchill predicted that "safety will be the sturdy child of terror, and survival the twin brother of annihilation."

Deterrence rested on the ability to eradicate the enemy within a matter of days, as in the actual war plans drawn up by the Strategic Air Command and no doubt by its Soviet counterpart. The most effective plan, all strategists agreed, would be the most extreme: a First Strike. Many past wars had started with an all-out sneak attack, and the threat was particularly familiar to Americans with their memories of Pearl Harbor and to Russians with their memories of Hitler's 1941 surprise invasion. Now the goal of strategy was to deter such a First Strike. For this a nation must possess, in the analysts' new jargon, "survivable" and "credible" forces that could wreak "assured destruction" in a "second strike."

This doctrine was one of the many abstract intellectual concepts that could be built in steel. An American fleet of submarines with Polaris missiles, a survivable, credible, assured-destruction, second-strike force, went to sea beginning in 1960, later joined by similar Soviet, British, French, and Chinese ships. The missiles were barely accurate enough to find an urban area. They were not aimed at traditional military targets, but at the minds of enemy leaders.

Deterrence was so far from normal military strategy that, according to some, it did not even require a nation to possess a stronger force than the enemy had. By the early 1960s this concept of "sufficiency" was mentioned in official United States policy, while in practice the British, French, and Chinese built only enough weapons, as the French delicately put it, to tear off an enemy's arm. American and particularly Soviet planners were not content to stop there, however. Each wanted to be the nation with the most weapons, if only to keep the enemy from hoping that after a war he could rule over the survivors.

The desire to have a multitude of weapons was reinforced from the late 1950s on by strategists and statesmen who pointed out that it might not be easy to deter a nation from grabbing a little slice of territory. Would [President John F.] Kennedy really risk the destruction of Washington to keep

Russians out of Hamburg? The alternative was to blast invading troops directly with "tactical" nuclear weapons, that is, ones not more than a few times larger than the Hiroshima bomb. Amid fierce international debate, thousands of such weapons were emplaced in Europe and the Far East. Many strategists hoped that war with such armament would be a step down the ladder from total destruction.

For the Western Europeans across whose countryside the tactical bombs would explode, it was not far down. Their strategists advised backing down another step, building a defense that could stand without nuclear weapons. Perhaps a mental cordon could be raised against "first use" of the bombs; perhaps the moral horror of nuclear energy had become powerful enough all by itself to keep war inside traditional limits?

Soviet military doctrine discouraged such talk. The Soviets were sure that an army fighting for its life would use its most decisive weapons almost from the start, and they openly planned to do that. NATO itself never felt certain it could stand off the Red Army without "escalation" up the ladder to nuclear weapons. And in any case Europeans, recalling the deserts of rubble they had witnessed in 1945, found a conventional war scarcely more attractive than a nuclear one. NATO therefore stated what was the simple truth as a matter of policy—that any invasion might bring them to use nuclear weapons.

NATO's soldiers might still look like the brave warriors of yore, but they actually served less as traditional defenders than as a trip-wire, rigged to set off tactical bombs upon any serious incursion. And many thinkers, especially Soviet ones, insisted that on the day tactical nuclear weapons were used, all restraints would be dropped; the wise warrior must therefore begin with a First Strike. No matter how far strategists tried to climb down the ladder, the specter of total destruction followed.

Herman Kahn and the Paradox of Deterrence

The most famous student of this strange ladder was a young RAND physicist, Herman Kahn. He seemed the opposite of a military man with his exceedingly round stomach and thick glasses, but he could pour out sparkling ideas and neatly packaged historical anecdotes in a way that kept senior officers fascinated through hours of lectures. In 1960 he piled together his notes and published them as a volume entitled *On Thermonuclear War*. At once controversy erupted over Kahn's unfamiliar logic, as exemplified above all by his "Doomsday Machine."

This notional device would be set automatically to destroy the world if ever bombs exploded on the owner's territory: the ultimate in deterrence through assured destruction. Kahn was quick to admit that building a Doomsday Machine would be stupid and immoral. He insisted that nevertheless people ought to analyze it—for the United States and the Soviet Union, with their trip-wire troops and missile sub-

---

The Cold War on Film

Stanley Kubrick's 1964 film Dr. Strangelove, or How I Learned to Stop Worrying and Love the Bomb *remains one of the most telling documents of the Cold War. In this dark satirical comedy about a nuclear war "accidentally" begun by an insane American general named Jack Ripper, Kubrick points out the inherent dangers of the atomic age. In this scene, President Merkin Muffley and the president's military adviser, a former Nazi scientist named Dr. Strangelove (both played by Peter Sellers), discuss with the Soviet ambassador a secret Soviet "doomsday machine" using the language and logic of deterrence theory.*

MUFFLEY: Then you mean it is possible for them to have built such a thing?

STRANGELOVE: Mr. President, the technology required is easily within the means of even the smallest nuclear power. It requires only the will to do so.

MUFFLEY: But, how is it possible for this thing to be triggered automatically, and at the same time impossible to untrigger?

STRANGELOVE: Mr. President, it is not only possible, it is essential. That is the whole idea of this machine, you know. Deter-

marines and all, were building something ever more like a Doomsday Machine. Kahn had put his finger on a central problem. It had already been hinted at by Churchill, whose landmark 1955 speech noted that beyond a certain point deterrence meant "the worse things get the better." Churchill frankly called that a "paradox" he could not resolve.

In 1962 Kahn got to the heart of the paradox by borrowing an analogy from Bertrand Russell. The philosopher had drawn attention to the adolescent game of "chicken," in which two cars drive headlong toward each other until one driver swerves aside, losing the game. Kahn accepted the analogy to nuclear diplomacy. He added that the best way to win such a showdown would be "to get in the car drunk, wear dark glasses, and throw the steering wheel out of the window as soon as the car has gotten up to speed"; the op-

---

rence is the art of producing in the mind of the enemy . . . the fear to attack. And so, because of the automated and irrevocable decision making process which rules out human meddling, the doomsday machine is terrifying. It's simple to understand. And completely credible, and convincing. . . .

MUFFLEY: But this is fantastic, Strangelove. How can it be triggered automatically?

STRANGELOVE: Well, it's remarkably simple to do that. When you merely wish to bury bombs, there is no limit to the size. After that they are connected to a gigantic complex of computers. Now then, a specific and clearly defined set of circumstances, under which the bombs are to be exploded, is programmed into a tape memory bank. . . .

STRANGELOVE: Yes, but the . . . whole point of the doomsday machine . . . is lost . . . if you keep it a secret! Why didn't you tell the world, eh?

AMBASSADOR DESADESKI: It was to be announced at the Party Congress on Monday. As you know, the Premier loves surprises.

Dialogue transcribed from a videotape copy of *Dr. Strangelove, or How I Learned to Stop Worrying and Love the Bomb*, dir. and prod. Stanley Kubrick, Columbia Pictures, 1964.

ponent would surely give way. The game of chicken went even further than the Doomsday Machine in demanding that players give up responsible control.

Unable to refute the logic of this simplified system, some strategists decided that the only solution was to make the system complex, to keep as many rungs as possible on the escalation ladder between a border scuffle and total destruction. A nation must have plenty of everything—troops with rifles and tactical warheads and so on up to forces bordering on a Doomsday Machine. As practical advice this policy was publicly adopted by Kennedy and all later American presidents, and more quietly by every other nuclear-armed nation. Eventually certain leaders like Richard Nixon took Kahn's advice to its logical end, working to convince their enemies that they might use bombs irrationally. The whole system was bizarre but it seemed to work, precisely insofar as leaders, aware of the crazy uncertainty of all human affairs, feared to test even the first rung of the rickety ladder. In short, the system's success rested upon its very lack of sense.

This insoluble paradox in deterrence theory, this precarious logic of unreason, was not clearly understood until the 1980s, and even then the majority of military and diplomatic thinkers remained mired in its deliberate confusion. From the 1950s on the sharpest analysts left ambiguities, internal contradictions, and blind leaps of logic in their writings. Most writers changed their position from one year to the next and sometimes, it seemed, from one page to the next.

An example of the muddle was the failure of most writers to define clearly even the key term "deterrence." Sometimes it meant, as the French translated the term, "dissuasion." That meant arranging things so that enemies would deduce, like chess players, that they should not launch an attack because it was clear they would not win the game. Other times deterrence meant what the Russian translation frankly called "terrorization," which did not address the intellect at all. Of course, military logic on the one hand or an appeal to raw fear on the other might well require different strategies and even different hardware. But most thinkers mixed the two approaches, evading refutation in one mode of thought by shifting indiscriminately to the other. An even more surprising gap in the debate was that, caught up in the details of their argument, many strategists forgot to mention that nuclear weapons could never be used on cities in a way that would satisfy simple morality.

Is There Any Rational Excuse for Nuclear War?

The debates over ambiguous and dehumanized concepts bewildered the public. Popular thinking about strategy took on an Alice-in-Wonderland quality, amounting to a set of inconsistent clichés that reflected the internal contradictions of more sophisticated discussion. At the deeper level of belief and symbolism, the countless clever articles and books published in the late 1950s and early 1960s scarcely influenced how most people imagined nuclear war. Quite the reverse: the already widespread images of nuclear war influenced the strategists.

One example was that central theoretical concept, the all-out First Strike. A surprise attack had been a reasonable idea when Pearl Harbor was bombed, but in the nuclear age it would be less a military tactic than the slaughter of an entire people. Any child could see that only a uniquely powerful, totally evil, and downright insane person could commit such a crime. The First Strike of the theorists resembled nothing so much as the mad scientist's outburst.

The same theme infected discussion of the alternative policy, graduated deterrence. Theorists concentrated on how to keep escalation from climbing to full-scale warfare, or as they put it, from going out of control. To call what would be a deliberate decision of national authority, prepared long in advance and dutifully carried out with the cooperation of millions, "going out of control"—that too was less military logic than mad-scientist thinking. And the keystone of policy, mutual assured destruction, was still closer to old tales, as the Doomsday Machine made plain. Yet these fantastic ideas almost displaced the concept that had dominated traditional strategy: war as a continuation of politics. The genuine, and far from drastic, local conflicts of interest between the United States and the Soviet Union tended to disappear behind a fog of exclamations about an apocalyptic suicide pact.

Still more curious, most analysis halted at the point where deterrence failed. What would the political situation of the world be like a year after that? In other words, what rational human purposes would be served by a nuclear war? Almost every thinker tended to ignore this question. Even in professional strategy analysis the time beyond full-scale use of bombs usually resembled the space beyond midnight on the doomsday clock, that empty zone the mind could never enter. As one analyst later remarked, "My mind just stops there."

Chapter 3

Cold War II

Turning|Points

IN WORLD HISTORY

Détente Comes to an End

H.W. Brands

H.W. Brands is Distinguished Professor of History and Melbern G. Glasscock Chair in American History at Texas A & M University in College Station, Texas. He has written more than a dozen books on various subjects in American history, including several on the Cold War. In this excerpt, he examines the political and historical factors that came together during the latter years of Jimmy Carter's presidential tenure (1979–1980) and brought about the end of détente between the United States and Soviet Union. Brands concentrates on the situation in the United States, emphasizing the role that outspoken "present-dangerists" (those who feared that communism presented an imminent threat to the United States) played in steering Carter's foreign policy toward a more hostile, anti-Communist attitude in the wake of events like the Islamic Revolution in Iran and the Soviet invasion of Afghanistan, both of which occurred in 1979. Brands claims that the Soviets were largely responsible for ending détente because of their aggression in Afghanistan, but also argues that Carter's political foes in the United States criticized Carter's détente-era policies toward the Soviets as dangerously misguided in order to gain the presidency for Ronald Reagan in 1980.

The drumbeat of criticism mounted as [Jimmy] Carter entered office [in 1977], though for a time the Democratic president managed to ignore most of it. His rejection of an "inordinate fear of communism" convicted him, in present-dangerist minds, of stunning naïveté, and his preachings about human rights ignored the greatest danger to human rights of all: the prospect of a world communist state. During 1977 and 1978, Carter blunted the criticism with diplomatic progress in other areas, notably the Middle East. Carter's unrelenting and ultimately successful efforts to mediate a peace accord between Israel and Egypt appeared to prove, at least to those willing to be convinced, that there did indeed exist important problems that could be resolved if American leaders allowed themselves to look beyond the conceptual confines of the struggle against communism.

But in 1979 Carter's position disintegrated. The year began with the flight of Shah Pahlavi from Iran and the return of Ayatollah Khomeini from exile. By itself, the Iranian revolution should have had little effect on the debate in the United States over the nature of the communist threat, since Khomeini and the mullahs who now ruled Iran evinced no more affinity for the atheists of the East than for the Great Satan of the West. Yet the loss of a long-time ally in a crucial region of the world, together with Carter's vacillation in determining how to deal with the shah's collapse, reflected poorly on the administration's judgment. Americans waiting in gas lines to pay higher-than-ever prices had plenty of time to reflect on precisely this matter.

The summer of 1979 brought the overthrow of the Somoza [family] regime in Nicaragua [which had been in power since 1933, with strong economic and military support from the United States]. The Nicaraguan revolution seemed more closely related to the ideological contest between the United States and the Soviet Union, since the Sandinistas who controlled the successor government unabashedly took their inspiration from [Fidel] Castro's Cuba. Carter tried to avoid the mistakes he thought the Eisenhower administration had made with Castro, and he kept sending American aid. But the Sandinistas hadn't mounted their revolution to become bourgeois reformers. They took the Americans' food and money, and went about the business of remaking Nicaraguan politics and society along radical lines.

Making an Argument for Resuming the Cold War

The proponents of a revived Cold War capitalized on Carter's discomfiture over Iran and Nicaragua. In November 1979,

Commentary carried a withering assault on the administration's policies by CPD [Committee on the Present Danger, a strongly anti-communist group] member and political scientist Jeane Kirkpatrick. Under the title "Dictators and Double Standards," Kirkpatrick damned Carter for losing Iran and Nicaragua, much as conservatives thirty years earlier had damned [Harry S.] Truman for losing China. Kirkpatrick asserted that Carter's policies toward Pahlavi and [Anastasio] Somoza, two rulers who, though less than democratic, were better than what was certain to follow, could hardly have been more perverse. "In each country," Kirkpatrick asserted, "the Carter administration not only failed to prevent the undesired outcome, it actively collaborated in the replacement of moderate autocrats friendly to American interests with less friendly autocrats of extremist persuasion."

Kirkpatrick drew what she deemed a crucial distinction between authoritarian autocracies of the right, like those of Somoza and Pahlavi, and totalitarian autocracies of the left, like those found in communist countries. The former allowed the continued existence of traditional social institutions, which served to shelter individuals from the oppressive power of the state. The latter tolerated no interference with state power. On account of this difference, the former offered greater hope for liberalization—which was to say, some hope as opposed to none. "Although there is no instance of a revolutionary 'socialist' or Communist society being democratized," Kirkpatrick wrote, "right-wing autocracies do sometimes evolve into democracies—given time, propitious economic, social and political circumstances, talented leaders, and a strong indigenous demand for representative government."

Kirkpatrick contended that the Carter administration employed a double standard in dealing with dictators. In stressing the need to move beyond the Cold War, the administration displayed an unsettling tendency to destabilize American allies, while leaving communist dictatorships firmly in place. "The American commitment to 'change' in the abstract ends up by aligning us tacitly with Soviet clients and irresponsible extremists like the Ayatollah Khomeini or, in the end, Yasir

Arafat." (With other neoconservatives, Kirkpatrick considered Israel a strong ally against radicalism.) She continued, "So far, assisting 'change' has not led the Carter administration to undertake the destabilization of a *Communist* country. The principles of self-determination and nonintervention are thus both selectively applied. We seem to accept the status quo in Communist nations (in the name of 'diversity' and national autonomy), but not in nations ruled by 'right-wing' dictators or white oligarchies.". . .

Kirkpatrick's article caught the attention of at least one person whose opinion mattered— or would matter soon. Ronald Reagan read the piece, and decided that its author would fit well into a Reagan administration. As things turned out, Kirk-

Jimmy Carter

patrick got a job as Reagan's representative to the United Nations, and the distinction between redeemable authoritarians and irredeemable totalitarians provided the basis for much American foreign policy during the 1980s.

While Reagan was trying to figure out what job to give Kirkpatrick, another pair of events significantly enhanced his prospects of becoming the nation's top job-giver. In the process, they contributed to the resurrection of the Cold War. The seizure of several dozen hostages from the American embassy in Tehran [in November 1979], though as unrelated to the superpower rivalry as the rest of the Iranian revolution, seemed further evidence of American impotence in the face of global challenge. Carter handled the matter reasonably well from a humanitarian standpoint, and the fact that all the hostages eventually returned unharmed [in January 1981] resulted largely from his refusal—with the glaring exception of a botched rescue mission—to do anything rash. From a political standpoint, though, he could hardly have handled the matter worse. By making the hostages the center of his attention, he paralyzed his administration. He gave the hostage-holders less incentive than they might have had to release them, and afforded his domestic opponents an easy target. With reason, many Americans considered intolerable a situation in which the United States found itself helpless in the face of extreme provocation by the medieval-minded government of a third-rate country. Increasingly, they heeded those who promised to restore American dignity and power.

Afghanistan and the End of Detente

Detente's coup de grace came in December 1979, when the Soviet Union invaded Afghanistan. Moscow's move probably followed less from a grand design upon the Persian Gulf or the Indian Ocean than from a desire to keep the Islamic fundamentalism that had taken control of Iran from doing the same to Afghanistan and sweeping into the Muslim republics of the Soviet Union. All the same, Carter chose to interpret the move as a direct challenge. Whatever reality underlay the tumultuous situation in the Middle East, political circumstances in the United States left him almost no choice. Republicans continued to rebuke him for ineptitude and flaccidity in dealing with Iran and Nicaragua. And increasing numbers of Democrats were following suit. The SALT [Strategic Arms Limitation Talks] II treaty, signed by Carter and [Soviet premier Leonid] Brezhnev in Vienna in June 1979, had stalled in the Senate. [Senator] Henry Jackson, showing no more respect for detente as pursued by a president of his own party than he had for the Republican version, described Carter's policy as "appeasement in its purest form." In August, another Democrat, Senator [Frank] Church, had announced the discovery of a Soviet "combat brigade" in Cuba. The unit in question had in fact been in Cuba for several years at least, but Church hadn't been facing a tough re-election campaign in conservative Idaho then, and no one had paid attention. Now everyone paid attention. In responding to Church's announcement, the Carter administration attempted the delicate task of demonstrating its determination not to allow a threat to develop in Cuba, and at the same time reassuring Americans that the matter was nothing to worry about. It failed on both counts. After declaring the status quo unacceptable, it ended up leaving matters essentially as they stood.

Within the administration itself, hardliners were gaining the ascendancy. For nearly three years, the moderate [Secretary of State Cyrus] Vance had tried to offset the reactive anti-Sovietism of Carter's national security adviser, Zbigniew Brzezinski. For most of that period, Carter had listened to both men. But the events of 1979—as they occurred overseas, and as they were interpreted at home—pushed the president irrevocably toward Brzezinski. With an impolitic ingenuousness that only made his problems worse, Carter declared, on the final day of 1979, "My opinion of the Russians has changed more drastically in the last week than in the two and one-half years before that." Not to be mistaken, Carter repeated himself: "The action of the Soviets has made a more dramatic change in my opinion of what the Soviets' ultimate goals are than anything they've done in the previous time that I've been in office."

In two sentences, Carter conceded victory to the antidetentists. He confessed to the naïveté they had been charging him with since 1976, and he implicitly endorsed their call for a return to confrontation. He made the endorsement explicit during the next month. He withdrew the SALT II treaty from Senate consideration. He embargoed grain exports to the Soviet Union, beyond those already committed. He barred the sale of high-technology products to the Soviets. He suspended Russian fishing privileges in American waters. He canceled a variety of academic and cultural exchange programs. He ordered the withdrawal of the American team from the 1980 summer Olympic games in Moscow.

And in his State of the Union speech in late January 1980, he set forth what came to be called the Carter Doctrine. After recapitulating the critical moments of the Cold War, with emphasis on the measures his predecessors had taken to block Soviet expansionism, Carter placed himself squarely in their footsteps. The Soviet invasion of Afghanistan, he explained, had brought Moscow's forces "to within 300 miles of the Indian Ocean and close to the Straits of Hormuz—a waterway [in the Persian Gulf] through which most of the world's oil must flow." Russian entrenchment in Afghanistan would pose "a grave threat" to the flow of Middle Eastern oil. In the most direct language possible, Carter warned the Kremlin against further advances. "Let our position be absolutely clear. An attempt by any outside force to gain control of the Persian Gulf region will be regarded as an assault on the vital interests of the United States of America, and such an assault will be repelled by any means necessary, including military force." To add weight to this last statement, Carter conspicuously announced an increase for defense in the federal budget he was proposing for fiscal 1981. . . .

At this point, the only question that remained was how cold the new Cold War would get.

Who Killed Detente?

Actually, there *was* another question, but one that would be of greater interest to historians and other after-the-facters than it was to Carter, the present-dangerists [i.e., members of the CPD or those who agreed with it], and those struggling to make policy at the time. This question involved causation, to wit: Who killed detente? For Carter and the rest in 1980, it was sufficient that detente was dead. They could leave the autopsy to those without care for hostages, oil supplies, and elections.

The obvious answer was that the Soviets killed detente, chiefly by their invasion of Afghanistan. By blatantly violating the principles of restraint that were supposed to have governed superpower relations since the Moscow summit of 1972, the Kremlin left the United States no choice but to retaliate. Carter exaggerated when he called the Soviet invasion of Afghanistan "the greatest threat to peace since the Second World War." He must have been forgetting Korea and Vietnam, which not only threatened but shattered peace, and the Cuban missile crisis. But the president's overall response wasn't out of line with the provocation.

Obvious answers usually contain some truth, and this one about the Soviet role in detente's demise is no exception. Yet if the Soviets hadn't dispatched detente in December 1979, it probably wouldn't have survived the American election campaign of 1980. No viable Republican presidential candidate was about to go anywhere near detente, and, considering the condition of Carter's political fortunes, the president almost certainly would have been forced to back away from what remained of the policy. The SALT II treaty had little chance of gaining Senate approval even before the Afghanistan affair—which, in fact, gave the Carter administration an excuse to pull the treaty and blame the Russians. As Brzezinski commented in urging such a strategy on the president, "If we blame the Soviet invasion of Afghanistan for the delay of SALT, it will be less a political setback for us."

Although it would be a mistake (albeit a common one, for Americans) to attribute too much influence to American actions in determining what the Soviet Union did, the Soviets understood American politics well enough to realize that detente probably had only a few months left to live. They certainly didn't go into Afghanistan *because of* the beating detente was taking in the United States, but, to the extent they considered the likely American reaction to an invasion, they must have calculated that they had little to lose on detente's score. Afghanistan or not, the Kremlin faced a rough time in America in the upcoming election campaign. A miracle might save Carter, but communists aren't supposed to believe in miracles. In any case, his salvation might well have been at Moscow's expense. A Republican victory promised even less.

Fully as much as the Soviets, the present-dangerists were responsible for the death of detente. They didn't deny the charge. On the contrary, they embraced it. Since the early 1970s, the likes of [Senator Henry] Jackson, [journalist/editor Norman] Podhoretz, [longtime statesman Paul] Nitze, and Kirkpatrick had opposed any relaxation between the superpowers, and their opposition had only increased as the decade aged. Taking their cue from Winston Churchill's attacks on appeasement during the 1930s, they strove mightily to destroy detente forty years later, and they considered themselves patriots for their efforts.

The Reasons for Detente's Demise

Why did they succeed? For a number of reasons. In the first place, the Soviets cooperated in acting the villain. The invasion of Afghanistan was the clearest case of villainy, but from the beginning of detente, the Kremlin had persisted in activities that sorely tested the 1972 understanding that the superpowers should avoid actions that disrupted international affairs. In Angola and in the Horn of Africa (where the Russians backed leftist coup-makers in Ethiopia and Somalia), directly and through Cuban proxies, the Soviet Union continued to play the Cold War game of beggar-thy-superpower-neighbor [i.e., force the United States to spend time and money fighting communism around the world]. During the 1973 Middle East war [primarily between Egypt and Israel], Moscow had been so far from cooperating in calming matters that the Nixon White House—that den of detentists—had felt required to place American military forces on alert to warn the Kremlin away from intervening on Egypt's side. Needless to say, the Soviets believed they had justification for acting as they did, but even detente's supporters in America often found the Kremlin's arguments flimsy.

In the second place, the attack on detente succeeded because detente's proponents oversold their product. Most Americans had never gotten used to the fact that friction exists between great powers even in the best of times. Recalling, historically if not personally, the days of America's relative isolation in the nineteenth century, when the United States had had much of a hemisphere more or less to itself, Americans found it difficult to adjust to the shrunken-globe world politics of the twentieth century. (This was one reason why the Cold War had come as a surprise to many Americans in the late 1940s.) When Nixon went to China and the Soviet Union in 1972, laughing with and toasting [Chinese premier] Mao [Zedong] and Brezhnev, and when the president spoke of a new era in international relations, it was easy for Americans to gain the impression that affairs among the great powers would be as friendly as the meetings of their leaders seemed to be. In Beijing in 1972 Nixon asserted, "This was the week that changed the world." He spoke too optimistically, and his excess optimism came back to cost detente.

In the third place, detente died because the Carter administration did a dismal job directing it. Through his first three years in office, Carter failed to resolve the difference of opinion that separated the Brzezinski camp in his administration from the Vance group. The result of this failure was a policy that sometimes exhibited a split personality. One notable address by Carter at the United States Naval Academy in June 1978 left everyone puzzling over what the administration was up to. "We must avoid excessive swings in the public mood in our country, from euphoria when things are going well to despair when they are not, from an exaggerated sense of compatibility with the Soviet Union to open expressions of hostility," the president declared. Then he proceeded to demonstrate just such a swing. "Detente between our two countries is essential to world peace," he said, before adding, "To the Soviet Union, detente seems to mean a continuing aggressive struggle for political advantage and increased influence." The latter statement wasn't much of a recommendation for something defined as essential to world peace. Carter didn't help detente's case when he presented it to Moscow as a take-it-or-leave-it proposition. "The Soviet Union can choose either confrontation or cooperation. The United States is adequately prepared to meet either choice."

The Soviets responded by declaring Carter's speech "strange." Washington reporters, despite readier access to administration officials, had no better luck figuring out what was going on. The *Washington Post* subtitled its account of the address "Two Different Speeches." The *New York Times*, said the speech seemed "contradictory." The *Los Angeles Times's* diplomatic correspondent called the message "as ambiguous as the conflicting policies and complex circumstances from which it sprang." Syndicated columnist Mary McGrory asked, "What was Carter saying?" and concluded, "All he said was that he doesn't even know what he thinks."

The Second Cold War

Fred Halliday

The improved relations that existed between the United States and Soviet Union for the better part of the 1960s and 1970s came to an end in 1979 as a number of factors caused renewed antagonism between the two superpowers. Fred Halliday, professor of international relations at the London School of Economics and Political Science in London, England, calls the tense years that followed the end of détente "Cold War II." Halliday argues that the post-WWII confrontation between the United States and the Soviet Union initially peaked from 1946 to 1953 (a period he calls "Cold War I") and then moderated until the late 1970s. Halliday reserves the use of the term "cold war" specifically for periods when the two superpowers focused their military, rhetorical, and ideological energies directly on each other (as opposed to deflecting them onto secondary, or "client," conflicts like the Vietnam War). In this viewpoint (written in 1983 as Cold War II was ongoing), Halliday compares the two Cold Wars in terms of not only the international events that helped to bring them about, but also the ways that interaction between the two rival nations differed during these years of heightened conflict. The most important similarity for Halliday is the superpowers' tendency to see all global issues during these periods as part of an unresolvable ideological division between communism and capitalism.

Cold War II developed, like its predecessor Cold War I, from the breakdown of relations between the major capitalist states and the USSR that were to some degree more cooperative. On the basis of its first four years, 1979–1982, it

Excerpted from *The Making of the Second Cold War*, by Fred Halliday (London: Verso, 1983). Copyright © 1983 by Fred Halliday. Reprinted by permission of the publisher.

can be seen how it partook, with some significant variations, of the characteristics that marked off Cold War I [1946–1953] as a distinct period of postwar history.

The most obvious index of Cold War is a greater sense of the danger of war. Cold War II involved an increased emphasis by both sides upon the likelihood of war and on the need for military preparations against possible attacks from the enemy. The rise of the peace movement certainly served to draw greater attention to this issue, and it, for the first time, achieved a significant audience inside the USA. But the development of resistance to nuclear weapons policies in the west from 1979 onwards was not only a response to the sustained accumulation of weapons over the past two decades. It was also a reaction to the specific increases in military expenditure and changes in weapons deployment associated with the late 1970s, i.e. to a military buildup that got under way at the start of Cold War II.

Western governments had, since 1978, been calling for a new military capacity, stressing the need to expand military expenditure and highlighting the legitimacy of the use of force in international relations. [President Jimmy] Carter pledged himself in 1978 to a 3 per cent real increase in US military spending; the Republican Party Manifesto of 1980 committed itself to restoring US military superiority. Speaking to cadets at the US military academy of West Point in 1981, on the dangers of the 'Treaty Trap', [President Ronald] Reagan promised to expand America's military strength: 'No nation that placed its faith in parchment or paper while at the same time it gave up its protective hardware ever lasted long enough to write many pages in history', he said. Reagan's first Secretary of State, Alexander Haig, stated on many occasions during the first months after coming into office that the Administration's priority was, in his phrase, 'the restoration of US economic and military strength'. He told one audience that some things were more valuable than peace. This emphasis upon the need for a new military capacity vis-à-vis the USSR went together with greater belligerency in third world policies—with increased preparations for intervention there, with warnings about a renewed US willingness to intervene in key states (e.g. Saudi Arabia) and with threats of force against such targets as Libya, Cuba and Nicaragua. The increased level of US military readiness, imitated to a greater or lesser degree by its European allies, was the most evident practical symbol of the changes in the west attendant upon the Second Cold War.

There was not a commensurate hardening of policy on the Soviet side. Indeed western politicians justified their shift as a response to a continuous Soviet buildup over the 1970s. But force came to play a more prominent part in Soviet foreign policy, most notably in the Soviet intervention in Afghanistan of December 1979, the first time Soviet troops were used in combat outside the Soviet sphere of influence since 1945. The Soviet Union attained a level of military preparedness never seen before and had introduced new [intermediate range] missiles into the European theatre, the SS-20S. In response to the declarations of the Reagan Administration Soviet leaders increasingly stressed that they were prepared to match western military innovations and, if necessary, to fight to defend their interests when attacked. Whilst not overtly bellicist [warlike] in tone, as US statements often were, Soviet foreign policy statements certainly became distinctly more martial with the onset of the Second Cold War. Soviet officials also, on occasion, adopted a hectoring and minatory tone in addressing public opinion in countries that were seen as particularly facilitating the US buildup—Japan and West Germany.

The Intensified War of Words

Cold War II was also accompanied by new waves of that ideological contestation so characteristic of the earlier period. In the west, this involved emphasis upon such questions as the weakness of the Soviet economy, the plight of dissidents, the rate of Soviet arms expenditure and production, and the global implications of Soviet foreign policy. These are all serious issues meriting discussion; but the manner in which they were conventionally discussed was of a highly speculative and polemical kind, one that often bore little relationship to the truth or to historical proportion. With the advent of the Reagan Administration the USSR was repeatedly accused of backing 'international terrorism', and even of attempting to assassinate the Pope. Reagan's remark that the Russian 'are prepared to lie, cheat and steal' to further their goal epitomised this mood. Very few commentators associated with the Reagan Administration appeared to know much about Soviet society, or to seek to understand the motivations of Russia's leaders or population. What is striking is that many of the problems identified in this propaganda had, if anything, been alleviated in the 1970s. They could not justify the *intensified* vilification to which the USSR was subjected in the climate of the Second Cold War.

The Soviet side did, for different reasons, show less of a change in tone. One factor was that in the Detente period, Soviet writers were less accomodating to the capitalist viewpoint than many western writers were to the USSR, and the switch back to a more polemical tone involved less drastic changes. Another factor is that greater control of the press means that if Soviet writers reveal less of the truth about their opponents, they also retail less untruth and abuse. But the US Administration did not continue to enjoy the favour shown to it in the period of [Richard] Nixon and [Gerald] Ford, and the USA was now held responsible for a wide range of militaristic initiatives towards the USSR. Whereas US foreign policy was treated more indulgently in the past, it was now charged with counter-revolutionary activities in Afghanistan, Cambodia, Central America and Poland in a replay of the polemics [disputes] characteristic of the earlier Cold War.

Cold War II was accompanied by a dramatic cooling in bilateral relations between east and west, and in particular in negotiations between the USSR and the USA. There was certainly a contrast with the First Cold War, when no talks at all took place and discussions on arms control were completely blocked. In 1982, three years into the Second Cold War, east-west talks were taking place in Geneva, on intermediate-range nuclear weapons and on strategic arms reductions, in Madrid, at the Conference on Security and Co-operation in Europe [CSCE], a sequel to the Helsinki Agreement of 1975, and in Vienna, on Mutual and Balanced

Forced Reductions [MBFR] in Europe. The 'Hot Line' remained in place and data on space exploration were being
exchanged. But on the western side the political intent of
such talks seemed to be as much to reduce criticism and
force concessions on the USSR as it was to seek compromise;
and, whatever the outcome of these talks, the fact remained
that there was from the mid-1970s onwards, i.e. before the
onset of Cold War II proper, a standstill in east-west negotiation. SALT [Strategic Arms Limitations Treaty]-II did not
follow on from SALT-I signed back in 1972. The CSCE and
MBFR discussions appeared to be going nowhere and were
used primarily as occasions to pillory the other side. In
strategic matters a similar lack of agreement was evident—
on such issues as the Arab-Israeli question, security in the
Persian Gulf, the Horn of Africa, Afghanistan and the Indian
Ocean. Economic ties between east and west were maintained and there was not a complete shutting off of the financial and commercial bonds built up in the 1970s; but as
far as the USA was concerned, trade itself became an area of
conflict. A series of boycotts and cancellations of agreements
in the period from 1979 onwards served to subordinate economic links to the dictates of Cold War.

Overall, the flow of meetings and talks during Cold War II
served to mask the similarity with Cold War I whereas the
underlying reality of bilateral impasse served to confirm it.
Cold War I involved a standoff in Europe, with the exception
of Greece, but major conflicts in the Far East. Cold War II
has not led to any direct conflict in Europe either, but during
the 1970s there were massive social upheavals in all three
continents of the third world and these helped both to cause
and to sustain Cold War II. . . . [O]ne of the main reasons for
Cold War II was the wave of third world revolutions which
from 1974 onwards engulfed the South, from Saigon [Viet-
nam] to Managua [Nicaragua], and thereby provoked deep
anxiety in the advanced capitalist states. The response of the
USA and its allies was to blame these developments on the
USSR, and to instigate counter-attacks in Central America,
Western Sahara, the Persian Gulf, Afghanistan and Cambodia. None of these third world crises equalled the high point

of Cold War I—the Chinese Revolution of 1949—in scale, but once again the massive but paralysed tensions of Europe, the 'Central Front' of NATO [North Atlantic Treaty Organi-

---

Reagan Signals the End of Détente

On January 29, 1981, in his first official news conference as president, Ronald Reagan left no doubt that he intended to end any remaining détente-era policies and resume a tough policy stance toward the Soviet Union. His responses to a reporter's questions about the possibilities of a resumption of détente both echo his tough anticommunist campaign rhetoric and presage his policies over the next several years.

Q. Mr. President, what do you see as the long-range intentions of the Soviet Union? Do you think, for instance, the Kremlin is bent on world domination that might lead to a continuation of the cold war? Or do you think that under other circumstances détente is possible?

A. Well, so far détente's been a one-way street the Soviet Union has used to pursue its own aims. I don't have to think of an answer as to what I think their intentions are: They have repeated it.

I know of no leader of the Soviet Union, since the revolution and including the present leadership, that has not more than once repeated in the various Communist Congresses they hold, their determination that their goal must be the promotion of world revolution and a one world Socialist or Communist state—whichever word you want to use.

Now, as long as they do that and as long as they, at the same time, have openly and publicly declared that the only morality they recognize is what will further their cause: meaning they reserve unto themselves the right to commit any crime; to lie; to cheat, in order to obtain that and that is moral, not immoral, and we operate on a different set of standards, I think when you do business with them—even at a détente—you keep that in mind.

New York Times, "Transcript of President's First News Conference on Foreign and Domestic Topics," January 30, 1981, p. A10.

zation] designation, were displaced onto third world theatres where no such paralysis was to be found.

The Effect of Cold War II on Dissent

The USA and the USSR sought to accompany the heightened level of confrontation with each other by greater controls on dissent within their own ranks, both within their own societies and within their own alliance systems. Within western society the previous two decades witnessed a substantial erosion of traditional ideological and social systems of domination—along lines of class, race, sex and age. The Second Cold War was linked to a wide-ranging conservative rollback in most spheres of social policy, both in the USA and Europe. In economic matters this took the form of monetarist [a theory of economics that believes growth to be dependent on a steady increase in the money supply] macroeconomic policies and the devastations of supply-siders. In social policy, this rollback involved the reversal through fund-cutting and legislation of the gains made by trades union organizations and by movements of women, gays and blacks during the 1970s. A combination of direct confrontation and unemployment was also used to undermine trades unions. The reassertion of internal unity and hegemony was, however, but a concomitant of the re-establishment of a new international unity, with in this case the reassertion by Washington of US hegemony as forcefully as circumstances allowed. This reinforcement of the US position was most evident in military matters—pressure on allies for expenditure increases, stationing of Cruise and Pershing-II missiles in Europe, demands for support for US initiatives in the third world. But it was also extended to encompass inter-capitalist economic policy, aid and trade policies towards the third world, and negotiating postures towards the USSR. In both internal and international issues, the postulation of an external threat was combined with alarm about the erosion of pre-existing values to foster mobilisation for a new Cold War.

In the USSR the party leadership had, from the early 1960s onwards, brought about a steady reduction in arbitrary and terroristic acts by the state security forces. Only in one area, the use of psychiatric clinics to intern political dissenters, was there a subsequent net deterioration. But the Kremlin accompanied this with an erratic policy towards those outspokenly critical of the system. This suppression of the overtly critical began in the early 1970s and by the late 1970s the dissident movement had to a large extent been driven underground; a few publicised trials had been used both to intimidate critics within the USSR and to demonstrate to their western supporters that the Soviet system was not going to tolerate their interference. The onset of Cold War II nevertheless led to an increase in hostility to internal opposition as contacts between east and west lessened. Jewish emigration was cut by 95 per cent between 1980 and 1982; direct telephone links to western Europe were severed in the latter year, and the mailing of books abroad was impeded. This went together with an attempt to stimulate greater patriotic sentiment in the USSR and with an emphasis on the need to educate the young in the necessities of military discipline. A small independent peace group set up in June 1982 was harassed. In the broader context of eastern Europe, special attention was given by the CPSU [Communist Party of the Soviet Union] leaders to Poland, where opposition was greatest, and in December 1981 martial law was declared there by the Polish army in order to contain and reverse the movement that had grown up around Solidarity. Polemics against 'pluralism' [i.e., political movements other than Soviet-style communism], even under socialism, became common. While there was no return in Moscow during Cold War II to the levels of control associated with the Stalin period, involving show trials and political executions, repression of dissent in both the USSR and eastern Europe was notably greater than during earlier periods of tolerance.

Cold War II and a New Policy Focus

Cold War II involved a concerted and sustained attempt by the USA to subordinate the various dimensions of its foreign policy, and that of its allies, to confrontation with the USSR. The image of a 'Soviet Threat' was used not merely to elicit increased vigilance against the Soviet Union, but also to create strategic framework within which other issues should be seen and given their due proportion and to mobilise the European allies and Japan for economic pressure on the USSR. The emphasis was on facing up to the USSR, rather than on seeking compromise, and on giving priority to this, rather than on the relative distinctness of the different issues dividing the states of the world.

It is relevant to recall how different this was from the dominant tone of western political discourse in the earlier part of the 1970s. Then the Soviet Union was not seen as the *radix malorum*, the root of all international evil, that it was later to become. A revival of the Cold War was no more foreseen than the resurgence of politicised religion, a world-wide recession, or the combative regionalism of western Europe. Speaking in 1974, Secretary of State [Henry] Kissinger was able to say: 'the biggest problem American foreign policy confronts right now is not how to regulate competition with its enemies . . . but how to bring our friends to a realisation there are greater common interests than simple self-assertiveness'. In a major foreign policy speech at Notre Dame University in 1977 President Carter called on America to 'get away from the unhealthy obsession' with the USSR that had marked previous Administrations. For a while Carter espoused the viewpoint associated with the Trilateral Commission [a group of prominent businessmen, academics, and politicians to which Carter belonged] which placed priority on the need to restructure relations between capitalist states rather than on the bipolar US-Soviet conflict.

This disaggregation of the problems of foreign policy was accompanied by a belief that the USA and the USSR could find common ground on the major issues of the day. Thus Kissinger sought to involve the Soviet Union in agreements that would encourage it to reduce its arms production and restrain itself in the third world. Typical of this period was the view of the noted foreign affairs specialist. Alistair Buchan, writing in 1973: 'The Soviet Union and the United States will develop a series of specific understanding to keep their strategic relationship stable and to attempt to restrain conflict in areas where they cannot escape commitment, notably Europe and the Middle East'. Similarly, the Washington correspondent of the *Sunday Times* [of London], Henry Brandon wrote of the USA and USSR as 'confined by a mutual vulnerability of which they have become well aware' and which would ensure that the 1970s would see a lessening of international tensions. This expectation was widely held at the time. Hence, if Detente involved the twin beliefs of a multipolar world and the possibility of compromise with the USSR on the basis of shared interest, in Cold Wars I and II western leaders have laid stress upon the bipolar and antagonistic character of world politics and on the need to marshal all the forces at the west's disposal for a confrontation with the opposite camp.

Beginning of the End: The Eastern European Revolutions of 1989

John Feffer

Mikhail Gorbachev's reforms in the mid-1980s were not intended to end the dominance of communism in the Soviet Union and its Eastern European satellite states. John Feffer, author of a number of books dealing with contemporary European politics, argues that the twin policies of glasnost and perestroika were nevertheless the stimulus for the democratic revolutions that unexpectedly spread through Eastern Europe in the summer and fall of 1989. Feffer moves through the process chronologically, but also by country, beginning with Poland and Hungary, two countries he argues were primed for reform earlier than most of their neighbors. Feffer continues by contrasting countries such as Czechoslovakia, where the transition from communism to a more democratic government was accomplished peacefully, with those like Romania, where the overthrow of the despotic Ceausescu regime was accomplished only after considerable violence. The revolutions of 1989 essentially ended the Cold War in Europe, since (in principle) they erased the political antagonism between the Eastern and Western halves of the continent. In the end, Feffer does not credit Gorbachev with the decline and eventual demise of communism in Eastern Europe. However, his analysis suggests that the process was both significantly accelerated and less likely to result in a violent backlash (like that which occurred in Tiananmen Square earlier in 1989) because of Gorbachev's active encouragement of reform from within.

In retrospect, historical outcomes always seem inevitable. The revolutions of 1989, viewed from the secure knowledge of the present, had to have happened. [Mikhail] Gorbachev was steering the Soviet Union in a new direction, protests were building throughout Eastern Europe, the communist governments in the region were looking shakier and more isolated each day. This bloc was about to burst apart. It was just a question of when.

But on June 4, 1989, when the Berlin Wall was still an implacable presence, with Nicolae Ceausescu still comfortably ensconced in his Romanian personality cult, and the revolutions of the fall a hot summer away, nothing seemed inevitable. True, from the Polish point of view, a new era was beginning. Voters throughout the country were turning out for their first (partially) free national elections in four decades, and the newly legalized [non-communist political party] Solidarity was heading for a resounding victory. But that same day, on the opposite side of the world, another historical path was being followed. The Chinese government had decided to put down the Beijing Spring with force, sending troops and tanks into Tiananmen Square, killing hundreds, and extinguishing for the time being not only revolution but democratic reform as well.

Even the Poles, in their post-election elation, eyed the Chinese "solution" warily. As they celebrated their own electoral victory that June, Poles remembered their experience with martial law eight years earlier: the defiance, the repressions, the move underground, the ineffectual foreign response. It had happened once. Why not again? The opposition in Poland had been repressed so many times that its pessimism, bordering on paranoia, seemed reasonable when measured against this historical background.

If the Poles still harbored lingering fears, so much greater were the worries of their neighbors. The words "Tiananmen Square" would be the negative reference point, the worst-case scenario for the emerging opposition movements in the region in the fall of 1989. The possibility that any of the collapsing governments might use force—the truncheon of last resort—certainly diminished the "inevitability" of the radical change even as that change was occurring at breakneck speed. The proponents of change had lost before. In some countries, they had lost dozens of times. But in 1989, they were poised, finally, to win. And when the "Tiananmen Square" scenarios were finally pushed safely into the "might have been" and change became irreversible, the feeling was exhilarating. For people who had learned, as Polish literary critic Stanislaw Baranczak put it, to "breathe underwater," resurfacing in those first heady revolutionary moments was a narcotic like no other.

Revolution Begins in Poland and Hungary

The beginning of 1989 found Eastern Europe divided into roughly three groups. Poland and Hungary were in the forefront of reform. The communist governments in both countries had decided that to win public approval for an austerity package off economic reforms they would permit a degree of political pluralism and power-sharing with the opposition movement. In the second category were the damage controllers: East Germany and Czechoslovakia. Dismissive of the political and economic reforms favored by their reformist neighbors, the communist governments of the GDR [German Democratic Republic, or East Germany] and Czechoslovakia were more interested in controlling opposition than in repressing them outright (though explicit repression did happen too). These governments preferred to purchase the support of their populations with consumer goods and treated with great skepticism the flowering of *glasnost* ["openness"] and *perestroika* ["restructuring"] in the Soviet Union. In the third category, as the Stalinist holdover, Romania maintained a well-developed police state that waged an internal war against its population. Straddling these categories, the Bulgarian Communist Party was rather schizophrenic adopting reformist programs based on Gorbachev's *perestroika* and yet violently repressing its ethnic Turkish community. In Yugoslavia, an Eastern Europe in miniature, all three categories were represented as each republic prepared to strike off in different directions.

The differences among these countries in 1989 were not

something new. Eastern Europe had never been the undifferentiated ring of satellites referred to in Cold War shorthand as the Soviet "bloc." Regional animosites underscored the heterogeneity. Romania and Hungary clashed politically over ethnic and territorial issues; Bulgaria and Yugoslavia feuded over Macedonia; Poland and East Germany continued to trade complaints over their common border and adjacent territorial waters. This was no happy family of socialist nations. This was a region whose leaders were forced to settle for unhappy compromises for fear of the geopolitical implications of a rancorous divorce.

This era of unhappy compromises—among communist states as well as between the governments and the political oppositions—came to an abrupt end in 1989. Ironically, the new age was heralded by a compromise—between Poland's Communist Party and the outlawed Solidarity trade union movement. In the years after martial law, Solidarity's membership and influence had declined significantly, in part because its moderation irritated younger, more militant workers. Those workers took the lead in 1988, spearheading two key strikes. Meanwhile, in the fall of that year, after continued economic decline, a new communist government led by Mieczyslaw Rakowski came to power declaring that the Party had two choices: institute reform now or be surprised by revolution later. With the Party leaning toward rapprochement and the workers raising their voices, [Lech Walesa] the electrician from Gdansk who had vaulted to the leadership of Solidarity in 1980 returned to the spotlight. In December 1988, Lech Walesa formed the Citizens' Committee, a group, largely intellectuals, brought together to negotiate with the communist government in the roundtable talks announced at the beginning of 1989.

These talks lasted a mere eight weeks, but in that short time Polish history was rewritten. Formerly implacable enemies sat down together to draft an agreement legalizing Solidarity and establishing a timeline for the first partially free national elections in over four decades. What had seemed for so long to be an unbridgeable gap between a communist government and a non-communist opposition was, albeit with many mutual reservations, gradually bridged. Governments and opposition movements in neighboring countries could look to Poland for inspiration in negotiating out of corners as they had once looked with a mixture of pity and fear at how both sides in Poland had negotiated themselves into them in 1980–81.

Hungary was the first country to follow suit. Throughout the spring of 1989, a series of events—an unofficial celebration of the 1848 revolution, an alternative May Day—demonstrated the depth of public support for change. In June, the reburial of Imre Nagy, the martyred leader who stood up to the Soviets in 1956, brought out 250,000 Hungarians and was treated to an eight-hour television broadcast. (At a similar commemoration the previous year considered unlawful by the government, the police quickly dispersed the few hundred brave demonstrators.) Begun nine days after the success of Solidarity's Citizens' Committee in the Polish elections, the Hungarian roundtable negotiations legalized underground parties as in Poland but also laid the groundwork for entirely free elections in 1990.

An informal competition had begun between the two countries: who would be in reform's absolute vanguard? Poles could boast of Solidarity and its decade-long struggle; Hungarians emphasized that their revolution was being accomplished not only nonviolently but virtually without strikes or mass demonstrations. Poland sponsored the first roundtable talks; Hungary would schedule the first entirely free elections. By the time Hungary issued its final roundtable document, Poland had again moved into the lead when Tadeusz Mazowiecki formed the first non-communist government in Eastern Europe. The Polish government in September 1989 was no longer controlled by the Polish Communist Party. The options for opposition movements had just widened: not simply power-sharing on a junior basis but power-controlling.

The Revolutionary Movement Spreads to East Germany

It is not hard to imagine the shock and horror with which the governments of East Germany, Czechoslovakia, Bulgaria, and Romania viewed these deviations and heresies. Yet, throughout the changes of the first half of 1989, they maintained an "it-can't-happen-here" attitude. After all, these more orthodox regimes had not permitted massive trade unions in their midst as in Poland or well-developed semi-official movements of civil society as in Hungary. This security proved illusory indeed. The misplaced confidence of these communist leaders certainly contributed to triggering the revolutions of the fall. Their refusal to reform left revolution the only alternative.

The first country to join Poland and Hungary in the camp of radical reform was East Germany. Pastors from the Lutheran Evangelical Church, the largest religious denomination in the GDR, had been conducting peace vigils in the southern city of Leipzig for the better part of the 1980s. In the fall of 1989, these vigils gave birth to the Monday demonstrations which, in the context of the Polish changes and the emigration of GDR citizens, rapidly grew in size. The hemorrhaging of the GDR that August and September amounted to tens of thousands of people. Meanwhile, police repression of nonviolent protesters increased in several cities. The aging East German communist leader Erich Honecker decided that it was time for a Chinese solution. Honecker notified the army, and preparations were made for confrontation in Leipzig. An isolated government willing to use force to compensate for declining legitimacy squared off against an overwhelming majority of the population.

Honecker's order to use force on October 9 in Leipzig was ultimately countermanded. The demonstration proceeded peacefully. A civic group, New Forum, formed in mid-September, took advantage of the large turnout to call for negotiations with the government. By October 23, demonstrations in Leipzig had swelled to 200,000 people. The chants, which at the height of the exodus were "we want to go," had changed to the infinitely more provocative "we want to stay." Although travel restrictions to the West were lifted on October 20, the rallies continued to grow. The determination of the East German protesters caught the communist leadership by surprise.

But the biggest surprises were yet to come. On November 7, the entire political leadership of the GDR resigned. Then, while the new communist government was still adjusting to the situation, the mayor of East Berlin gave an order on November 9 that was subsequently misinterpreted. He asked the border guards at the Berlin Wall to allow people to cross over for that night only in order to relieve some of the political pressure. The border guards opened the Wall that night—and never closed it again. From that moment on, with the Wall no longer separating East from West, the pace of change quickened. Roundtables proliferated at all levels throughout the country, the hated security police (Stasi) were neutralized, and national elections were planned for the following spring.

"Velvet" Revolutions in Czechoslovakia and Bulgaria

As the Polish government prepared for roundtable negotiations at the beginning of 1989, the Czechoslovak government was busy arresting 800 opposition activists, among them playwright and dissident Vaclav Havel. Later, as Poles were anticipating their first semi-free elections, one of Havel's plays made its Warsaw debut. Communist Prime Minister Rakowski attended the opening night performance while Havel himself was still sitting in jail. The night East and West Germans danced on the Berlin Wall, toasting each other with champagne, Czechs and Slovaks did some soul-searching. First Poland, then Hungary, now East Germany: why not here? Czechs and Slovaks would soon answer their own question. A week after the fall of the Berlin Wall, police confronted a line of students marching toward the center of Prague. The students placed their candles at the feet of the riot police and calmly sat down on the street. After a tense stand-off, the police attacked with truncheons, breaking arms and legs and sending many students to the hospital. As the attack of Birmingham police on Black school children had galvanized the US Civil Rights Movement in 1963, the beating of unarmed young people pushed Prague workers and intellectuals into further non-violent action.

The following Monday, 300,000 people massed in Wenceslas Square to listen to playwright Havel publicly proclaim the very messages for which he had been repeatedly jailed. A general strike was planned, an opposition movement was united under the name Civic Forum, and demands were presented to a government as taken aback by the protests as Honecker and his cronies had been a month earlier in East Germany. In the space of six weeks, the demonstrators executed a "velvet" revolution—peaceful, nonviolent, often humorous—that toppled the communist government, installed an interim government with Vaclav Havel as its interim president, and instituted roundtable negotiations that would detail the elections to come that following spring.

Bulgarian leaders had now seen enough. Sufficiently warned, Party reformers replaced long-time ruler Todor Zhivkov in November, initiating limited changes from above. Too little, too late. For a country that had had no significant opposition movement for four decades, a broad-based coalition of protesters came into existence with surprising speed. Within a week of Zhivkov's ouster, 50,000 people were demonstrating in Sofia pressing for further change. Various opposition movements pulled together in December to form the Union of Democratic Forces and to prepare for eventual elections. But in Bulgaria, as in Yugoslavia, the legalization of parties outside the Party would have to wait until early 1990.

The Last Holdouts: Albania and Romania

Entering the last month of 1989, it looked as though the convulsions in Eastern Europe had subsided. Two countries remained relatively unaffected by the changes, Romania and Albania, Eastern Europe's truly disadvantaged. Albania wouldn't undergo any substantial change until 1990. In Romania, meanwhile, Nicolae Ceausescu and his Communist Party, considering their positions secure, expected to live out the century in the leader's proclaimed Years of Light. They were not given the chance to revise their estimates.

The Romanian revolution began in Transylvania, home of the mythic Dracula and, more importantly, a sizable Hungarian minority. An outspoken ethnic Hungarian pastor, Laszlo Tokes, was removed from his church by the Romanian authorities, touching off large-scale demonstrations in the regional capital, Timisoara. The Tiananmen Square scenario, which had been successfully averted in every other Eastern European country, quickly became reality for Romania. A combination of security police and army personnel killed hundreds of people in Timisoara. Undaunted by early reports of thousands massacred, protesters took to the streets in Bucharest. When Ceausescu appeared at the balcony of the Party building to greet the crowds at an orchestrated pro-government rally on December 21, he heard the chants of opposition activists for the first time. The surprise on his face was clearly visible. Four days later, on Christmas day, Ceausescu and his wife were dead, executed after a cursory trial by order of a provisional government. The reports of tens of thousands killed have since been amended—896 killed, 2,100 injured. . . .

Gorbachev's Role in the Eastern European Revolutions

1989 was Eastern Europe's year of living dangerously. It began with relatively sedate negotiations and ended with bloody revolution. In between came a series of more or less "velvet" transitions. The pace and suddenness of the changes seemed to indicate that they had come from nowhere. Newspaper coverage emphasized the singularity of the events of 1989, their almost ahistorical character. But the revolutionary changes certainly had their sources, whether in the region's history of opposition and reform or in the developing context of East-West relations.

The "great man" theory of history has often been the recourse of hurried journalists and conservative historians. While certainly the Caesars, Napoleons, and Washingtons have had their impact on history, excessive attention paid to their personal roles often obscures the roles of other actors and underestimates the impact of structural and collective forces. With this caveat established, however, the role of Soviet leader Mikhail Gorbachev in the changes in Eastern Europe must be recognized. Upon coming to power in 1985, Gorbachev received what could only be considered a lukewarm reception in the West. Even as he consolidated control within the Party and began the political and economic reforms that would shake up and eventually destroy the Soviet Union, Gorbachev was still treated with great suspicion by Western politicians, journalists, and Sovietologists.

Regardless of the domestic future of the post-Soviet Union, Gorbachev's reforms in foreign policy have changed the direction of European and world history. Not only did Gorbachev resurrect Khrushchev's doctrine of "separate paths to socialism," but he, unlike Khrushchev, held to the principle. Khrushchev encouraged reform in Eastern Europe only to step backward in 1956 and order Soviet troops to put down the Hungarian experiment. By contrast, Gorbachev spoke of "separate paths to socialism" as early as 1986 and watched in 1989 as the countries of Eastern Europe took very separate paths indeed, and none of them toward a stated goal of socialism.

In fact, Gorbachev did more than simply watch. Domestically he pushed through reforms, specially in the area of cultural freedom that inspired movements in Eastern Europe to demand similar changes. Not content to work by example, Gorbachev took an interventionist stance as well, actually accelerating changes along his western border. He telephoned Party members in Poland to "encourage" them to compromise. In October 1989, as demonstrations swelled in East Germany, Gorbachev deliberately underscored his previous position in a speech in Finland, declaring that "the Soviet Union has no moral or political right to interfere in the affairs of its East European neighbors." It marked, as his government spokesperson phrased it, the replacement of the Brezhnev Doctrine (which justified Soviet intervention into the affairs of neighboring powers) with the "Sinatra Doctrine" (which allowed countries to do things "their way"). Two days before the initial student demonstration in Czechoslovakia in November, Gorbachev gave high-level advice to the Communist Party there: change, or else.

Although he was important, one man did not change

everything. Gorbachev removed the struts from beneath the communist parties in Eastern Europe, leaving them vulnerable but not necessarily on the verge of collapse. Western economic institutions also contributed to weakening the various governments by saddling them with large debts and encouraging them to leave the Soviet bloc. The CIA funneled money and equipment covertly to anti-communists in the region through such organizations as the National Endowment for Democracy and even enlisted the Vatican's assistance in the case of Poland. But toppling these governments still remained the task of public movements.

The Last Years of the Soviet Union

David S. Mason

As the democratization of former Communist states in Eastern Europe accelerated in the late 1980s and Mikhail Gorbachev's twin policies of glasnost (openness) and perestroika (restructuring) changed Soviet citizens' attitudes toward their government, the Soviet Union began rapidly to disintegrate. In this selection, David S. Mason examines how the external momentum of the Eastern European revolutions and the internal attempts at reform within the Soviet system combined to bring about the ultimate demise of the USSR, and thereby to end the Cold War. Mason begins by discussing Gorbachev's last-ditch efforts to maintain the Soviet Union's status as a Communist superpower. He then looks at the creation of the Commonwealth of Independent States in 1991 as an attempt to salvage some of the political and economic ties between the increasingly autonomous former Soviet republics. Finally, he analyzes the effect of the Soviet Union's rapid decline and disappearance on its former client states in Eastern Europe, on the United States, and on the wider global political situation. Mason is professor of political science at Butler University in Indianapolis, Indiana. He has written five books on various aspects of Eastern European politics at the end of the 20th century.

The rebirth of East-Central Europe coincided with the gradual decay and disintegration of the Soviet Union. The reorientation of East-Central Europe toward the West was made both desirable and possible because of the dramatically weakened international position of the USSR. This situation was an irony for the [Mikhail] Gorbachev leadership, which had unleashed the changes in Eastern Europe with its own glasnost and perestroika in the Soviet Union. In what Berkeley historian Martin Malia has called "the boomerang effect from Central Europe," the Eastern European revolutions doubled back on the Soviet Union and accelerated the disintegration of that system too.

The Eastern European Impact on the Soviet Union

The symbiosis of change that had toppled one government after another in Eastern Europe began in 1990 to affect the Soviet Union as well. In both politics and economics, precedents from East-Central Europe were adopted in the Soviet Union. During the five years of perestroika [Gorbachev's policy of "restructuring" Soviet society to make it more democratic and market-oriented] for example, Gorbachev had always insisted on maintaining the leading role of the Communist party. But the collapse of communism in Eastern Europe weakened Gorbachev's resolve and his ability to maintain this commitment to party dominance. In February 1990, he told the party's Central Committee that the party had to earn its leading role through the ballot box and in competition with other parties. The next month, the Congress of Peoples' Deputies amended Article 6 of the Constitution to eliminate the party's political monopoly, as most of the ECE [East-Central European] states had already done.

The decentralization and fragmentation of the Soviet Union were also hastened by the Eastern European revolutions. A 1988 election law in the Soviet Union had allowed semicompetitive elections for the new national legislature (the Congress of Peoples' Deputies) in March of 1989. But the real electoral revolutions occurred in republican and local elections between December 1989 and March 1990, after the collapse of communist governments in Eastern Europe. In the Russian republic, radical forces under the banner of the Democratic Russia Movement won over one-third of the seats in the legislature and were then able to elect Boris Yeltsin to the republican presidency in May. The next month, the Russian Parliament declared Russia sovereign. At the local level, Gavriil Popov and Anatolii Sobchak were elected as mayors of Moscow and Leningrad, respectively. Soon after that, Yeltsin, Popov, and Sobchak all resigned from the Communist party.

In the other republics, the forces of change were more nationalistic than democratic, although the two often went together. Nationalistic forces in the Baltic republics, in particular, seemed to take courage from the democratic revolutions to their west. Independence-minded popular fronts swept the republican parliamentary elections in Lithuania, Estonia, and Latvia in early 1990 and coincided with the increasingly radical demands for sovereignty in those states. In March 1990, the Lithuanian parliament formed a noncommunist coalition government, following a precedent set by neighboring Poland the previous summer and establishing a precedent that was later followed by other Soviet republics.

In the economic sphere, too, the rapid moves toward the market in East-Central Europe prodded the Soviets to accelerate perestroika. The Gorbachev leadership all along had favored a gradual reform of the Soviet economic system. But with the application of shock therapy to the Polish economy in January 1990, this strategy quickly became a subject of discussion in Moscow. By the summer of 1990, Stanislav Shatalin and Grigory Yavlinsky had introduced their own 500-day plan for rapid transition to the market. The Shatalin plan was rejected by Gorbachev at the time, but elements of it were revived in Yeltsin's Russia after the collapse of the Soviet Union.

By 1990, the Soviet economy was near collapse. The limited decentralization of perestroika had basically destroyed the vertical chain of command of the plan without yet replacing it with the horizontal exchanges among producers and consumers characteristic of the market. Furthermore, the political liberalization had fatally undermined popular trust in government, paralyzing its efforts to make more radical economic changes. Increasingly, the national economy ground to a halt; most economic activity was taking place only at the republican or local level. These problems were reflected in increasingly gloomy economic statistics and precipitous declines in GNP and production. The dismal economic scene within the Soviet Union raised concern outside the country as well. Increasingly, Western governments insisted on substantial economic reform as a precondition for further aid.

The Commonwealth of Independent States

The mounting economic problems, however, made it increasingly unlikely that "the country" would continue to exist as an integrated unit as centrifugal nationalistic forces accelerated. Gorbachev had hoped to delay the country's fragmentation with a new union treaty with nine of the fifteen republics. On the eve of the meeting to sign the new treaty, conservative forces in the leadership attempted to oust Gorbachev and reestablish order, control, and central authority. The failure of the August 1991 coup, however, simply accelerated the fragmentation of the country. By the end of the year, the Soviet Union was officially dissolved and the Commonwealth of Independent States [CIS] emerged in its place, minus the Baltic states and Georgia.

The CIS was created, in large measure, to stave off the even worse economic disaster that would occur if each of the former Soviet republics went their own way. But the end of communism and the Soviet Union did not mean the end of political and economic problems for the peoples and governments of the former union. As we have seen, the economic problems promised to worsen, at least in the short run, and new conflicts of pride and national identity threatened the harmony of the commonwealth. A virtual civil war in Georgia and a violent revival of the conflict over Nagorno-Karabakh (the Armenian enclave in Azerbaijan) were worrisome harbingers for the postcommunist era.

The disintegration of so large a country would have dramatic consequences outside the commonwealth as well. It would entail a redrawing of, and perhaps some negotiation over, the former country's western borders. It would also mean yet another redrawing of the map of Europe with the emergence of new, small and vulnerable states. It would further complicate the efforts of the states in East-Central Europe to align and integrate themselves with the West. The multitude of new, poor states in the commonwealth would additionally stretch the financial aid resources of the industrialized countries and would probably reduce those available to the ECE states outside the commonwealth. It would also pose a host of new issues for the West: those concerning economic aid and trade, new security arrangements, political stability, and membership in the UN [the United Nations], EC [the European Community] NATO, [the North Atlantic Treaty Organization] and other multilateral institutions.

Like so many other changes in East-Central Europe, the decline of the Soviet Union was two-edged in terms of its impact on other states. On the one hand, the Eastern European revolutions were made possible by Moscow's turn inward and its efforts to reverse its own long economic decline. On the other hand, the economic decline and political fragmentation of the USSR posed new problems for its postcommunist neighbors. The biggest of these problems was the economic one.

Under the old system of intrabloc trade coordinated by Comecon [the Council for Mutual Economic Assistance, a Soviet-era organization that dictated economic policy to Eastern European nations] goods were traded with little consideration for quality or cost, and transactions were conducted with the "transferable ruble," an artificial currency that was of less value than even the ordinary Soviet ruble. A joke in Poland described this system of exchange as "one dead dog for two dead cats." The system was not very efficient, perhaps, but it did promote high amounts of trade among the European communist states; goods that might not have been marketable in the West could be sold to other bloc states.

This whole system, however, was destroyed with the dissolution of Comecon and with the Soviet decision, effective in January 1991, to conduct all foreign trade on a hard currency basis and to sell its own products (especially energy) at world market prices. This was part of the Kremlin's effort to rationalize its own foreign trade and to integrate the Soviet economy more closely with global trade. Nevertheless, the impact on East-Central Europe was immediate and negative and worked in both directions. From the Soviet side, now that they were buying with hard currency there was no advantage to buying inferior goods from their former Comecon partners. For the countries of East-Central Europe, the new rules meant that Soviet oil and natural gas, which they had previously purchased at subsidized prices, were now much more expensive and were available only for scarce hard currency. Furthermore, the galloping economic collapse of the Soviet Union and then of the commonwealth states dras-

Gorbachev Resigns

On Christmas Day 1991, Mikhail Gorbachev resigned as president of the Soviet Union. Within six days the USSR completely ceased to exist, marking the unquestioned end of the Cold War, if not necessarily of the issues that caused it. In his resignation speech, Gorbachev expressed both his hope that the CIS would maintain some semblance of the old Soviet Union, without Communist domination, and his desire for a democratic future in Russia.

The process of renovating this country and bringing about drastic change in the international community has proven to be much more complicated than anyone could imagine. However, let us give its due to what has been done so far.

This society has acquired freedom. It has been freed politically and spiritually, and this is the most important achievement that we have yet fully come to grips with. And we haven't, because we haven't learned to use freedom yet.

However, an effort of historical importance has been carried out. The totalitarian system has been eliminated, which prevented this country from becoming a prosperous and well-to-do country a long time ago. A breakthrough has been effected on the road of democratic change. . . .

As the economy is being steered toward the market format, it is important to remember that the intention behind this reform is the well-being of man, and during this difficult period

tically reduced their own abilities to trade. Consequently, the postcommunist governments, while struggling to revive their domestic economies, suddenly lost their most lucrative export markets. In the first quarter of 1991, Poland's exports to the Soviet Union declined 80 percent from the year before and was responsible for a quarterly trade deficit of $300 million. In the same three months Czechoslovakia's exports to the Soviet Union declined by 36 percent and Hungary's by 85 percent. The loss of Soviet markets meant the closure of many industries in those countries, exacerbating the already difficult problem of unemployment. The new govern-

everything should be done to provide for social security, which particularly concerns old people and children. . . .

We're now living in a new world. An end has been put to the cold war and to the arms race, as well as to the mad militarization of the country, which has crippled our economy, public attitudes and morals. The threat of nuclear war has been removed. . . .

I consider it vitally important to preserve the democratic achievements which have been attained in the last few years. We have paid with all our history and tragic experience for these democratic achievements, and they are not to be abandoned, whatever the circumstances, and whatever the pretexts. Otherwise, all our hopes for the best will be buried. I am telling you all this honestly and straightforwardly because this is my moral duty.

I am very much concerned as I am leaving this post. However, I also have feelings of hope and faith in you, your wisdom and force of spirit. We are heirs of a great civilization and it now depends on all and everyone whether or not this civilization will make a comeback to a new and decent living today. . . .

Of course, there were mistakes made that could have been avoided, and many of the things that we did could have been done better. But I am positive that sooner or later, some day our common efforts will bear fruit and our nations will live in a prosperous, democratic society.

New York Times, "End of the Soviet Union; Text of Gorbachev's Farewell Address," December 26, 1991, p. A12.

ments in East-Central Europe were expecting a reorientation of their trade to the West, but they had been hoping that the reduction in Soviet trade would be more gradual. This sudden thrust out of the nest and into the global market would be an important test of their ability to survive on their own. It would also make them even more dependent on Western largess.

The Soviet decay and collapse most immediately affected its neighbors in the economic sphere, but it also raised national security concerns in East-Central Europe. The new governments in the region were delighted to remove themselves from Soviet domination and gladly cooperated in the dismantling of the Warsaw Pact. Extricated from this Eastern alliance, but unable to join NATO, the postcommunist states found themselves without alliances or solid security guarantees. Even before the disappearance of the Soviet Union, there was concern in the ECE states about instability in that country. Some feared that efforts by Soviet republics to leave the union would allow the return of a hardline and authoritarian leadership in Moscow. Such a situation almost materialized with the August coup attempt. There was also concern over the possibility of civil war or ethnic conflicts that could possibly spill over into East-Central Europe. None of these concerns disappeared with the termination of the Soviet Union.

Even without this worst-case scenario, the breakup of the Soviet Union could have severe consequences for the ECE countries. The combination of the economic breakdown and the relaxation of emigration restrictions in the fomer Soviet Union led to a huge new flow of migrants to both eastern and western Europe from the Soviet successor states. These came on top of the already substantial population flow from eastern to western Europe (especially Germany), which had contributed to the rise of right-wing xenophobia in Germany, France, and elsewhere. There was also concern over the possible revival of national animosities between the former Soviet republics and their western neighbors. Poland, for example, was concerned about possible revival of anti-Polish sentiment in the former western Soviet republics of Byelorussia and

Ukraine (both of which contained territory taken away from Poland after World War II). All of these concerns intensified the efforts of the ECE governments to seek closer association and assurances from the West and from NATO.

The End of the Cold War

The Cold War had been based on mutual fear; the United States feared aggression by the Soviet Union and therefore created a huge military establishment, which in turn intimidated the Soviet Union and led it to fortify its defenses. This vicious circle of distrust and suspicion spun off an arms race, with each side fearful of falling behind the other. In nuclear arsenals in particular, this led to an enormous "overkill" capacity on both sides. The United States, for example, had enough strategic nuclear weapons to strike every large- and medium-sized Soviet city *forty times*—enough "to make the rubble bounce."

The accelerating decline of Soviet power and the Gorbachev regime's commitment to new thinking sharply reduced the Soviet threat to the United States and the West, which in turn reduced its belligerent stance toward the Soviet Union. The vicious circle of threats and distrust was replaced by a new spiral of trust and reassurance. At first, many Westerners did not put much faith in Gorbachev's new thinking, insisting that rhetoric alone did not justify a lowering of Western defenses. Over time, however, the actions did match the words as the Soviet Union reduced its armaments, withdrew its troops from Afghanistan, and cut its commitments to leftist movements and regimes in the Third World. The major test of new thinking, however, was in Eastern Europe, the region of primary strategic concern to the Soviet Union. Here too, Moscow's actions followed its rhetoric. When Poland's communist government fell apart after the elections of June 1989, Moscow reacted with equanimity and promises of support for the new government of Tadeusz Mazowiecki. It was now apparent that the Brezhnev Doctrine [Soviet policy of maintaining ideological and political uniformity in Eastern Europe] was no longer in force. The Polish precedent gave heart to reformers and revolutionaries elsewhere in the region as one communist regime after another began to fall apart. The Moscow leadership watched its empire collapse and did nothing. If the Soviet Union could not prevent the collapse of communism in Eastern Europe, it certainly would not attempt to impose communism on more distant countries. The Cold War started in Eastern Europe and it ended there.

In the United States, the collapse of communism in Europe and the end of the Cold War initially brought a sense of euphoria, exhilaration, and optimism. Some felt that the United States had "won" the Cold War, and now it faced no obstacles to the spread of Western institutions and ideas. Others saw in the collapse of the Soviet threat an unprecedented opportunity to rethink U.S. national security policy and to reshape domestic priorities. There was much discussion of a peace dividend that could be realized from reductions in defense spending. Savings from the huge defense budget could be committed to pressing domestic needs: education, the environment, poverty, drug abuse, and medical care.

The disappearance of the communist threat, however, left the United States in a "conceptual vacuum." The Cold War had always provided a framework for U.S. foreign policy and had dictated its foreign, military, and national security policies. In terms of U.S. relationships with other states, that policy was governed primarily by a country's orientation toward communism. The United States supported governments or movements that opposed communism and opposed those that did not. The most important U.S. allies were usually also democratic, but in many cases the U.S. effort to contain communism led the country to support governments that were repressive or dictatorial (e.g., South Vietnam, Taiwan, South Africa, El Salvador) or to subvert governments that were leftist but freely elected (the Dominican Republic in 1965, Chile in 1973, Nicaragua in the 1980s.)

With containment of communism no longer necessary after 1989, the United States lost this conceptual framework for its foreign policy. There were many voices that suggested a rethinking of U.S. foreign and national security policy. Theodore Sorensen, a former adviser to President [John]

Kennedy, argued for redefining national security around two major goals: the preservation of the country's economic effectiveness and the peaceful promotion of democracy around the world. In his view, this would entail reduced efforts to project U.S. military power and greater attention to reducing the country's trade deficit and debt, to strengthening its global economic competitiveness, and this would also mean increased foreign aid for fledgling democracies. Sorensen was concerned, however, that without strong executive leadership a rethinking of U.S. priorities would be lost in a "mishmash of political considerations." Military budget reductions, for example, would "reflect not actual needs but log-rolling among the services as well as pressures on the Congress from local defense plants and bases."

In the United States, the [Ronald] Reagan and [George] Bush administrations struggled to fill the conceptual vacuum left by the waning threat of communism. President Reagan frequently evoked terrorism as the new global threat and accused Libya's President Muammar Khadafy of being a major sponsor of terrorism. In April 1986, Reagan ordered an air raid on Libyan military installations, hoping in the process to kill Khadafy himself. Khadafy survived, but his adopted infant daughter perished in the air attacks. President Bush identified yet another global threat in international drug traffickers. He also employed military force, sending U.S. Marines to take over Panama in December 1989. The major target was Panamanian strongman Manuel Noriega, whom the United States accused of supporting drug shipments to the United States. But these were shadowy and elusive enemies that did not evoke the unanimity and fear in the American public that communism had. As Congressman Les Aspin put it, "The old world was good guys and bad guys. The new world is gray guys." There was no basis here for a new U.S. foreign policy.

The Persian Gulf War in a Cold War Context

President Bush developed a bolder and more visionary approach in September 1990 when he announced to a joint session of Congress his concept of a "new world order," which was strikingly similar to Gorbachev's vision of global interdependence and peaceful resolution of disputes. This new framework seemed to work well in the face of the threat posed by Iraq's invasion of Kuwait in August 1990. Meeting with President Bush in Helsinki in early September, President Gorbachev expressed strong support for the U.S. position, denounced the Iraqi invasion, and called for Iraq's unconditional withdrawal from Kuwait. The Soviet Union also backed the successive resolutions of the United Nations Security Council that imposed an embargo on Iraq and, by November, authorized member states "to use all means necessary" to effect Iraq's withdrawal from Kuwait. This behavior led Secretary of State [James] Baker to characterize the Soviets as "very reliable partners" in the Persian Gulf crisis. For the first time since World War II, the superpowers were working together rather than against each other in a major Third World crisis.

This easy condominium began to erode, however, as the Bush administration increasingly escalated its demands on Iraq and steadily moved toward a military solution. The Soviet leadership was uncomfortable with Bush's unstated but clear intention to eliminate Iraq as a major power in the region—a goal that went far beyond the UN resolutions calling simply for the removal of Iraq from Kuwait. The Soviet military, especially, became increasingly alarmed as the United States massed a half million troops in the Persian Gulf, only 500 miles from the southern borders of the Soviet Union. Gorbachev and his advisers repeatedly attempted to negotiate a peaceful settlement of the issue. Gorbachev's adviser, Yevgeniy Primakov, visited the Gulf three times. But the Bush administration was strongly opposed to these efforts and insisted on Iraq's full compliance with all UN resolutions. In the absence of any concessions from Saddam Hussein, the United States unleashed a furious aerial bombardment of Kuwait on January 15, softening up the Iraqi forces for a massive U.S.-led ground assault six weeks later. Operation Desert Storm lasted just 100 hours and resulted in a humiliating surrender by Saddam Hussein.

The war was also a humbling experience for Gorbachev.

The outbreak of the war increasingly marginalized the Soviet Union, especially because Gorbachev continued to strive for a negotiated settlement. During the combat, the Kremlin leadership looked on as superior U.S. weaponry outclassed and destroyed Iraqi materiel, much of which had been supplied by the Soviet Union. The war strengthened the voice and the hand of the antiperestroika conservatives in Moscow, who complained of the eclipse of Soviet power and influence in world affairs. In December, on the eve of the air war, foreign minister Eduard Shevardnadze tendered his resignation and warned of a possible right-wing coup d'état in the country. The conservative newspaper *Sovetskaia Rossiia* [*Soviet Russia*] contended that Moscow's participation in the U.S.-led alliance against Iraq "ended the U.S.S.R.'s existence as a superpower." This perception almost certainly contributed to the coalition of military and security forces that attempted to oust Gorbachev from power in the failed coup of August 1991.

The war also seemed to place the new world order on the back burner. The furious attack on Saddam Hussein's forces seemed to belie Bush's dedication to a world of diplomacy and peaceful settlement of disputes. The predominance of the United States in the anti-Iraq coalition and in the combat operation raised questions about the U.S. commitment to multilateral diplomacy, especially as far as the other "superpower" was concerned. However, it was clear by the end of the war, if not before, that there now was only one superpower. Both friends and foes of the United States began to talk of the replacement of the "bipolar" world with a "unipolar" one. The Gulf War also did nothing to slow U.S. military spending; the Bush administration asked Congress for $291 billion for the Pentagon in 1992, compared to $286 billion in 1991, and this did not include a $15 billion "supplemental" request to cover part of the Gulf War costs. The Center for Defense Information, a coalition of retired U.S. military officers, argued that a military budget of $200 billion would suffice in the post–Cold War era. But the U.S. fascination with the high-tech weapons of the Gulf War and the Bush administration's preoccupation with foreign affairs over domestic seemed to offer little hope to those who expected an early "peace dividend."

Chapter 4

Reflections on the Cold War

Turning|Points

IN WORLD HISTORY

The Cold War Was a Relatively Stable Peace

Eric Hobsbawm

Eric Hobsbawm, one of the most noted historians of the twentieth century and a lifelong Marxist, is professor emeritus of economic and social history at Birkbeck College of the University of London in England. Hobsbawm argues that the Cold War was a much more stable arrangement of power than it seemed to be, despite the unquestionable climate of hostility that existed between the United States and Soviet Union. Hobsbawm contends that the military reality of the Cold War rarely matched the dire propaganda that both sides used against each other. With the exception of a competition for influence in the unclaimed territory of the so-called Third World, the Cold War represents for Hobsbawm a general acceptance of the balance of power between the Communist East and capitalist West as it existed at the end of World War II. He claims that both superpowers inflated their rhetoric of ideological antagonism for domestic purposes, but that both countries also clearly understood the potential consequences of direct armed confrontation and thus sought to avoid it at all costs.

The forty-five years from the dropping of the atom bombs to the end of the Soviet Union do not form a single homogeneous period in world history. . . . [T]hey fall into two halves, the decades on either side of the watershed of the early 1970s. Nevertheless, the history of the entire period was welded into a single pattern by the peculiar international situation which dominated it until the fall of the U.S.S.R.: the constant confrontation of the two superpowers which emerged from the Second World War, the so-called "Cold War."

The Second World War had barely ended when humanity plunged into what can reasonably be regarded as a Third World War, though a very peculiar one. For, as the great philosopher Thomas Hobbes observed, "War consisteth not in battle only, or the act of fighting: but in a tract of time, wherein the will to contend by battle is sufficiently known." The Cold War between the two camps of the U.S.A. and the U.S.S.R., which utterly dominated the international scene in the second half of the Short Twentieth Century, [i.e., 1914–1991] was unquestionably such a tract of time. Entire generations grew up under the shadow of global nuclear battles which, it was widely believed, could break out at any moment, and devastate humanity. Indeed, even those who did not believe that either side intended to attack the other found it hard not to be pessimistic, since Murphy's Law is one of the most powerful generalizations about human affairs ("If it can go wrong, sooner or later it will"). As time went on, more and more things were there which could go wrong, both politically and technologically, in a permanent nuclear confrontation based on the assumption that only the fear of "mutually assured destruction" (correctly concentrated into the acronym MAD) would prevent one side or the other from giving the ever-ready signal for the planned suicide of civilization. It did not happen, but for some forty years it looked a daily possibility.

The peculiarity of the Cold War was that, speaking objectively, no imminent danger of world war existed. More than this: in spite of the apocalyptic rhetoric on both sides, but especially on the American side, the governments of both the superpowers accepted the global distribution of force at the end of the Second World War, which amounted to a highly uneven but essentially unchallenged balance of power. The U.S.S.R. controlled, or exercised predominant influence in one part of the globe—the zone occupied by the Red Army and/or other communist armed forces at the end of the war, and did not attempt to extend its range of influence further by military force. The U.S.A. exercised control and predominance over the rest of the capitalist world as well as the western hemisphere and the oceans, taking over what remained of the old imperial hegemony of the former colonial powers. In return, it did not intervene in the zone of accepted Soviet hegemony.

A View of the World in 1945

In Europe the demarcation lines had been drawn in 1943–45, both by agreement at various summit meetings between [President Franklin] Roosevelt, [British prime minister Winston] Churchill and [Soviet premier Joseph] Stalin, and by virtue of the fact that only the Red Army could actually defeat Germany. There were a few uncertainties, notably about Germany and Austria, which were solved by the partition of Germany along the lines of the Eastern and Western occupation forces, and the withdrawal of all ex-belligerents from Austria. The latter became a sort of second Switzerland—a small country committed to neutrality, envied for its persistent prosperity and therefore described (correctly) as "boring." The U.S.S.R. accepted West Berlin as a Western enclave inside its German territory with reluctance, but was not prepared to fight the issue.

The situation outside Europe was less clear-cut, except for Japan, where the U.S.A. from the start established a completely unilateral occupation that excluded not only the U.S.S.R. but any other co-belligerent. The problem was that the end of the old colonial empires was predictable, and indeed in 1945 plainly imminent on the Asian continent, but the future orientation of the new post-colonial states was by no means clear. . . . [T]his was the zone in which the two superpowers continued, throughout the Cold War, to compete for support and influence, and hence the major zone of friction between them, and indeed the one where armed conflict was most likely, and actually broke out. Unlike Europe, not even the limits of the area under future communist control could be predicted, let alone agreed by negotiation in advance, however provisionally and ambiguously. Thus the U.S.S.R. did not much want a communist takeover in China, but it took place nevertheless.

However, even in what soon came to be called the "Third World," the conditions for international stability began to emerge within a few years, as it became clear that most of the new post-colonial states, however unsympathetic to the U.S.A and its camp, were non-communist, indeed mostly anti-communist in their domestic politics, and "non-aligned" (i.e. outside the Soviet military bloc) in international affairs. In short, the "communist camp" showed no sign of significant expansion between the Chinese revolution and the 1970s, by which time Communist China was no longer in it.

The Odd Stability of the Cold War World

In effect, the world situation became reasonably stable soon after the war and remained so until the middle 1970s, when the international system and its component units entered another period of lengthy political and economic crisis. Until then both the superpowers accepted the uneven division of the world, made every effort to settle demarcation disputes without an open clash between their armed forces that might lead to a war between them, and, contrary to ideology and Cold War rhetoric, worked on the assumption that long-term peaceful coexistence between them was possible. Indeed, when it came to the point, both trusted one another's moderation, even at times when they were officially on the brink of, or even engaged in, war. Thus during the Korean War of 1950–53, in which the Americans were officially involved, but not the Russians, Washington knew perfectly well that up to 150 Chinese planes were actually Soviet planes flown by Soviet pilots. The information was kept dark, because it was correctly assumed that the last thing Moscow wanted was war. During the Cuban missile crisis of 1962, as we now know, the main concern on both sides was how to prevent warlike gestures from being misinterpreted as actual moves to war.

Until the 1970s this tacit agreement to treat the Cold War as a Cold Peace held good. The U.S.S.R. knew (or rather learned) as early as 1953 that the U.S. calls to "roll back" communism were mere radio histrionics, when Soviet tanks were quietly allowed to re-establish communist control against a serious working-class revolt in East Germany. From then on, as the Hungarian revolution of 1956 confirmed, the West would keep out of the region of Soviet domination. The Cold War that actually tried to live up to its own rhetoric of a struggle for supremacy or annihilation was not the one in which basic decisions were taken by governments, but the shadowy contest between their various acknowledged and unacknowledged secret services, which in the West produced that most characteristic spin-off of the international tension, the fiction of espionage and covert killing. In this genre the British, through Ian Fleming's James Bond and John le Carré's sour-sweet heroes—both had served their time in the British secret services—maintained a steady superiority, thus compensating for their country's decline in the world of real power. However, except in some of the weaker countries of the Third World, the operations of KGB, CIA and their like were trivial in terms of real power politics, though often dramatic.

Was there, under these circumstances, a real danger of world war at any time during this long period of tension—except, of course, by the sort of accident which inevitably threatens those who skate long enough on sufficiently thin ice? It is hard to say. Probably the most explosive period was that between the formal enunciation of the "Truman Doctrine" in March 1947 ("I believe that it must be the policy of the United States to support free peoples who are resisting attempted subjugation by armed minorities or by outside pressures") and April 1951, when the same U.S. president dismissed General Douglas MacArthur, commander of the U.S. forces in the Korean War (1950–53), who pushed military ambition too far. This was the period when the American fear of social disintegration or revolution within the non-Soviet parts of Eurasia were not wholly fantastic—after all, in 1949 the communists took over China. Conversely, the U.S.S.R. found itself faced with a U.S. which enjoyed the monopoly of nuclear arms and multiplied militant and threatening declarations of anti-communism, while the first cracks appeared in the solidity of the Soviet bloc as [Marshal Josip] Tito's Yugoslavia broke away (1948). Moreover, from 1949 on

China was under a government which did not merely plunge readily into a major war in Korea, but—unlike all other governments—was willing to envisage actually fighting and surviving a nuclear holocaust. Anything might happen.

Once the U.S.S.R. acquired nuclear weapons—four years after Hiroshima in the case of the atom bomb (1949), nine months after the U.S.A. in the case of the hydrogen bomb (1953)—both superpowers plainly abandoned war as an instrument of policy against one another, since it was the equivalent of a suicide pact. Whether they seriously envisaged nuclear action against third parties—the U.S.A. in Korea in 1951, and to save the French in Vietnam in 1954; the U.S.S.R. against China in 1969—is not quite clear, but in any case the weapons were not used. However, both used the nuclear threat, almost certainly without intending to carry it out, on some occasions: the U.S.A. to speed peace negotiations in Korea and Vietnam (1953, 1954), the U.S.S.R. to force Britain and France to withdraw from Suez in 1956. Unfortunately, the very certainty that neither superpower would actually *want* to press the nuclear button tempted both sides into using nuclear gesticulation for purposes of negotiation or (in the U.S.A.) for domestic politics, confident that the other did not want war either. This confidence proved justified, but at the cost of racking the nerves of generations. The Cuban missile crisis of 1962, an entirely unnecessary exercise of this kind, almost plunged the world into an unnecessary war for a few days, and actually frightened even the top decision-makers into rationality for a while.

Soviet Expansionism Caused the Cold War

Robert Conquest

Robert Conquest is one of the most prolific American scholars of Russian history and a senior research fellow at the Hoover Institution at Stanford University in Palo Alto, California. Conquest was an outspoken critic of the Soviet regime throughout its existence and this excerpt from his retrospective look at twentieth-century history reflects this perspective. Conquest argues that the Soviet leaders who replaced Nikita Khrushchev in 1964 mounted an "ideological offensive" against the capitalist West and asserts that this tactic was largely responsible for continuing the Cold War in the decades after the Cuban Missile Crisis. Not at all the call for peaceful coexistence that many Western leaders interpreted it to be, Conquest discusses this ideological offensive as both a substitute for and perhaps a precursor to military expansionism. Thus, Conquest interprets even a seemingly cooperative policy such as détente as only a diversionary tactic that in no way signaled a diminished will on the part of the Soviet Union to spread communism throughout the world. It was, he maintains, this consistent, if occasionally masked, will to expand that demanded the opposition of the West until the Soviet Union eventually crumbled in the late 1980s.

The period between [Joseph] Stalin's death in 1953 and the emergence of the [Leonid] Brezhnev regime in 1964 saw continued progress in Soviet armaments: the detonation of the first deliverable hydrogen bomb in 1953, the launching of the first satellite in 1957—the latter marking the achieve-

Excerpted from *Reflections on a Ravaged Century*, by Robert Conquest (New York: W.W. Norton and Company, 2000). Copyright © 2000 by Robert Conquest. Reprinted with permission.

ment of an intercontinental ballistic missile.

The satellite launch, followed by other Soviet space achievements, had a major propaganda effect. There was a strong impression that the Soviet Union deployed a superior science and technology. And this was, of course mistakenly, thought to have produced a "missile gap" in which the United States was outgunned—though in fact the Soviet Union had not really caught up in terms of effective deployment.

The Cuban missile crisis in 1962 was, in this context, an attempt to outflank America's general superiority. The Soviet retreat was accompanied by much, though unpublicized, comment in Moscow military and political circles to the effect that the USSR would never again be caught in a position of weakness. The period that ensued and that only ended in the Soviet collapse at the end of the 1980s saw the continuity of the totalitarian mind-set. In one sense, the Soviet leaders, especially after [Nikita] Khrushchev's fall, were not red-hot ideologists. On the other hand, their minds were such that they had no other way of conceiving, or even justifying, their role. Even if doubts had entered one or another mind—as, however minimally and vaguely, they seem to have entered Khrushchev's—they could barely find expression. His successors were men who—unlike Khrushchev and his generation—had had no experience whatever of pre-Soviet times. They were all mere products of the apparatus. They had no other way of "thinking." Their view of the world remained that of sectarian hostility to all other sources of political ideas and political power, and an almost ineradicable conviction that struggle on a world scale was their historical mission.

Tactics, and the assessment of opportunity, varied with Marxist assessments of the balance of forces. So in the mid-1960s, the time when Stalin had, in fact, foreseen that the USSR would be in a position to "have another go," [i.e., have recovered militarily and economically from the devastation of World War II] we entered the second main phase of the Cold War—on which we shall go into more detail. For it is at about this time that a decision seems to have been made in the Kremlin to take on the West in armaments and on a world scale.

The Soviets Launch an Ideological Offensive

The expression "offensive against the positions of imperialism" began to appear regularly in the Soviet press in 1965. The first use of the phrase seems to have been by Brezhnev in an address to the congress of the Romanian Communist Party on 20 July 1965, when he noted that "some years ago" the Communist Parties had already concluded that the relation of forces had shifted in their favor, and that in the meantime this had reached such a stage that "the progressive forces are now on the offensive." The call for this "offensive" was formalized in the manifesto of the Communist Parties in November.

As to the scope of Soviet ambitions, in June 1968 Foreign Minister Andrei Gromyko flatly asserted in his speech to the Supreme Soviet:

> The Soviet Union is a great power situated on two continents, Europe and Asia, but the range of our country's international interests is not determined by its geographical position alone. . . . [T]he Soviet people do not plead with anybody to be allowed to have their say in the solution of any question involving the maintenance of international peace, concerning the freedom and independence of the people and our country's extensive interests. . . . During any acute situation, however far away it appears from our country, the Soviet Union's reaction is to be expected in all capitals of the world.

Though, of course, equivalent Western reaction to events in Poland was illegitimate.

One would have thought Gromyko's claim to a place in the sun was unequivocal. Yet some Westerners extracted a fairly harmless intent from it. They argued that all Gromyko urged, and so all the Soviet Union wanted, was the status of a global power coequal with the United States. On this argument, the Soviet Union for decades put in an enormous effort and overstrained its economy for the right to have its opinion "listened to" in discussions of world problems! And if we interpreted it as meaning that the Kremlin simply wanted a half share with the West in every sphere, it remained nonsense. Were we really to envisage a peaceable world in which every country was ruled by a stable coalition of Communists and democrats? Or alternate countries that were Communist and non-Communist, with no attempt to spread the power of the former into the latter?

The idea that Soviet expansionism was in later years simply a "great power" matter hardly holds up. We need not, indeed we cannot, sort out the components of the expansionist motivations. We certainly cannot exclude an "imperialist" element in the mix, but there are a number of arguments against overstressing it. First, the expansion, except in Afghanistan, was not in the Russian interest area. And in fact, the army leadership, naturally the keepers of strategic tradition, still thought in terms of Europe and Asia and resisted the new trend. The various Soviet adventures overseas were, of course, tied up with the enormous naval expansion of the Khrushchev and post-Khrushchev era, both effect and cause of this new transoceanic colonialism—though, as ever, rational thinking on naval deployment seems to have been lacking. A prominent official of the period once asked me exasperatedly how they could have built a big fleet in a sea it could not get out of. The navy was extremely expensive, and contributed greatly to the economic burden of military production. And that level of production was itself an argument against any but a commitment to arms at all costs.

And meanwhile, all theoretical pronouncements, both public and secret, gave the essentials of Soviet foreign policy, as enumerated by Gromyko in his book *The Foreign Policy of the Soviet Union* (Moscow, 1975):

> The Communist Party subordinates all its theoretical and practical activity in the sphere of foreign relations to the task of strengthening the positions of socialism, and the interests of further developing and deepening the world revolutionary process.

Was Détente a Diversionary Tactic?

But the USSR, and the whole Soviet bloc, were still economically far weaker than the USA and the West. In that context, further steps were taken to persuade the West not to match the Soviet armament drive. This was the Soviet concept of "détente."

[In 1967,] Brezhnev stated the political results he sought from "détente" clearly enough: "In conditions of international tension, in bourgeois countries, the reactionary elements become active, the military raise their heads, anti-democratic tendencies and anti-Communism are strengthened. And conversely, the past few years have shown quite clearly that, in conditions of slackened international tension, the pointer of the political barometer moves left."

Translated out of Sovietese, this signified that from the Soviet viewpoint, détente was intended to weaken Western vigilance, making it easier for appeasers and pro-Soviet elements to come to power.

The ideological struggle, Soviet leaders often insisted, should be continued, and even intensified, during a period of détente. As Brezhnev put it, "Our Party has always warned that in the ideological field there can be no peaceful coexistence, just as there can be no class peace between the proletariat and the bourgeoisie." On 27 June 1972, at a dinner for [Cuban leader] Fidel Castro, he added:

> While pressing for the assertion of the principle of peaceful coexistence, we realize that successes in this important matter in no way signify the possibility of weakening our ideological struggle. On the contrary, we should be prepared for an intensification of this struggle and for its becoming an increasingly acute form of struggle between the two social systems.

Soviet insistence on the continuation of the ideological struggle was often misunderstood. As [historian] Walter Laqueur remarked, in the West "Soviet insistence on the continuation of the ideological struggle is all too often not taken seriously"—because the concept of such struggle is alien to Western thought. People were, Laqueur arged, inclined to think that Soviet pronouncements were merely a matter of lip service to doctrine. In fact, however, "ideological struggle is not something which concerns the philosophers. It is a synonym for political struggle, and political struggle, needless to say, means power, not only the power of ideas, but also some far more tangible things." Laqueur added that the notion sometimes held by Western statesmen, that Soviet policy was difficult to understand (and he quotes [West German] Chancellor Willy Brandt directly to that effect) was only the case "if one refuses to take seriously what Soviet leaders are saying" and if one refused to compare their sayings with their actions.

Thus, this "ideological struggle" was not a matter of winning well-conducted philosophical debates at international congresses—though even as to theoretical argument, [Vladimir] Lenin cogently said that his controversial methods were "calculated to evoke in the reader hatred, aversion and contempt . . . calculated not to convince, but to break up the ranks of the opponent, not to correct the mistake of the opponent, but to destroy him."

Through the entire "détente" period, the Soviet "ideological" offensive went ahead. At home in the USSR, there was a continuous flow of propaganda (the viciousness of whose tone is still perhaps not sufficiently appreciated abroad) against the internal evils and the international aggressiveness and militarism of the West, blanketing the country with harsh abuse and plain lies. Abroad, every possible medium was employed to blacken the Western governments and their friends, to assist their enemies, and to undermine their military defenses and their political will.

During the last years of the regime, Soviet officials, including spokesmen for the Central Committee's Foreign Department, wrote that the Brezhnevite "détente" was a deception; that the Soviet stance remained expansionist; but that the Western governments' reaction prevented any substantial gains—i.e., that in spite of all their efforts, our policies remained effective.

World War II and the Cold War in Comparison

Stephen E. Ambrose

Stephen E. Ambrose is one of the most influential American historians of the twentieth century, having written extensively on a diverse range of topics such as the Civil War, the white settlement of the American West, World War II, Dwight D. Eisenhower, and Richard Nixon. He also served as a professor of history for more than thirty-five years, retiring in 1995 to devote himself more fully to writing and research. In this selection, Ambrose compares World War II with the Cold War (which had only recently concluded when this essay was written in 1991) in order to retrospectively evaluate the latter's place in American history. Ambrose not only compares the motivations that guided American participation in both conflicts, but also discusses a number of historical precedents from World War II that he feels greatly affected the way in which the Cold War—as well as some of its "hot" subconflicts—was conducted. Ambrose's historical perspective is generally less ideological in nature than that of Marxists such as Eric Hobsbawm or conservatives such as Robert Conquest; as a result, his initial assessment of the Cold War represents a "middle-of-the-road" alternative. Ambrose ultimately believes the Cold War to have been a just cause, but questions the validity of the way in which a number of these precedents were applied to the conflict against communism.

World War II pitted freedom and democracy—and Communism—against Nazism, fascism and Japanese militarism. When the latter surrendered unconditionally, the victorious

Excerpted from *Americans at War*, by Stephen E. Ambrose (Jackson: University Press of Mississippi, 1997). Copyright © 1997 by University Press of Mississippi. Reprinted with permission.

allies went after each other: the Cold War pitted freedom and democracy against Communism. In many ways, that struggle continues; still, it is obvious that freedom and democracy won some major battles [in the late 1980s, and early 1990s]. The real winners in those battles were the Poles, the East Germans, the Czechs, the Hungarians. These were stunning victories, comparable to the ones in 1945. Churchill said that the Nazi surrender was the signal for the greatest outburst of joy in the history of mankind, and he was right; but the tearing down of the Berlin Wall was not far behind. Can there be anyone among us who was not deeply moved when that hateful thing came down?

How does our contribution to the victories won in Central and Eastern Europe in 1989 compare to our contribution to the victories of 1945? In World War II, we sent planes, tanks, ships and fighting men to Europe, and aid to our allies. In the Cold War, we gave precious little support to the democratic forces in Poland, East Germany, Czechoslovakia, Yugoslavia and Hungary, and none at all to Bulgaria, Rumania and Albania. We refused to recognize the Soviet annexation of the Baltic states but we also failed to give those countries any support whatsoever, other than rhetorical "captive nations" resolutions. The truth is, those nations in the region who are free liberated themselves. Neither George Patton's Third Army nor its successors were anywhere to be seen.

The right wing in American politics is arguing today [in the early 1990s] that we did make the essential contribution, by speeding up the arms race during the Reagan presidency. They claim that the Soviets were bankrupted by the attempt to keep up and thereby were forced to retreat from the advanced positions the Red Army had occupied in 1945. The Reagan build-up left us with a $3 trillion debt, but the right wing argues that that is a small price to pay for such a great victory.

This seems to me to be a strange argument for right-wingers to make. I would turn it around and say that Communism failed because it is a rotten system, and that it lasted as long as it did, in part, because the dictators could convince their people that they were under a threat from the West comparable to the threat from Hitler. (Parenthetically, the single redeeming feature of Communism is that it stopped Hitler; never forget that nine out of every ten Wehrmacht [German armed forces] soldiers killed in World War II were killed by the men and women of the Red Army.)

Three Major Differences Between World War II and the Cold War

In World War II we used every weapon in our arsenal, including atomic bombs, to force our enemies into unconditional surrender. In the Cold War, we used our weapons only in Korea and Vietnam, and even there we refused to make war as we had in World War II. One example will suffice: in World War II we bombed enemy cities without compunction, deliberately killing civilians by the hundreds of thousands. Very few voices were raised in objection. In the Vietnam War, when we bombed Hanoi in December 1972, the air force took care to avoid civilian targets, and civilian casualties were fewer than two thousand, which in 1945 would not even have rated a back-page one-paragraph story in the newspapers. But in 1972 there was a worldwide howl of protest, most of all from within the U.S.

Why the difference? The most basic cause for the moral revulsion over the Christmas bombing [the bombing of the North Vietnamese capital Hanoi in late December 1972] was the nature of the war itself. Between 1942 and 1945 the United States and her allies were fighting for their lives against foes who were not only pure evil but also powerful enough to threaten the entire world. In World War II there were no ongoing negotiations with the Germans and Japanese, only a demand for their unconditional surrender. In 1942–1945 the Allies were bombing in order to hasten that surrender.

But in 1972 no one believed that the United States was fighting for its life, or that the North Vietnamese could conquer the world, or that there could be no end to the war until Hanoi surrendered, or that more bombing would bring a quicker end to the war.

This brings up another contrast between World War II

and the Cold War: until the fighting began in 1939, the Western democracies consistently, perversely, underestimated the Japanese and German threats. In the Cold War, when the fighting between the main antagonists never did begin, the United States consistently, perversely overestimated the Communist threat. This is one of those cases in which one generation applied the wrong lesson from the preceding generation; in the same way, the American leaders in the pre–World War II period had applied the wrong lesson from their predecessors, thinking that the United States had make a mistake when it entered World War I, and that it had done so because American businessmen and bankers had sold so much and loaned so much to Britain and France that they had to protect their investment. Thus the pre–World War II leaders passed the various neutrality acts, forbidding trading with or loaning money to nations at war, which was a good way to avoid World War I but a terrible way to deal with the world crisis of 1938–1941. Let future leaders beware: whatever the lessons of the Cold War are, they will not apply to the crises of the future.

Another obvious major difference between World War II and the Cold War is that in the former we went on the offensive all around the world, contributing to the liberation of China and Southeast Asia, making possible the liberation of the Philippines, Korea, North Africa, and Western Europe. In the Cold War, we stayed on the defensive. Except for a brief foray into North Korea in 1950, we never attempted to liberate anyone. Containment, not liberation, was our policy. In the longest war in our history, we fought with self-imposed constraints. We never sent troops into North Vietnam, despite severe provocation; only once did we send troops into Cambodia, and then for less than two months. . . .

The reason for the restraint was the development of the atomic bomb and intercontinental missiles. That was also the reason for the remarkable fact that from 1945 to 1989, the U.S. and the Soviet Union spent enormous sums on military weapons without ever once firing even one of them against the enemy they were chiefly built to use against. The superpowers built tens of thousands of nuclear weapons, doing so with the hope that they would never be used. (It is my hunch that neither side ever gave serious consideration to a first strike.)

The Defining Legacies of World War II

Four legacies from World War II dictated the manner in which the Cold War was waged. The first, actually dating to prewar years, had to do with the need to stand up to aggression. The second was fear of a surprise attack. The German invasion of the Soviet Union in June 1941 and the Japanese attack on Pearl Harbor in December of that year caught the U.S.S.R. and the U.S.A. completely by surprise. The leaders of the two countries throughout the Cold War were middle-aged or young men in 1945. Barbarossa [the surprise Nazi invasion of the USSR] and Pearl Harbor were burned into their souls. They vowed that never again would their countries be caught unprepared and by surprise.

The third legacy was technological: rockets and atomic weapons. Combined, they made a potential World War III so obviously suicidal that it was unthinkable. But of course that was a judgment that was valid only so long as the other side had a rational leader, and the fourth legacy from World War II was Tojo's and Hitler's: the stark fact that great nations sometimes have insane murderers for leaders, men who are willing to destroy their own people rather than submit to superior force or logic. So the leaders of the superpowers built weapons they hoped/prayed/believed would never be used.

They have not been used. They have cost huge sums and made the world far more dangerous. But they have also prevented World War III, and acted as a constraint on the superpowers as they fought small wars against Third World countries, the U.S. in Korea and Vietnam, the Soviets in Afghanistan. (It is remarkable that nations powerful enough to destroy the world were defeated, or held in check, by the North Koreans, the North Vietnamese, and the Afghans.)

Thus a fifth legacy from World War II has been spurned throughout the Cold War, that of unconditional surrender. In 1941 the American people looked at Nazi Germany and militarist Japan and said, "These are evil nations imposing an unspeakably cruel, criminal dictatorship on their own

Post–Cold War Europe

DENMARK

BRITAIN

NETHERLANDS

Berlin •

POLAND

BELGIUM

GERMANY

CZECH REPUBLIC

LUXEMBOURG

SLOVAKIA

SWITZERLAND

AUSTRIA HUNGARY

SLOVENIA

FRANCE

ITALY

CROATIA

ROMANIA

BOSNIA SERBIA

SPAIN

ALBANIA

people and those they have conquered. They must be crushed." In the Cold War, the American people looked at the Communists ruling the Soviet Union and said, "Theirs is an evil regime imposing an unspeakably cruel, criminal dictatorship on the territories of its own people and those they have conquered—and they must be contained."

The different reactions could not have been greater and they led to much frustration. The Republicans in the late forties and early fifties denounced containment as "cowardly." They wanted liberation—that is, total victory. But when Eisenhower became president, in 1953, he ignored advice that he go over to the offensive, liberate North Korea, and then go to war against Communist China. Instead, he made peace, and then kept the peace. He explained to congressional leaders, "This Cold War is a continuous crisis that we will have to live with. Our most realistic policy is holding the line until the Soviets manage to educate their people. By doing so, they will sow the seeds of destruction of Communism. This will take a long time."

Eisenhower's counsel of patience, adopted by all his successors, has worked in Western Europe, South Korea, and Japan, but so far has been an utter failure in China and Vietnam, and it doomed two generations of Central and Eastern Europeans to slavery.

The Pros and Cons of Cold War Restraint

Because of the failures, the temptation to use the military option, up to and including nuclear weapons, was always there. But even our two most belligerent presidents resisted the temptation. John Kennedy came into office full of bellicose rhetoric. He wanted to go on the offensive worldwide and was ready to pay any price, bear any burden, to insure the triumph of freedom everywhere. He sponsored an invasion of Cuba—but then backed down at the critical moment. He took a strong stance on Berlin—and then backed down when Khrushchev built the wall. He faced down Khrushchev in the Cuban missile crisis—but only by paying a cost that has been a calamity for the Cuban people, his pledge that the U.S. would never invade, which has left them under Castro's control for thirty years. It is astonishing that the United States has spent trillions on her armed forces in those thirty years, and tolerated a sassy, provocative dictatorship that provides military bases to our enemy ninety miles off our coast.

Until he became president, Richard Nixon had been America's leading anti-Communist. In every crisis he raised his voice for more fire power, now. He wanted to liberate North Korea in 1953, to use atomic weapons against the Communists at Dien Bien Phu in 1954 and in China in 1955. He called for victory in Vietnam in 1964 and for the next four years was Johnson's leading critic—not for doing too much, but for doing too little.

But when he became president, he took the U.S. out of Vietnam, far short of victory. He decided the U.S. should aim for sufficiency, not superiority, in nuclear weapons and entered into the first arms control agreement of the Cold War, SALT I [Strategic Arms Limitation Talks]. He established detente with the Soviet Union. After twenty-two years of the most unrelenting hostility toward Communist China, he went to Peking to exchange toasts with Mao Tse-tung and Chou En-lai.

American presidents in the Cold War, including Kennedy and Nixon, have—in general and on the really big issues—followed a policy of realistic restraint. The one great exception was Vietnam. There we entered on a wave of hubris. We were completely unrealistic about the nature of the war and what we needed to do to win it. We exhibited a remarkable, and, since we had gone to war, foolish restraint—for example, by going along with the fiction that the war was limited to South Vietnam and that Laos and Cambodia were neutral. As noted, we fought with a restraint that stands in the sharpest possible contrast with how we fought World War II, but we fought in a way that exposed us to worldwide condemnation (the same can be said about the Red Army in Afghanistan).

During the Cold War, we built the most powerful armed forces we have ever had, but in forty-five years, while they won some battles, they never won a war. The first American victory since 1945 came in 1991, and then it was over Iraq in a war that had nothing to do with the Cold War for which the armed forces were built. But we can turn that around: we built armed forces that were so powerful in order to deter, to avoid war—and it worked.

This brings to the fore [a] question about the Cold War: what was the cost? As compared to World War II, it was trivial. In World War II, nearly 50 million people died, among them more than a quarter-million American soldiers and sailors, but most of them Russians, Jews, Poles, Yugoslavs, Germans, Japanese, Chinese and Filipinos. In the Cold War, casualties were not nearly so high; only in Korea and Vietnam did the fighting even approach the intensity of World War II. In those two wars, about a hundred thousand U.S. soldiers and sailors were killed, a terrible price to pay to be sure, but not so high as World War II. [As of 1991], the Cold War has left the U.S. with a $3 trillion debt, a much greater sum than after World War II, when the national debt was $270 billion but, when adjusted for inflation, about the same.

A legacy from both wars has been the relative militarization of American society. Although the American defense establishment is much less pervasive than the Soviet Union's, or than Europe's had been in the late nineteenth and first four-and-a-half decades of the twentieth century, it is far more intrusive in the daily lives of Americans than had ever been the case before 1941. After World War II, while the Europeans were spending money on social welfare, the Americans were spending it on what has been called military welfare. This has led to a quip: after World War II the Americans were Prussianized while the Germans were Americanized.

Was the Cold War worth the cost? Unquestionably. No one can ever prove that the Truman doctrine of containment, and its chief implementing policies, NATO and the Marshall Plan, saved Western Europe from Communism—because we cannot know what would have happened had they not been implemented—but I believe it did. No one can ever prove that Communism would have collapsed in Central and Eastern Europe and the Soviet Union had there not been the Voice of America and Radio Free Europe and a consistent refusal by every Cold War president to accept as legitimate the Soviet domination of Central and Eastern Europe—but I believe those were significant factors, and cite in evidence the polls that indicate that VOA and Radio Free Europe were the most popular radio programs in Eastern and Central Europe [from the 1950s through the 1980s]. No one can ever prove that American leadership was even helpful to, much less critical to, the triumphs of democracy that have taken place in many parts of the world in the past few years—but I believe it was.

Was the Cold War inevitable? Nothing in human affairs is inevitable; people must make choices. The West could have acquiesced in the Communist enslavement of the peoples of the Soviet Union and Eastern Europe; the policy is called appeasement. It is the policy we have followed with the Communist rulers who have enslaved China and Tibet. As the Chinese example shows, mortal combat between capitalism and freedom on the one hand and Communism and slavery on the other is not inevitable.

The Danger of Stalinist Communism Was Both Real and Exaggerated

Vojtech Mastny

Born in the former Czechoslovakia, Vojtech Mastny is a senior research scholar at the Woodrow Wilson International Center for Scholars and a senior fellow at the National Security Archive, in Washington, D.C. He has written extensively on the politics of Eastern Europe and the Soviet Union during the Cold War. Mastny argues that the perceived threat that the USSR posed to the United States was inconsistent at best over the course of the five decades of the Cold War. Mastny claims that Soviet leaders throughout the Cold War implicitly understood that nuclear conflict with the United States was unwinnable, but that their overconfidence during periods of relative prosperity prompted more aggressive rhetoric toward the United States than the reality of their situation dictated. Mastny identifies Joseph Stalin as the leader most responsible for this inconsistent foreign policy, partly because of his desire for total control over the Soviet Union and partly because of political miscalculations in Europe and the Far East. In Mastny's view, the Cold War was justified despite the overstatement of the threat of actual war between the United States and Soviet Union, because totalitarian government as embodied by Stalin had to be resisted. Furthermore, Mastny claims that Western Europe indirectly benefited from conducting a lengthy struggle against communism by reevaluating and strengthening its democratic principles.

Excerpted from *The Cold War and Soviet Insecurity*, by Vojtech Mastny (New York: Oxford University Press, 1996). Copyright © 1996 by Vojtech Mastny. Reprinted by permission of the publisher.

The Soviet sense of insecurity that bred the Cold War also provided the constraints that kept it within bounds. The inside evidence of Moscow's capabilities and intentions no longer leaves a doubt that its leaders never wanted to overstep the limits. This is not to say that the threat the West perceived was an empty one. In their quest for security, Stalin and his successors were inclined to take greater risks whenever they saw the correlation of forces turning in their favor. In estimating their own strengths and the weaknesses of their adversaries, they were prone to miscalculations. These were enhanced by their ideological preconceptions, which postulated the ultimate victory of their system despite temporary setbacks.

In the course of the forty-year contest, domestic considerations determined Soviet international behavior far more than most contemporaries, misled by the Kremlin's not having to account for its action to anyone, were prepared to believe. As long as [Joseph] Stalin was in charge, those considerations were more general than specific—his need to maintain his autocratic power and an economy that would sustain it. Only later did they entail a clash of specific interests resulting in alternative policies articulated by different individuals or groups. During Stalin's lifetime, Soviet policy was for all intents and purposes his policy, on the whole conforming to [Nikita] Khrushchev's description of the despot as someone behaving "like Almighty God with a host of angels and archangels. He might listen to us, but the main thing was that he spoke and we listened. He did not explain his reasoning, but passed down the word to lesser mortals. They did what they were told when he wanted it done." This was the time when the Soviet system came the closest to the ideal model of totalitarian autocracy; in the real world, however, the autocrat's control was less than total, his policy often inconsistent, and its results not always commensurate with expectations.

As the Soviet empire spread, it became more difficult to manage simply because of its sheer size and complexity. There were more problems than someone of more systematic working habits than Stalin could effectively handle in one day—and his preferred nighttime schedule was anything but normal nor was his reliance on superior memory rather than on paperwork a guarantee of efficiency. The situation sometimes allowed subordinates at the intermediate level—rather than those in his main entourage—to exert a greater impact on policy than might be expected from the nature of the system, though never against his will.

In trying to divine Stalin's wishes from the not always clear signals those "lesser mortals" were receiving from him, subordinates applied the Marxist categories that they held in common with their superiors. In doing so while preventively protecting themselves against accusations of slackness, they were prone to err on the militant side. Their resulting initiatives were sometimes rejected as too risky, sometimes adopted; when the often indecisive despot was unable or unwilling to decide, they might be implemented by default.

In waging the Cold War, Stalin relied mainly on the *political* cohesion of the terroristic system he had created and its presumed comparative advantage over what he regarded in Marxist terms as inherent disarray among his capitalist enemies—only to see these unite as never before and himself bequeath to his heirs a system both untenable in its original form and unreformable in the long run. Afterward Khrushchev counted more on what he believed was the *economic* superiority of Soviet-style socialism—its supposed ability to outperform Western capitalism—only to strain the inherited system by lopsided expenditure of scarce resources for short-term effects and risky improvisations that undercut its performance and eventually cost him power. Under [Leonid] Brezhnev and his weak successors, the Soviet Union finally came to bank for all intents and purposes mainly on the strength inherent in its *military* power—to attain parity and preferably superiority in advanced weaponry in relation to the United States, thus offsetting its own diminishing capability to compete in nearly all other fields—only to strain the backward system to the extent of effectively paralyzing it. In the end its last manager, [Mikhail] Gorbachev, presided over its collapse after realizing that the prohibitively expensive military might could not be translated into political strength.

Stalin's Foreign Policy Weakened the USSR

Ironically, the Soviet Union was the least dangerous when it appeared to be the most—at the peak of the Cold War, when it acted the most hostile. The paradox was due not so much to U.S. nuclear superiority, whose utility for policy Stalin rightly discounted, as to his sense of internal and external vulnerability that existed for other reasons. He could neither bring his despotism to the level of perfection he considered necessary in order to feel safe nor could he believe that his capitalist enemies would ever be appeased. Somehow and somewhere, the insurmountable tension would therefore lead to a showdown, for which his country was not yet prepared.

Stalin's foreign policy has been aptly described as not so much "inexplicable in its parts as incoherent in its whole." This was the result of its being so thoroughly dominated by a single man who managed to project the image of prescience and omnipotence but was in fact a mere caricature of the Almighty God whom he tried to imitate. The more that is known about Stalin, the less he looks like the shrewd calculator and hard-boiled realist, for which supposed qualities he was respected even by his adversaries. He was given to illusions and wishful thinking to an extraordinary degree, repeatedly overestimating the extent of discord among his adversaries that might allow him to dictate his terms from a position of relative strength—something that his country never attained and could not have attained.

This chronic error of judgment accounted particularly for the persistence of Stalin's belief that Germany could be united on the foundations established in the eastern part of it that he controlled. Admittedly, the German question would have taxed the dexterity of any Russian statesman. More important than the magnitude of Stalin's problems, however, was his propensity to pile them up and make them worse by bungling. Such blunders as the Berlin blockade or the row with [Yugoslavian leader Josip] Tito would have been sufficient for Stalin to be sacked if he had been the head of a responsible government. Since he was not, he could afford to merely cut his losses and proceed with more blunders—none greater than his lending support to [communist leader and

future premier of North Korea] Kim Il Sung's adventure in
Korea. His opening of the "second front" in Asia in collusion
with the Chinese was a development of much greater importance than outsiders had grown accustomed to believe before
the vast new evidence of its inner workings became available.

The Korean War was important not so much because it
strained Soviet relations with the Chinese—which it did only
in the long run, whereas at the time Stalin's control over

Exaggerating the Communist Threat Justified U.S. Military Spending

*George F. Kennan was certainly not one to ascribe a benevolent in-
tention to the Soviet Union throughout his lengthy career as a diplomat and a scholar; in fact, his Long Telegram of 1946 encouraged
Truman to take a more outspoken position against the Soviets. However, in this excerpt from an introduction to Norman Cousins's 1987
book* The Pathology of Power, *Kennan claims that the might of the
Soviet Union was often intentionally overstated by representatives of
the U.S. "military-industrial complex" to justify continuation of the
high level of military spending. Eisenhower had warned about such a
scenario in his farewell speech early in 1961 as well.*

[The arms race] has led to the emergence of a military-
industrial establishment of such dimensions that it has become
the greatest single factor in our economic life, overshadowing
the peaceful and constructive elements of the American economy and in some respects encroaching on them and replacing
them. It is an establishment outside the perimeter of democratic control, as Eisenhower so clearly perceived it might become. . . . Were the Soviet Union to sink tomorrow under the
waters of the ocean, the American military-industrial complex
would have to remain, substantially unchanged, until some
other adversary could be invented. Anything else would be an
unacceptable shock to the American economy. . . .

So vast a peacetime defense establishment has demanded, of
course, as a counterpart indispensable to its rationale, an adversary proportionate to it—proportionate in its alleged iniquity,

them and their willing submission to him were much greater than they later cared to admit—as because Stalin was conducting by proxy a real war, not only the cold one, against the United States—and could not win it. The benefits he derived from its stalemate paled in comparison with his growing frustration, so evident during his last years of life.

By then, Soviet foreign policy all but came to a standstill as he concentrated on solving all his real and imaginary secu-

---

in the presumed intensity of its hostility, and in the immensity of the armed power with which it was supposed to confront us. This counterpart was found in the form of the Soviet Union; and the forbidding image has been assiduously built up and nurtured, as it had to be, over the course of several decades. It was not that the reality of Soviet power provided no sustenance at all for the development of this image. The Soviet Union did indeed present problems for the statesmen of the West. The apparently inordinate size of its armed forces; its postwar position astride the eastern half of the continent; its fading but still perceptible world-revolutionary rhetoric; . . . and the persistent presence within its political-military establishment of an element no less militarized in its thinking and no less inclined to think in terms of some ultimate military showdown than some of those who confronted it on our side of the line; all these were real phenomena. What was wrong was not that they should be taken into account, as they had to be. What was wrong was that they became subject, at the hands of those who cultivated this image, to a regime of oversimplification, exaggeration, misinterpretation, and propagandistic distortion that had the cumulative effect of turning a serious but not unmanageable problem into what appeared to many people to be a hopeless, insoluble one—insoluble, that is, other than by some sort of apocalyptic military denouement.

George F. Kennan, "Foreword to *The Pathology of Power* by Norman Cousins (1987)" in *At a Century's Ending: Reflections, 1982–1995*. New York: Norton, 1996, pp. 118–19.

rity problems at home. His manner of doing so was singularly counterproductive. Having decimated his faithful disciples in Eastern Europe, he generated even among his closest associates in the Kremlin a fear for their lives that may well have precipitated his death as a result of conspiracy, though not soon enough to prevent considerable damage to the cause of communism and to the empire he had created.

In his insatiable quest for security at the price of everybody else's insecurity, Stalin made the people he controlled accessories to his crimes. In Eastern Europe the complicity destroyed any moral claim for leadership by the communist parties—the pillars of Soviet power in the area. The attempt by Stalin's successors to shift the responsibility for his and their own crimes onto their chief executor, [Soviet Minister for State Security Lavrentii] Beriia, helped them to proceed with a partial repudiation of Stalinism's debilitating legacy but did not enable them to overcome it.

The unbridgeable chasm between Stalinist and Western values was also the ultimate reason why the post-Stalin leadership could not be brought to entertaining the idea of genuine accommodation with the West even if the West had tried. Dismal though this may sound, [Dean] Acheson and other U.S. policymakers were unfortunately right not allowing into their "minds the idea that unilateral concessions . . . would change, by ameliorating, Soviet policy." What he and his contemporaries were not right about was estimating the scope and nature of the Soviet threat.

If that threat has been widely misunderstood, there cannot be any misunderstanding about the sheer evil of Stalinism. The depth of that evil was, if anything, underestimated even by its foreign critics, who otherwise correctly saw it as inherent in the system and its sustaining ideology, and could only be adequately grasped once the particulars have been attested to by witnesses and documents from its homeland. These have fully substantiated the notion that the Soviet Union under Stalin was not a normal state but one run by a criminal syndicate at the service of a bloody tyrant hungry for power and ready to abuse it whenever he could do so without paying too high a price.

The Cold War Was Justified

If the empire Stalin created was in fact every bit as evil as suspected, and much more, then those who waged the Cold War against it need not apologize for the effort. The pertinent question, rather, is whether they did the best they could. Certainly, the U.S. policy based on [American diplomat George] Kennan's premise that Soviet expansionism could be contained until the system that propelled it would collapse under the weight of its own sins has been vindicated—but only after forty years. The cost of delay might seem to make more commendable the ostensibly realistic alternative once advocated by the liberal publicist Walter Lippmann and shared as well by Winston Churchill, who believed that because of its weakness Moscow could be compelled much earlier to accept a deal favorable to the West. Yet not only did the way the Soviet power eventually collapsed in 1989-91 defy the canons of realism, but Stalin was also not realistic enough to entertain such a deal in the first place.

There was, in theory, the third alternative of the United States using its superior military and moral power to topple Stalin's tyranny by war or a threat of war—just as he feared it might. And the whole rotten edifice could well have come tumbling down—just as he feared it might. Such an outcome would have been most probable during the time of paralyzing great fear that preceded his death. But it could never be certain, for the house Stalin built had withstood, after all, the assault by [Adolf] Hitler, who, too, had wielded great military power though not the moral power the West had. In any case, preventive war was never part of U.S. policy, nor would the American system of government have allowed it.

The United States did challenge the enemy by conducting unconventional war through its propaganda and covert operations. While their precise extent remains uncertain—because of the American rather than Russian archival restrictions—they were more extensive than has so far been officially admitted. Although they were not effective enough to achieve the intended destruction of Soviet power, they sufficiently advertised this intention as to generate the impression of being more dangerous than they actually were.

Magnified by the communists' presumption of implacable capitalist hostility and the subversion they invented to justify preventive repression, the fear in their hearts was genuine, not merely pretended.

That fear was not the original cause but an important contributing one to the terror Stalin unleashed in Eastern Europe against mostly imaginary subversives at the height of the Cold War. Its conspicuous victims were not so much his real enemies, who had already been made harmless before, as the communist elites. Although their periodic purging was part and parcel of his system, the Western psychological warfare added to its impact by nourishing—both deliberately and unwittingly—the despot's growing insecurity. Thus the West, though not destroying the enemy power, succeeded in impairing it. Yet the United States did not try to exploit this success during the critical time before Stalin's death, and later on the conditions were no longer so favorable.

Benefits—Intentional and Otherwise—of the Cold War

If the Soviet threat had been disposed of already in Stalin's time rather than in 1991, with it would have gone not only the additional costs of the Cold War but also some of its benefits. The Eastern Europeans, to be sure, could not claim any, having had to endure communism against their will for another thirty-five years. At least the unsuccessful attempts during this period to reform the system to reconcile it with their preferences as well as with modern times proved that this was impossible. In contrast, for the West, the years of the Cold War were those of unprecedented accomplishments and rewards—though ultimately less so for the United States than for Western Europe.

Meeting the Soviet threat as a moral challenge was congenial to the American mentality. What was not congenial was doing so over a prolonged period of time, with self-restraint, and by avoiding military force to achieve a clear decision. In view of these limitations, the Marshall Plan and NATO [the North Atlantic Treaty Organization] were monuments to creative and imaginative statesmanship, which in effect decided the outcome of the Cold War already by 1949, although the accomplishment would not become clear until all was over. In the meantime, the futile arms race exacted a price from the United States as the key member of the alliance that disproportionately bore the brunt of the military competition with the Soviet adversary. Its unexpected disappearance found Americans unprepared, disoriented about the purpose of their redundant military power, and groping for a better foundation of their role in the world.

In Western Europe, the perceived Soviet threat prompted an historic reckoning by a generation that had in its lifetime experienced firsthand an extraordinary series of catastrophes: the suicide of nationalist Europe during World War I, the debacle of capitalism in the Great Depression, the subsequent defeat of democracy by fascism amid the destruction of World War II, and finally Stalin's travesty of socialism. The pragmatic response to these calamities amalgamated what was the best in nationalism and internationalism, capitalism and socialism, liberalism and conservatism, democracy and meritocracy. It promoted national reconciliation within the movement for European unity, helped launch the first successful democracy on German soil, and gave Western Europe an unprecedented prosperity, which after the Cold War would serve as the enviable model for Eastern Europe as well.

A larger benefit of the Cold War was the demonstration that a conflict so intense could nevertheless be managed without getting out of hand, thus contributing to the growing belief that war as such may have become obsolete. At first, its avoidance was a matter of choice more for the Americans than for Stalin, who could less afford it. He was therefore never tempted to use his military force, particularly not the atomic bomb, against the West, while the United States was prepared to use even the bomb if provoked, although the Soviet self-perception of inferiority never provided the provocation. So, despite Stalin's Korean miscalculation, not so much the Soviet threat as that of a major war was contained.

In ensuring the critical margin of stability, the penetration of Western governments by Soviet spies, which the counter-intelligence services tried so desperately but unsuccessfully to prevent, was a benefit in disguise. The information thus received offered Stalin the necessary minimum of reassurance about enemy intentions to convince him that war was not imminent but only impending. The longer it failed to materialize, the more difficult it was sustaining the belief that it ever would.

After Stalin the situation was reversed. The advent of the "nuclear balance of terror" effectively ruled out America's resorting to the doomsday weapon in defending Europe. In contrast, the perceived strategic parity enabled the Soviet Union, or its increasingly influential military men, to entertain dangerous notions about the utility of conventional, if not nuclear, weapons in advancing Soviet power and influence also into Western Europe. And the gratuitous attempts to advance them by force in other parts of the world, motivated by ideological preconceptions to a much greater degree than suspected, made the Cold War stability a good deal more precarious than the superficial détente of those years made Europeans to believe.

Appendix of Documents

Document 1: The Declaration of the Three Powers, December 1, 1943

Roosevelt, Churchill, and Stalin met for the first time in the Iranian capital of Tehran late in 1943 to coordinate their war strategy. Not only did they discuss a two-front counterattack against Germany, but they also began making plans for the order of the world after the end of the war. This declaration puts forth some of the points that would be discussed (and disagreed upon) more specifically in later conferences at Yalta and Potsdam.

We the President of the United States, the Prime Minister of Great Britain, and the Premier of the Soviet Union, have met these four days past, in this, the Capital of our Ally, Iran, and have shaped and confirmed our common policy.

We express our determination that our nations shall work together in war and in the peace that will follow.

As to war—our military staffs have joined in our round table discussions, and we have concerted our plans for the destruction of the German forces. We have reached complete agreement as to the scope and timing of the operations to be undertaken from the east, west and south.

The common understanding which we have here reached guarantees that victory will be ours.

And as to peace—we are sure that our concord will win an enduring Peace. We recognize fully the supreme responsibility resting upon us and all the United Nations to make a peace which will command the goodwill of the overwhelming mass of the peoples of the world and banish the scourge and terror of war for many generations.

With our Diplomatic advisors we have surveyed the problems of the future. We shall seek the cooperation and active participation of all nations, large and small, whose peoples in heart and mind are dedicated, as are our own peoples, to the elimination of tyranny and slavery, oppression and intolerance. We will welcome them, as they may choose to come, into a world family of Democratic Nations. . . .

Emerging from these cordial conferences we look with confidence to the day when all peoples of the world may live free lives, untouched by tyranny, and according to their varying desires and their own consciences. We came here with hope and determination. We leave here, friends in fact, in spirit and in purpose.

A Decade of American Foreign Policy: Basic Documents, 1941–49 Prepared at the request of the Senate Committee on Foreign Relations by the Staff of the Committee and the Department of State. Washington, DC: Government Printing Office, 1950. Also available online: www.yale.edu/lawweb/avalon/wwii/tehran.htm.

Document 2: Declaration of Liberated Europe, February 13, 1945

The Big Three Allied leaders met again in Yalta on the Soviet Black Sea coast early in 1945. With the Axis nearing defeat in Europe, the planning for the fate of liberated territories was now much more specific. In this section of a much longer series of agreements, the leaders stated their goals for the normalization of Europe after the end of the war. In the years immediately after the war, Britain and the United States would frequently accuse the Soviets of violating the spirit of this declaration by their actions in Eastern Europe.

The establishment of order in Europe and the rebuilding of national economic life must be achieved by processes which will enable the liberated peoples to destroy the last vestiges of nazism and fascism and to create democratic institutions of their own choice. This is a principle of the Atlantic Charter—the right of all people to choose the form of government under which they will live—the restoration of sovereign rights and self-government to those peoples who have been forcibly deprived to them by the aggressor nations.

To foster the conditions in which the liberated people may exercise these rights, the three governments will jointly assist the people in any European liberated state or former Axis state in Europe where, in their judgment conditions require,

(a) to establish conditions of internal peace; (b) to carry out emergency relief measures for the relief of distressed peoples; (c) to form interim governmental authorities broadly representative of all democratic elements in the population and pledged to the earliest possible establishment through free elections of Governments responsive to the will of the people; and, (d) to facilitate where necessary the holding of such elections.

The three Governments will consult the other United Nations and provisional authorities or other Governments in Europe when matters of direct interest to them are under consideration.

When, in the opinion of the three Governments, conditions in any European liberated state or former Axis satellite in Europe make such action necessary, they will immediately consult together on the measure necessary to discharge the joint responsibilities set forth in this declaration.

By this declaration we reaffirm our faith in the principles of the Atlantic Charter, our pledge in the Declaration by the United Nations and our determination to build in cooperation with other peace-loving nations world order, under law, dedicated to peace, security, freedom and general well-being of all mankind.

A Decade of American Foreign Policy: Basic Documents, 1941–49 Prepared at the request of the Senate Committee on Foreign Relations by the Staff of the Committee and the Department of State. Washington, DC: Government Printing Office, 1950. Also available online: www.yale.edu/lawweb/avalon/wwii/yalta.htm.

Document 3: Proclamation Defining Terms for Japanese Surrender, July 26, 1945

Having been given the information of the successful test of the atomic bomb in Alamogordo, New Mexico, President Harry S. Truman used the meeting of the Allies at the German city of Potsdam to issue a call for Japan's surrender. This proclamation was appended to a larger group of agreements about the collective administration of the postwar world. Its language—which omits any mention of Soviet participation—marks a clear shift away from the strategy that had been put forth at Yalta, at which time the Soviet Union had been asked to join the war against Japan as soon as the war in Europe ended.

(1) We—The President of the United States, the President of the National Government of the Republic of China, and the Prime Minister of Great Britain, representing the hundreds of millions of our countrymen, have conferred and agree that Japan shall be given an opportunity to end this war.

(2) The prodigious land, sea and air forces of the United States, the British Empire and of China, many times reinforced by their armies and air fleets from the west, are poised to strike the final blows upon Japan. This military power is sustained and inspired by the determination of all the Allied Nations to prosecute the war against Japan until she ceases to resist.

(3) The result of the futile and senseless German resistance to the might of the aroused free peoples of the world stands forth in awful clarity as an example to the people of Japan. The might that now converges on Japan is immeasurably greater than that which, when applied to the resisting Nazis, necessarily laid waste to the lands, the industry and the method of life of the whole German people. The full application of our military power, backed by our resolve. All mean the inevitable and complete destruction of the

Japanese armed forces and just as inevitably the utter devastation of the Japanese homeland.

(4) The time has come for Japan to decide whether she will continue to be controlled by those self-willed militaristic advisers whose unintelligent calculations have brought the Empire of Japan to the threshold of annihilation, or whether she will follow the path of reason. . . .

(10) We do not intend that the Japanese shall be enslaved as a race or destroyed as a nation, but stern justice shall be meted out to all war criminals, including those who have visited cruelties upon our prisoners. The Japanese Government shall remove all obstacles to the revival and strengthening of democratic tendencies among the Japanese people. Freedom of speech, of religion, and of thought, as well as respect for the fundamental human rights shall be established. . . .

(13) We call upon the government of Japan to proclaim now the unconditional surrender of all Japanese armed forces, and to provide proper and adequate assurances of their good faith in such action. The alternative for Japan is prompt and utter destruction.

A Decade of American Foreign Policy: Basic Documents, 1941–49 Prepared at the request of the Senate Committee on Foreign Relations by the Staff of the Committee and the Department of State. Washington, DC: Government Printing Office, 1950. Also available online: www.yale.edu/lawweb/avalon/decade/decade17.htm.

Document 4: A Letter from Henry L. Stimson to President Truman, September 11, 1945

In the immediate aftermath of the use of the atomic bomb on Hiroshima and Nagasaki, a debate ensued among Truman's advisers as to whether or not the knowledge about constructing the bomb should be shared with the Soviets, who were technically still allied with the United States. This letter from Henry L. Stimson, the secretary of war, represents the more diplomatic side, which believed that the bomb could be used not as a threat but as a diplomatic tool to encourage democratic reforms within Soviet society.

In handing you today my memorandum about our relations with Russia in respect to the atomic bomb, I am not unmindful of the fact that when in Potsdam I talked with you about the question of whether we could be safe in sharing the atomic bomb with Russia while she was still a police state and before she put into effect provisions assuring personal rights of liberty to the individual citizen.

I still recognize the difficulty and am still convinced of the importance of the ultimate importance of a change in Russian attitude toward individual liberty but I have come to the conclusion that it would not be possible to use our possession of the atomic bomb as a direct lever to produce the change. I have become convinced that any demand by us for an internal change in Russia as a condition of sharing in the atomic weapon would be so resisted that it would make the objective we have in view less probable.

I believe that the change in attitude toward the individual in Russia will come slowly and gradually and I am satisfied that we should not delay our approach to Russia in the matter of the atomic bomb until that process is completed. . . . Furthermore, I believe that this long process of change in Russia is more likely to be expedited by the closer relationship in the matter of the atomic bomb which I suggest and the trust and confidence that I believe would be inspired by the method of approach which I have outlined.

"Henry L. Stimson to President Truman, September 11, 1945," Truman Presidential Museum and Library website, www.trumanlibrary.org/whistlestop/study_collections/bomb/small/mb15. htm.

Document 5: A Letter from Senator Kenneth McKellar to President Truman, September 27, 1945

In sharp contrast to Secretary of War Henry Stimson's advocacy of sharing knowledge of the atomic bomb with the Soviets (see Document 4), the following letter from Senator Kenneth McKellar to Truman outlines some of the twenty reasons McKellar gave for not giving atomic secrets to any other nation. Truman eventually adopted this tougher stance, a decision that helped make the atomic bomb a major divisive issue in the Cold War.

It seems to me unwise, impolitic, and dangerous to our nation's defense, provocative of war, and dangerous to peace, to give this formula to Russia, England, Canada or to any other nation.

In passing, I want to say that I have not a single unkind feeling toward Russia or the Russian people. I think both Russia and the people made a wonderful record in the late war. . . .

It is on their account indeed that I take this stand that if we give this formula to England or Canada we are in duty bound and in honor bound to give it to Russia and to China and our other Allies also.

I am going to try succinctly to give my reasons why this bomb, or the formula for making it, should not be given away to other nations:

(1). Russia as a government nor as a people did not give us material aid in discovering this formula and, therefore, is not entitled to the use of it or property rights in it on this account. . . .

(8). This formula may or may not be important industrially as well as in a military way. It may wholly revolutionize the use of force and power in this nation and, therefore, it should not be given away to any one for any purpose until we know its value and worth. . . .

(10). From a military standpoint, from actual experience with it, it is the greatest military power or force in the world today and, therefore, it may be and probably is the greatest foe of peace and the greatest promoter of war ever known in the world.

(11). Every nation great or small and ambitious for other nations' territory, whether a defeated or victorious nation in this war, upon becoming the owner of this formula will at once become imbued with the ambition that with the use of this formula they can acquire other nations' property and thereby increase the likelihood of war. . . .

(17). Given such a dangerous weapon or the formula for it, each and every nation will at once get their scientists busy with it and the most of them will think that they have improved it in a better and more effective way than any other nation and it won't be long before they will want to go to war to prove that they have got the best bomb in the world, and unless they change their past thousand years [of] history, a war of bombs will soon be fought. *To give the formula for this weapon to other nations or to any other nation without money and without price would be to invite them to get busy and prepare for another world war.*

"Letter to the President from Senator Kenneth McKellar outlining 20 reasons why the United States should not release to any nation the formula for making an atomic bomb, September 27, 1945," Truman Presidential Museum and Library website, www.trumanlibrary.org/whistlestop/study_collections/bomb/large/background/bmb7-1.htm.

Document 6: Kennan's Long Telegram, February 22, 1946

Early in February 1946, the State Department sent an urgent message to its Moscow embassy chief, George Kennan, requesting his interpretation of recent developments in Soviet policies. In his detailed response, part of which is excerpted here, Kennan outlined the direction in which he believed the Soviets to be heading. Truman and his closest advisers interpreted Kennan's summary as clear evidence of the Soviet leadership's unrelentingly hostile position. Kennan's so-called Long Telegram helped push Truman toward the policy of containment that defined U.S. relations with the Soviets for most of the next two decades, although Kennan himself proposed a much less adversarial response than the Truman Doctrine eventually became.

We have here a political force committed fanatically to the belief that with us there can be no permanent *modus vivendi*, that it is desirable and necessary that the internal harmony of our society be disrupted, our traditional way of life be destroyed, the international authority of our state be broken, if Soviet power is to be secure. This political force has complete power of disposition over energies of one of the world's greatest peoples and resources of the world's richest national territory, and is borne along by deep and powerful currents of Russian nationalism. In addition, it has an elaborate and far-flung apparatus for exertion of its influence in other countries, an apparatus of amazing flexibility and versatility, managed by people whose experience and skill in underground methods are presumable without parallel in history. Finally, it is seemingly inaccessible to considerations of reality in its basic reactions. For it, the vast fund of objective fact about human society is not, as with us, the measure against which outlook is constantly being tested and reformed, but a grab bag from which individual items are selected arbitrarily and tendentiously to bolster an outlook already preconceived. This is admittedly not a pleasant picture. The problem of how to cope with this force is undoubtedly greatest task our diplomacy has ever faced and probably the greatest it will ever have to face. It should be the point of departure from which our political general staff work at the present juncture should proceed. It should be approached with same thoroughness and care as solution of major strategic problem in war, and if necessary, with no smaller outlay in planning effort. I cannot attempt to suggest all the answers here. But I would like to record my conviction that the problem is within our power to solve—and that without recourse to any general military conflict. . . .

I think we may approach calmly and with good heart the problem of how to deal with Russia. As to how this approach should be made, I only wish to advance, by way of conclusion, the following comments: . . .

4. We must formulate and put forward for other nations a much more positive and constructive picture of the sort of world we would like to see than we have put forward in the past. It is not enough to urge the people to develop political processes similar to our own. Many foreign peoples, in Europe at least, are tired and frightened by experiences of the past, and are less interested in abstract freedom than in security. They are seeking guidance rather than responsibilities. We should be better able than the Russians to give them this. And unless we do, the Russians certainly will.

5. Finally, we must have courage and self-confidence to cling to our own methods and conceptions of human society. After all, the greatest danger that can befall us in coping with this problem of Soviet communism is that we shall allow ourselves to become like those with whom we are coping.

Foreign Relations of the United States, 1946, vol. VI: Eastern Europe, The Soviet Union. Department of State Publication 8470. Washington, DC: Government Printing Office, 1969. Also available online: www.mtholyoke.edu/acad/intrel/longtel.html.

Document 7: Novikov's Telegram to Molotov, September 27, 1946

Less than seven months after George Kennan sent his Long Telegram to Truman, the Soviet ambassador to Washington, Nikolai Novikov, sent a similar message to Soviet foreign minister Vyacheslav Molotov. Novikov interpreted U.S. foreign policy as increasingly bent on eliminating the Soviet Union as a rival by any means, including military.

The foreign policy of the United States, which reflects the imperialist tendencies of American monopolistic capital, is characterized in the postwar period by a striving for world supremacy. This is the real meaning of the many statements by President Truman and other representatives of American ruling circles: that the United States has the right to lead the world. All the forces of American diplomacy—the army, the air force, the navy, industry, and science—are enlisted in the service of this foreign policy. For this purpose broad plans for expansion have been developed and are being implemented through diplomacy and the establishment of a system of naval and air bases stretching far beyond the boundaries of the United States, through the arms race, and through the creation of ever newer types of weapons. . . .

The "hard-line" policy with regard to the USSR announced by [Secretary of State James] Byrnes after the rapprochement of the reactionary Democrats with the Republicans is at present the main obstacle on the road to cooperation of the Great Powers. It consists mainly of the fact that in the postwar period the United States no longer follows a policy of strengthening cooperation among the Big Three (or Four) but rather has striven to undermine the unity of these countries. The objective has been to impose the will of other countries on the Soviet Union. This is precisely the tenor of the policy of certain countries, which is being carried out with the blessing of the United States, to undermine or completely abolish the principle of the veto in the Security Council of the United Nations. This would give the United States opportunities to form among the Great Powers narrow groupings and blocs directed primarily against the Soviet Union, and thus to split the United Nations. Rejection of the veto by the Great powers would transform the United Nations into an Anglo-Saxon domain in which the United States would play the leading role. . . .

The present policy of the American government with regard to the USSR is also direct at limiting or dislodging the influence of the Soviet Union from neighboring countries. In implementing this policy in former enemy or Allied countries adjacent to the USSR, the United States attempts, at various international conferences or directly in these countries themselves, to support reactionary forces with the purpose of creating obstacles to the process of democratization of these countries. . . .

The numerous and extremely hostile statements by American government, political, and military figures with regard to the Soviet Union and its foreign policy are very characteristic of the current relationship between the ruling circles of the United States and the USSR. These statements are echoed in an even more unrestrained tone by the overwhelming majority of the American press organs. Talk about a "third war," meaning a war against the Soviet Union, even a direct call for this war—with the threat of using the atomic bomb—such is the content of the statements on relations with the Soviet Union by reactionaries at public meetings and in the press. . . . The basic goal of this anti-Soviet campaign of American "public opinion" is to exert political pressure on the Soviet Union and compel it to make concessions.

"Telegram by Soviet N. Novikov to Moscow, 27 September 1946," Cold War International History Project of the Woodrow Wilson International Center for Scholars website, http://cwihp.si.edu.

Document 8: The North Atlantic Treaty, April 4, 1949

The North Atlantic Treaty helped solidify the military alliances that would face off against one another in Europe during the Cold War. The twelve original signatories, including the United States, Canada, and most other Western European democracies, sought a collective self-defense treaty against Soviet incursions in the Western bloc, overcoming congressional concerns that the United States was risking harmful foreign entanglements.

The Parties to this Treaty reaffirm their faith in the purposes and principles of the Charter of the United Nations and their desire to live in peace with all peoples and all governments.

They are determined to safeguard the freedom, common heritage and civilization of their peoples, founded on the principles of democracy, individual liberty and the rule of law. They seek to promote stability and well-being in the North Atlantic area.

They are resolved to unite their efforts for collective defense and for the preservation of peace and security. They therefore agree to this North Atlantic Treaty:

Article 1: The Parties undertake, as set forth in the Charter of the United Nations, to settle any international dispute in which they may be involved by peaceful means in such a manner that international peace and security and justice are not endangered, and to refrain in their international relations from the threat or use of force in any manner inconsistent with the purposes of the United Nations.

Article 2: The Parties will contribute toward the further development of peaceful and friendly international relations by strengthening their free institutions, by bringing about a better understanding of the principles upon which these institutions are founded, and by promoting conditions of stability and well-being. They will seek to eliminate conflict in their international economic policies and will encourage economic collaboration between any or all of them. . . .

Article 4: The Parties will consult together whenever, in the opinion of any of them, the territorial integrity, political independence or security of any of the Parties is threatened.

Article 5: The Parties agree that an armed attack against one or more of them in Europe or North America shall be considered an attack against them all and consequently they agree that, if such an armed attack occurs, each of them, in exercise of the right of individual or collective self-defense recognized by Article 51 of the Charter of the United Nations, will assist the Party or Parties so attacked by taking forthwith, individually and in concert with the other Parties, such action as it deems necessary, including the use of armed force, to restore and maintain the security of the North Atlantic area.

American Foreign Policy 1950–1955, Basic Documents, Volume 1, Department of State Publication 6446. Washington, DC: Government Printing Office, 1957. Also available online: www.nato. int/docu/basictxt/treaty.htm.

Document 9: The Warsaw Pact, May 14, 1955

Separated from the North Atlantic Treaty by six years but essentially performing the same function for Eastern bloc nations, the Warsaw Pact's language intentionally mirrored that of the North Atlantic Treaty (see Document 8) in several sections, especially when invoking UN principles as the basis for alliance.

The Contracting Parties, reaffirming their desire for the establishment of a system of European collective security based on the participation of all European states irrespective their social and political systems, which would make it possible to unite their efforts in safeguarding the peace of Europe; mindful, at the same time, of the situation created in Europe by the ratification of the Paris agreements, which envisage the formation of a new military alignment in the shape of "Western European Union," with the participation of a remilitarized Western Germany and the integration of the latter in the North-Atlantic bloc, which increased the danger of another war and constitutes a threat to the national security of the peaceable states; being persuaded that in these circumstances the peaceable European states must take the necessary measures to safeguard their security and in the interests of preserving peace in Europe; guided by the objects and principles of the Charter of the United Nations Organization; being desirous of further promoting and developing friendship, cooperation and mutual assistance in accordance with the principles of respect for the independence and sovereignty of states and of noninterference in their internal affairs, have decided to conclude the present Treaty of Friendship, Cooperation and Mutual Assistance. . . .

Article 3: The Contracting Parties shall consult with one another on all important international issues affecting their common interests, guided by the desire to strengthen international peace and security. They shall immediately consult with one another whenever, in the opinion of any one of them, a threat of armed attack on one or more of the Parties to the Treaty has arisen, in order to ensure joint defence and the maintenance of peace and security. . . .

Article 5: The Contracting Parties have agreed to establish a Joint Command of the armed forces that by agreement among the Parties shall be assigned to the Command, which shall function on the basis of jointly established principles. They shall likewise adopt other agreed measures necessary to strengthen their defensive power, in order to protect the peaceful labors of their peoples, guarantee the inviolability of their frontiers and territories, and provide defense against possible aggression. . . .

Article 8: The Contracting Parties declare that they will act in a spirit of friendship and cooperation with a view to further developing and fostering economic and cultural intercourse with one another, each adhering to the principle of respect for the independence and sovereignty of the others and non-interference in their internal affairs.

American Foreign Policy 1950–1955, Basic Documents, Volume 1, Department of State Publication 6446. Washington, DC: Government Printing Office, 1957. Also available online: www.isn.ethz.ch/php/ documents/collection_3/PCC_docs/Treaty550514.htm.

Document 10: NSC 68: United States Objectives and Programs for National Security, April 14, 1950

Drafted by a group headed by Paul Nitze, the head of the State Department Policy Planning Staff, NSC 68 turned the Truman Doctrine into more specific recommendations for government policy. This lengthy document explicitly stated that the United States needed to bolster its military capabilties and its national resolve to help deter, and if necessary repel, an attack by the Soviets, which Nitze's group felt was increasingly more likely.

The objectives of a free society are determined by its fundamental values and by the necessity for maintaining the material environment in which they flourish. Logically and in fact, therefore, the Kremlin's challenge to the United States is directed not only to our values but to our physical capacity to protect their environment. It is a challenge which encompasses both peace and war and our objectives in peace and war must take account of it.

1. Thus we must make ourselves strong, both in the way in which we affirm our values in the conduct of our national life, and in the development of our military and economic strength.

2. We must lead in building a successfully functioning political and economic system in the free world. It is only by practical affirmation, abroad as well as at home, of our essential values, that we can preserve our own integrity, in which lies the real frustration of the Kremlin design.

3. But beyond thus affirming our values our policy and actions must be such as to foster a fundamental change in the nature of the Soviet system, a change toward which the frustration of the design is the first and perhaps the most important step. Clearly it will not only be less costly but more effective if this change occurs to a maximum extent as a result of internal forces in Soviet society.

In a shrinking world, which now faces the threat of atomic warfare, it is not an adequate objective merely to seek to check the Kremlin design, for the absence of order among nations is becoming less and less tolerable. This fact imposes on us, in our own interests, the responsibility of world leadership. It demands that we make the attempt, and accept the risks inherent in it, to bring about order and justice by means consistent with the principles of freedom and democracy. We should limit our requirement of the Soviet Union to its participation with other nations on the basis of equality and respect for the rights of others. Subject to this requirement, we must with our allies and the former subject peoples seek to create a world society based on the principle of consent. Its framework cannot be inflexible. It will consist of many national communities of great and varying abilities and resources, and hence of war potential. The seeds of conflicts will inevitably exist or will come into being. To acknowledge this is only to acknowledge the impossibility of a final solution. Not to acknowledge it can be fatally dangerous in a world in which there are no final solutions. . . .

There is no reason, in the event of war, for us to alter our overall objectives. They do not include unconditional surrender, the subjugation of the Russian peoples or a Russia shorn of its economic potential. Such a course would irrevocably unite the Russian people behind the regime which enslaves them. Rather these objectives contemplate Soviet acceptance of the specific and limited conditions requisite to an international environment in which free institutions can flourish, and in which the Russian peoples will have a new chance to work out their own destiny. If we can make the Russian people our allies in the enterprise we will obviously have made our task easier and victory more certain.

Foreign Relations of the United States, vol. 1, National Security Affairs; Foreign Economic Policy. Washington, DC: Government Printing Office, 1977. Also available online: www.mtholyoke.edu/acad/intrel/nsc-68/nsc68-1.htm.

Document 11: Eisenhower's "Atoms for Peace" Speech, December 8, 1953

Near the end of his first year as president, Eisenhower addressed the United Nations on the subject of atomic energy, convinced in part by J. Robert Oppenheimer, the former head of the Manhattan Project, that something needed to be done to reduce the nuclear arms race. His speech proposed a number of international cooperative projects in which scientists would seek to convert radioactive material that had been set aside for military purposes into power for civilian use. As such, it represented one of the earliest major disarmament proposals. Although warmly received by Eisenhower's audience, the plan was ultimately rejected by the Soviets.

The United States would be more than willing—it would be proud—to take up with others "principally involved" the development of plans whereby such peaceful use of atomic energy would be expedited.

Of those "principally involved" the Soviet Union must of course, be one. I would be prepared to submit to the Congress of the United States, and with every expectation of approval, any such plan that would:

First, encourage world-wide investigation into the most effective peacetime uses of fissionable material; and with the certainty that they had all the material needed for the conduct of all experiments that were appropriate;

Second, begin to diminish the potential destructive power of the world's atomic stockpiles;

Third, allow all peoples of all nations to see that, in this enlightened age, the great powers of the earth, both of the East and of the West, are interested in human aspirations first rather than in building up the armaments of war.

Fourth, open up a new channel for peaceful discussion and initiate at least a new approach to the many difficult problems that must be solved in both private and public conversations if the world is to shake off the inertia imposed by fear and is to make positive progress toward peace.

Against the dark background of the atomic bomb, the United States does not wish merely to present strength, but also the desire and the hope for peace.

The coming months will be fraught with fateful decisions. In this Assembly, in the capitals and military headquarters of the world; in the hearts of men everywhere, be they governed or governors, may they be the decisions which will lead this world out of fear and into peace.

To the making of these fateful decisions, the United States pledges before you—and therefore before the world—its determination to help solve the fearful atomic dilemma—to devote its entire heart and mind to find the way by which the miraculous inventiveness of man shall not be dedicated to his death, but consecrated to his life.

Public Papers of the Presidents of the United States: Dwight D. Eisenhower. Washington, DC: Government Printing Office, 1954–1961. Also available online: www.tamu.edu/scom/pres/speeches/ikeatoms.html.

Document 12: Khrushchev's "Secret Speech," February 25, 1956

At the twentieth Party Congress in Moscow, Khrushchev surprised the delegates with a speech delivered in closed session during the middle of the night. In this speech, Khrushchev denounced Stalin for having diverted the Soviet Union from the true path of Marxism to a "cult of personality" centered around Stalin himself. This criticism of the system marked a clear break with past tradition and began a period of relative liberalism in Soviet society known as "the Thaw." Later in 1956, though, Khrushchev ruthlessly suppressed several anti-Soviet uprisings in Eastern Europe that were seemingly encouraged by this speech.

After Stalin's death, the Central Committee began to implement a policy of explaining concisely and consistently that it is impermissible and foreign to the spirit of Marxism-Leninism to elevate one person, to transform him into a superman possessing supernatural characteristics, akin to those of a god. Such a man supposedly knows everything, sees everything, thinks for everyone, can do anything, is infallible in his behavior.

Such a belief about a man, and specifically about Stalin, was cultivated among us for many years. The objective of the present report is not a thorough evaluation of Stalin's life and activity. Concerning Stalin's merits, an entirely sufficient number of books, pamphlets and studies had already been written in his lifetime. Stalin's role of Stalin in the preparation and execution of the Socialist Revolution, in the Civil War, and in the fight for the construction of socialism in our country, is universally known. Everyone knows it well.

At present, we are concerned with a question which has immense importance for the Party now and for the future—with how the cult of the person of Stalin has been gradually growing, the cult which became at a certain specific stage the source of a whole series of exceedingly serious and grave perversions of Party principles, of Party democracy, of revolutionary legality. . . .

We have to consider seriously and analyze correctly this matter in order that we may preclude any possibility of a repetition in any form whatever of what took place during the life of Stalin, who absolutely did not tolerate collegiality in leadership and in work, and who practiced brutal violence, not only toward everything which opposed him, but also toward that which seemed, to his capricious and despotic character, contrary to his concepts.

Stalin acted not through persuasion, explanation and patient cooperation with people, but by imposing his concepts and demanding absolute submission to his opinion. Whoever opposed these concepts or tried to prove his [own] viewpoint and the correctness of his [own] position was doomed to removal from the leadership collective and to subsequent moral and physical annihilation.

Congressional Record: Proceedings and Debates of the *84th Congress, 2nd Session* (May 22, 1956–June 11, 1956). Washington, DC: Government Printing Office, 1956. Also available online: www.fordham.edu/halsall/mod/1956khrushchev-secret1.html.

Document 13: State Department Response to U-2 Incident, May 7, 1960

The United States had been using high-altitude U-2 planes to spy on the Soviets for several years when one crashed in the Soviet Union on May 1, 1960, touching off a diplomatic crisis between the superpowers. After initially claiming to have lost a "weather research plane" that may have accidentally strayed over the USSR, the State Department issued this statement in response to Khrushchev's angry accusation that the plane had been spying. The admission of espionage enraged Khrushchev and caused a lengthy rift in U.S.-Soviet relations that endured until after the Cuban Missile Crisis.

The Department has received the text of Mr. Krushchev's further remarks about the unarmed plane which is reported to have been shot down in the Soviet Union. As previously announced, it was known that a U-2 plane was missing. As a result of the inquiry ordered by the President it has been established that insofar as the authorities in Washington are concerned there was no authorization for any such flight as described by Mr. Khrushchev.

Nevertheless it appears that in endeavoring to obtain information now concealed behind the Iron Curtain a flight over Soviet territory was probably undertaken by an unarmed civilian U-2 plane.

It is certainly no secret that, given the state of the world today, intelligence collection activities are practiced by all countries, and postwar history certainly reveals that the Soviet Union has not been lagging behind in this field.

The necessity for such activities as measures for legitimate national defense is enhanced by the excessive secrecy practiced by the Soviet Union in contrast to the free world.

One of the things creating tension in the world today is apprehension over surprise attack with weapon of mass destruction.

To reduce mutual suspicion and to give a measure of protection against surprise attack the United States in 1955 offered its open-skies proposal—a proposal which was rejected out of hand by the Soviet Union. It is in relation to the danger of surprise attack that planes of the type of unarmed civilian U-2 aircraft have made flights along the frontiers of the free world for the past 4 years.

Department of State Bulletin, May 23, 1960. Also available online: www.mtholyoke.edu/acad/intrel/u22.htm.

Document 14: Note from U.S. Ambassador to Soviet Foreign Minister, August 17, 1961

An exchange of diplomatic notes in the wake of the Soviet closing of the border between East and West Berlin on August 13, 1961, demonstrates the difference of perspective between the Cold War opponents. The following U.S. protest centers around the legal issue of violating the existing agreement to collectively administer Berlin (see Document 15 for Soviet response). The lack of resolution in this conflict ultimately led to the establishment of the Berlin Wall, which effectively sealed the border for the next twenty-eight years.

On August 13, East German authorities put into effect several measures regulating movement at the boundary of the western sectors and the Soviet sector of the city of Berlin. These measures have the effect of limiting, to a degree approaching complete prohibition, passage from the Soviet sector to the western sectors of the city. These measures were accompanied by the closing of the sector boundary by a sizable deployment of police forces and by military detachments brought into Berlin for this purpose.

All this is a flagrant, and particularly serious, violation of the quadripartite status of Berlin. . . . The United States Government has never accepted that limitations can be imposed on freedom of movement within Berlin. The boundary between the Soviet sector and the western sectors of Berlin is not a state frontier. The United States Government considers that the measures which the East German authorities have taken are illegal. It reiterates that it does not accept the pretension that the Soviet sector of Berlin forms a part of the so-called "German Democratic Republic" and that Berlin is situated on its territory.

By the very admission of the East German authorities, the measures which have just been taken are motivated by the fact that an ever increasing number of inhabitants of East Germany wish to leave this territory. The reasons for this exodus are known. They are simply the internal difficulties in East Germany. . . .

The United States Government solemnly protests against the measures referred to above, for which it holds the Soviet Government responsible. The United States Government expects the Soviet Government to put an end to these illegal measures. This unilateral infringement of the quadripartite status of Berlin can only increase existing tension and dangers.

Department of State Bulletin, vol. 45, no. 1158, September 4, 1961. Also available online: http://oll.temple.edu/hist249/course/Documents/usa_and_ussr_on_Berlin.htm.

Document 15: Reply from Soviet Foreign Minister to U.S. Ambassador, August 18, 1961

In response to U.S. protest of the sealing of the border between East and West Berlin (see Document 14), the Soviet foreign minister justifies the closing of the border as necessary to stop subversives from infiltrating East Berlin and encouraging citizens of the Communist bloc to immigrate to the West on false pretenses.

In connection with the note of the Government of the United States of America of August 17, 1961, the Government of the Union of Soviet Socialist Republics considers it necessary to state the following:

The Soviet Government fully understands and supports the actions of the Government of the German Democratic Republic [GDR] which established effective control on the border with West Berlin in order to bar the way for subversive activity being carried out from West Berlin against the GDR and other countries of the socialist community.

West Berlin has been transformed into a center of subversive activity diversion, and espionage, into a center of political and economic provocations against the GDR, the Soviet Union, and other socialist countries. . . . However, West Berlin authorities and the occupation organs of the three powers did not lift a finger to put an end to this criminal activity. . . .

The Government of the USA attempts in its note to represent its effort to perpetuate the occupation of West Berlin (and this 16 years after the end of the war) as a concern for the Germans and almost as a concrete expression of the right to self-determination. Such attempts in the final analysis cannot be taken seriously. And if the taking of defensive measures on the GDR border with West Berlin creates certain temporary inconveniences for the city's population, blame for this rests entirely with the occupation authorities and the FRG [West German] government, which have done everything to prevent improvement of the atmosphere in this area in accordance with the legitimate interests of all states. Thus, the protest made in the note of the Government of the USA is without foundation and is categorically rejected by the Soviet Government.

Department of State Bulletin, vol. 45, no. 1158, September 4, 1961. Also available online: http://oll.temple.edu/hist249/course/Documents/usa_and_ussr_on_Berlin.htm.

Document 16: Kennedy's Cuban Missile Crisis Speech, October 22, 1962

After six days of secret negotiations, President John F. Kennedy rejected the possibility of negotiating with the Soviets on the placement of nuclear missiles in Cuba. Simultaneously fearing the possible escalation of a military strike, though, he made the following televised address to explain the course of action he had chosen, which was a complete naval blockade of Cuba. The standoff that ensued, ultimately more rhetorical than military, represented some of the most tense days of the Cold War, and Kennedy's grave description of the nuclear threat that Soviet missiles posed to the U.S. mainland helped transmit this tension to the American populace.

Good evening, my fellow citizens: This Government, as promised, has maintained the closest surveillance of the Soviet military buildup on the island of Cuba. Within the past week, unmistakable evidence has established the fact that a series of offensive Missile sites is now in preparation on that imprisoned island. The purpose of these bases can be none other than to provide a nuclear strike capability against the Western Hemisphere. . . .

The characteristics of these new missile sites indicate two distinct types of installations. Several of them include medium range ballistic missiles, capable of carrying a nuclear warhead for a distance of more than 1000 nautical miles. Each of these missiles, in short, is capable of striking Washington, D.C., the Panama Canal, Cape Canaveral, Mexico City, or any other city in the southeastern part of the United States, in Central America, or in the Caribbean area. . . .

Neither the United States of America nor the world community of nations can tolerate deliberate deception and offensive threats on the part of any nation, large or small. We no longer live in a world where only the actual firing of weapons represents an efficient challenge to a nation's security to constitute maximum peril. Nuclear weapons are so destructive and ballistic missiles are so swift, that any substantially increased possibility of their use or any sudden change in their deployment may well be regarded as a definite threat to peace.

For many years, both the Soviet Union and the United States, recognizing this fact, have deployed strategic nuclear weapons with great care, never upsetting the precarious status quo which insured that these weapons would not be used in the absence of some vital challenge. Our own strategic missiles have never been transferred to the territory of any other nation under a cloak of secrecy and deception; and our history—unlike that of the Soviets since the end of World War II—demonstrates that we have no desire to dominate or conquer any other nation or impose our system upon its people. Nevertheless, American citizens have become adjusted to living daily on the bull's-eye of Soviet missiles located inside the USSR or in submarines.

Public Papers of the Presidents of the United States, John F. Kennedy, 1962. Washington, DC: Government Printing Office, 1963. Also available online: www.tamu.edu/scom/pres/speeches/jfkcuban.html.

Document 17: Gulf of Tonkin Resolution, August 7, 1965

Justified by an alleged attack on U.S. surveillance ships by North Vietnam (the truth of this situation has since been questioned), this congressional resolution authorized President Lyndon Johnson to send U.S. troops into Vietnam without a formal declaration of war. Within the next three years, Johnson would commit nearly three-quarters of a million soldiers to fight Communist aggression in Vietnam, and the war spread to several neighboring countries by the early 1970s.

Whereas naval units of the Communist regime in Vietnam, in violation of the principles of the Charter of the United Nations and of international law, have deliberately and repeatedly attacked United States naval vessels lawfully present in international waters, and have thereby created a serious threat to international peace; and

Whereas these attacks are part of a deliberate and systematic campaign of aggression that the Communist regime in North Vietnam has been waging against its neighbors and the nations joined with them in the collective defense of their freedom; and

Whereas the United States is assisting the peoples of southeast Asia to protect their freedom and has no territorial, military or political ambitions in that area, but desires only that these peoples should be left in peace to work out their own destinies in their own way: Now, therefore, be it RESOLVED BY THE SENATE AND HOUSE OF REPRESENTATIVES OF THE UNITED STATES OF AMERICA IN CONGRESS ASSEMBLED, That the Congress approves and supports the determination of the President, as Commander in Chief, take all necessary measures to repel any armed attack against the forces of the United States and to prevent further aggression.

SEC 2. The United States regards as vital to its national interest and world peace the maintenance of international peace and security in southeast Asia. Consonant with the Constitution of the United States and the Charter of the United Nations and in accordance with its obligations under the Southeast Asia Collective Defense Treaty, the United States is, therefore, prepared, as the President determines, to take all necessary steps, including the use of armed force, to assist any member or protocol state the Southeast Asia Collective Defense Treaty requesting assistance in defense of its freedom.

SEC 3. This resolution shall expire when the President shall determine that the peace and security of the area is reasonably assured by international conditions created by action of the United Nations or otherwise, except that it may be terminated earlier by concurrent resolution of the Congress.

Department of State Bulletin, August 29, 1964. Also available online: www.isop.ucla.edu/eas/documents/tonkin.htm.

Document 18: Declaration of the Brezhnev Doctrine, September 26, 1968

After deposing Khrushchev late in 1964, the Soviet government headed by Leonid Brezhnev and Aleksey Kosygin gradually began reasserting a more authoritarian brand of government control in both the Soviet Union and Eastern Europe. After the "Prague Spring" uprising in Czechoslovakia early in 1968, Brezhnev felt compelled to issue this statement, which became known as the Brezhnev Doctrine, in which he reaffirmed the dominance of Communist ideology in the Soviet Union and its client states.

The measures taken by the Soviet Union, jointly with other socialist countries, in defending the socialist gains of the Czechoslovak people are of great significance for strengthening the socialist community, which is the main achievement of the international working class. . . .

The peoples of the socialist countries and Communist parties certainly do have and should have freedom for determining the ways of advance of their respective countries.

However, none of their decisions should damage either socialism in their country or the fundamental interests of other socialist countries, and the whole working class movement, which is working for socialism.

This means that each Communist party is responsible not only to its own people, but also to all the socialist countries, to the entire Communist movement. Whoever forgets this, in stressing only the independence of the Communist party, becomes one-sided. He deviates from his international duty. . . .

The sovereignty of each socialist country cannot be opposed to the interests of the world of socialism, of the world revolutionary movement. Lenin demanded that all Communists fight against small-nation narrow-mindedness, seclusion and isolation, consider the whole and the general, subordinate the particular to the general interest. . . .

Each Communist party is free to apply the basic principles of Marxism-Leninism and of socialism in its country, but it cannot depart from these principles (assuming, naturally, that it remains a Communist party).

Concretely, this means, first of all, that, in its activity, each Communist party cannot but take into account such a decisive fact of our time as the struggle between two opposing social systems—capitalism and socialism. This is an objective struggle, a fact not depending on the will of the people, and stipulated by the world's being split into two opposite social systems. Lenin said: "Each man must choose between joining our side or the other side. Any attempt to avoid taking sides in this issue must end in fiasco." . . .

Discharging their internationalist duty toward the fraternal peoples of Czechoslovakia and defending their own socialist gains, the USSR and the other socialist states had to act decisively and they did act against the antisocialist forces in Czechoslovakia.

"Sovereignty and the International Obligations of Socialist Countries," *Pravda*, September 26, 1968. Also available online: www.fordham.edu/halsall/mod/1968brezhnev.html.

Document 19: The Shanghai Communiqué, February 28, 1972

This announcement—issued together by the governments of the United States and the People's Republic of China—was made at the conclusion of Nixon's groundbreaking visit to China early in 1972. It represented one of the high points of détente, since its language promised a reconciliation in the future. Although the war in Southeast Asia was ongoing, the leaders of the United States and China had met and publicly announced their intentions to reduce the hostile atmosphere that had existed between the two nations since the Communist takeover in 1949.

There are essential differences between China and the United States in their social systems and foreign policies. However, the two sides agreed that countries, regardless of their social systems, should conduct their relations on the principles of respect for the sovereignty and territorial integrity of all states, non-aggression against other states, non-interference in the internal affairs of other states, equality and mutual benefit, and peaceful coexistence. International disputes should be settled on this basis, without resorting to the use or threat of force. The United States and the People's Republic of China are prepared to apply these principles to their mutual relations.

With these principles of international relations in mind the two sides stated that:

a) progress toward the normalization of relations between China and the United States is in the interests of all countries;

b) both wish to reduce the danger of international military conflict;

c) neither should seek hegemony in the Asia-Pacific region and each is opposed to efforts by any other country or group of countries to establish such hegemony;

d) neither is prepared to negotiate on behalf of any third party or to enter into agreements or understandings with the other directed at other states.

Both sides are of the view that it would be against the interests of the peoples of the world for any major country to collude with another against other countries, or for major countries to divide up the world into spheres of interest. . . .

Both sides view bilateral trade as another area from which mutual benefit can be derived, and agreed that economic relations based on equality and mutual benefit are in the interest of the peoples of the two countries. They agree to facilitate the progressive development of trade between their two countries.

"Joint Communique of the United States of America and the People's Republic of China," U.S. Department of State International Information Programs website, http://usinfo.state.gov/regional/ea/uschina/jtcomm.htm.

Document 20: The Helsinki Accords, August 1, 1975

In 1972 Richard Nixon and Leonid Brezhnev proposed a lengthy series of meetings called the Conference on Security and Cooperation in Europe, which began meeting in 1973. Two years later, at the conclusion of the meetings, this statement was issued, which balanced Soviet interests in official acknowledgment of the post–World War II borders of Eastern Europe with U.S. demands for greater attention to human rights. The latter provisions especially would be invoked repeatedly as the Cold War heated up again in the 1980s.

The participating States will respect each other's sovereign equality and individuality as well as all the rights inherent in and encompassed by its sovereignty, including in particular the right of every State to juridical equality, to territorial integrity and to freedom and political independence. They will also respect each other's right freely to choose and develop its political, social, economic and cultural systems as well as its right to determine its laws and regulations. . . .

The participating States will refrain in their mutual relations, as well as in their international relations in general, from the threat or use of force against the territorial integrity or political independence of any State, or in any other manner inconsistent with the purposes of the United Nations and with the present Declaration. No consideration may be invoked to serve to warrant resort to the threat or use of force in contravention of this principle. . . .

The participating States regard as inviolable all one another's frontiers as well as the frontiers of all States in Europe and therefore they will refrain now and in the future from assaulting these frontiers. . . .

The participating States will settle disputes among them by

peaceful means in such a manner as not to endanger international peace and security, and justice. They will endeavor in good faith and a spirit of cooperation to reach a rapid and equitable solution on the basis of international law.

For this purpose they will use such means as negotiation, enquiry, mediation, conciliation, arbitration, judicial settlement or other peaceful means of their own choice including any settlement procedure agreed to in advance of disputes to which they are parties. . . .

The participating States will refrain from any intervention, direct or indirect, individual or collective, in the internal or external affairs falling within the domestic jurisdiction of another participating State, regardless of their mutual relations.

They will accordingly refrain from any form of armed intervention or threat of such intervention against another participating State. . . .

The participating States will respect human rights and fundamental freedoms, including the freedom of thought, conscience, religion or belief, for all without distinction as to race, sex, language or religion.

They will promote and encourage the effective exercise of civil, political, economic, social, cultural and other rights and freedoms all of which derive from the inherent dignity of the human person and are essential for his free and full development.

"Final Act—Helsinki Summit 1975," Organization for Security and Cooperation in Europe website, www.osce.org/docs/english/1990-1999/summits/helfa75e.htm#Anchor-29952.

Document 21: Jimmy Carter's State of the Union Address, January 21, 1980

Facing increasing internal pressure from anti-Communist groups in the United States, Carter used his annual address to Congress in 1980 to vigorously protest the Soviet invasion of Afghanistan the previous year. Fearful that the Soviets intended to push toward the oil-rich Persian Gulf and thereby complicate a growing energy crisis in the United States, Carter announced economic sanctions against the Soviets and began sending military aid to Afghanistan and neighboring states, thereby ending any hope for a resumption of détente.

Now, as during the last 3½ decades, the relationship between our country, the United States of America, and the Soviet Union is the most critical factor in determining whether the world will live at peace or be engulfed in global conflict.

Since the end of the Second World War, America has led other nations in meeting the challenge of mounting Soviet power. This has not been a simple or a static relationship. Between us there has been cooperation, there has been competition, and at times there has been confrontation. . . .

We superpowers also have the responsibility to exercise restraint in the use of our great military force. The integrity and the independence of weaker nations must not be threatened. They must know that in our presence they are secure.

But now the Soviet Union has taken a radical and an aggressive new step. It's using its great military power against a relatively defenseless nation. The implications of the Soviet invasion of Afghanistan could pose the most serious threat to the peace since the Second World War.

The vast majority of nations on Earth have condemned this latest Soviet attempt to extend its colonial domination of others and have demanded the immediate withdrawal of Soviet troops. The Moslem world is especially and justifiably outraged by this aggression against an Islamic people. No action of a world power has ever been so quickly and so overwhelmingly condemned. But verbal condemnation is not enough. The Soviet Union must pay a concrete price for their aggression. . . .

While this invasion continues, we and the other nations of the world cannot conduct business as usual with the Soviet Union. That's why the United States has imposed stiff economic penalties on the Soviet Union. I will not issue any permits for Soviet ships to fish in the coastal waters of the United States. I've cut Soviet access to high-technology equipment and to agricultural products. I've limited other commerce with the Soviet Union, and I've asked our allies and friends to join with us in restraining their own trade with the Soviets and not to replace our own embargoed items. And I have notified the Olympic Committee that with Soviet invading forces in Afghanistan, neither the American people nor I will support sending an Olympic team to Moscow.

The Soviet Union is going to have to answer some basic questions: Will it help promote a more stable international environment in which its own legitimate, peaceful concerns can be pursued? Or will it continue to expand its military power far beyond its genuine security needs, and use that power for colonial conquest? The Soviet Union must realize that its decision to use military force in Afghanistan will be costly to every political and economic relationship it values.

Public Papers of the Presidents of the United States, Jimmy Carter, 1980–81, Book 1: January 1 to May 23, 1980. Washington, DC: Government Printing Office, 1980. Also available online: www.jimmycarterlibrary.org/documents/speeches/su80jec.phtml.

Document 22: Ronald Reagan's "Star Wars" Speech, March 23, 1983

Although the early years of Reagan's presidency featured a dramatic increase in military spending, Reagan's overall tenure includes several steps that were intended to end the arms race. The much-criticized Strategic Defense Initiative (SDI) that he announced in this speech was one such proposal. This visionary—some, especially those who derisively nick-named the proposal "Star Wars," would say impossible—proposal was a source of contention between the United States and the Soviet Union for the remainder of Reagan's presidency.

Since the dawn of the atomic age, we've sought to reduce the risk of war by maintaining a strong deterrent and by seeking genuine arms control. "Deterrence" means simply this: making sure any adversary who thinks about attacking the United States, or our allies, or our vital interests, concludes that the risks to him outweigh any potential gains. Once he understands that, he won't attack. We maintain the peace through our strength; weakness only invites aggression. This strategy of deterrence has not changed. It still works. But what it takes to maintain deterrence has changed. It took one kind of military force to deter an attack when we had far more nuclear weapons than any other power; it takes another kind now that the Soviets, for example, have enough accurate and powerful nuclear weapons to destroy virtually all of our missiles on the ground. Now, this is not to say that the Soviet Union is planning to make war on us. Nor do I believe a war is inevitable—quite the contrary. But what must be recognized is that our security is based on being prepared to meet all threats. . . .

If the Soviet Union will join with us in our effort to achieve major arms reduction, we will have succeeded in stabilizing the nuclear balance. Nevertheless, it will still be necessary to rely on the specter of retaliation, on mutual threat. And that's a sad commentary on the human condition. Wouldn't it be better to save lives than to avenge them? Are we not capable of demonstrating our peaceful intentions by applying all our abilities and our ingenuity to achieving a truly lasting stability? I think we are. Indeed, we must.

After careful consultation with my advisers, including the Joint Chiefs of Staff, I believe there is a way. Let me share with you a vision of the future which offers hope. It is that we embark on a program to counter the awesome Soviet missile threat with measures that are defensive. Let us turn to the very strengths in technology that spawned our great industrial base and that have given us the quality of life we enjoy today.

What if free people could live secure in the knowledge that their security did not rest upon the threat of instant U.S. retaliation to deter a Soviet attack, that we could intercept and destroy strategic ballistic missiles before they reached our own soil or that of our allies? . . .

Tonight, consistent with our obligations of the ABM treaty and recognizing the need for closer consultation with our allies, I'm taking an important first step. I am directing a comprehensive and intensive effort to define a long-term research and development program to begin to achieve our ultimate goal of eliminating the threat posed by strategic nuclear missiles. This could pave the way for arms control measures to eliminate the weapons themselves. We seek neither military superiority nor political advantage. Our only purpose is one all people share—is to search for ways to reduce the danger of nuclear war.

Public Papers of the Presidents of the United States, Ronald Reagan, 1983, Book 1: January 1 to July 1, 1983. Washington, DC: Government Printing Office, 1984. Also available online: www.tamu.edu/scom/pres/speeches/rrsecure.html.

Document 23: Mikhail Gorbachev's Address to the United Nations, December 7, 1988

Having already committed the Soviet Union to reductions in the number of nuclear weapons deployed in Europe and announced major reforms of Soviet society, Gorbachev was being hailed by 1988 as a different kind of Soviet leader. The tone and content of this address to the United Nations reflect Gorbachev's desire to reorganize the relationship between the superpowers not on the basis of ideological and military competition, but on genuine coexistence.

Further world progress is now possible only through the search for a consensus of all mankind, in movement toward a new world order. We have arrived at a frontier at which controlled spontaneity leads to a dead end. The world community must learn to shape and direct the process in such a way as to preserve civilization, to make it safe for all and more pleasant for normal life. It is a question of cooperation that could be more accurately called "co-creation" and "co-development." The formula of development "at another's expense" is becoming outdated. In light of present realities, genuine progress by infringing upon the rights and liberties of man and peoples, or at the expense of nature, is impossible. . . .

The de-ideologization of interstate relations has become a demand of the new stage. We are not giving up our convictions, philosophy, or traditions. Neither are we calling on anyone else to give up theirs. Yet we are not going to shut ourselves up within the range of our values. That would lead to spiritual impoverishment, for it would mean renouncing so powerful a source of development as sharing all the original things created independently by each nation. In the course of such sharing, each should prove the advantages of his own system, his own way of life and values, but not through words or propaganda alone, but through real deeds as well. That is, indeed, an honest struggle of ideology, but it must not be carried over into mutual relations between states. Otherwise we simply will not be able to solve a single world problem; arrange broad, mutually advantageous and equitable cooperation between peoples; manage rationally the achievements of the scientific and technical revolution; transform world economic relations; protect the environment; overcome underdevelopment; or put an end to hunger, disease, illiteracy, and other mass ills. Finally, in that case, we will not manage to eliminate the nuclear threat and militarism. . . .

Relations between the Soviet Union and the United States of America span 5½ decades. The world has changed, and so have the nature, role, and place of these relations in world politics. For too long they were built under the banner of confrontation, and sometimes of hostility, either open or concealed. But in the last few years, throughout the world people were able to heave a sigh of relief, thanks to the changes for the better in the substance and atmosphere of the relations between Moscow and Washington.

No one intends to underestimate the serious nature of the disagreements, and the difficulties of the problems which have not been settled. However, we have already graduated from the primary school of instruction in mutual understanding and in searching for solutions in our and in the common interests. The USSR and the United States created the biggest nuclear missile arsenals, but after objectively recognizing their responsibility, they were able to be the first to conclude an agreement on the reduction and physical destruction of a proportion of these weapons, which threatened both themselves and everyone else.

United Nations Doc. A/43/PV.72 (1988). Also available online: http://oll.temple.edu/hist249/course/Documents/gorbachev_speech_to_UN.htm.

Document 24: NATO's Declaration of the End of the Cold War, July 5, 1990

In the summer of 1990, with the literal Berlin Wall and the figurative Iron Curtain both gone, NATO secretary general Manfred Wörmer felt prepared to issue a declaration that the alliance officially considered the Cold

War to be over. In this speech, also known as the London Declaration, Wörmer announces the new priorities on which NATO would focus now that hostilities between it and the Eastern bloc appeared to have ended.

The Cold War belongs to history. Our Alliance is moving from confrontation to cooperation. We are building a new Europe, a Europe drawn together by the unfettered aspiration for freedom, democracy and prosperity. Never before has Europe had such a tangible opportunity to overcome the cycle of war and peace that has so bedevilled its past. . . .

In the past few weeks a series of ministerial meetings have drawn up the basis for this Alliance's contribution to the new Europe. Already we are responding to change with change and with initiative. We are adapting our Alliance, reaching out to all who wish to build the same Europe as we do. Today we will renew our offer of cooperation and give it concrete form. We look at the Soviet Union and the countries of Central and Eastern Europe as potential partners and friends. . . .

Europe is not yet immune from future risk or danger. This Alliance, which has contributed so much to overcoming Europe's painful division, must play its full part alongside other Western institutions in extending the stability and security we enjoy to all European nations. . . . We must bring the military situation rapidly into line with the new political realities of Europe. . . .

Our Alliance cannot be successful in its new tasks if it fails to fulfill the oldest and most fundamental one: the preservation of peace. We must retain a secure defense. It is not an obstacle to change but the very precondition for change, and our weapons never were, and never will be, a threat to anyone.

Neither North America nor Europe can be secure and successful unless they stay together. Now that Europe is stronger and more integrated it can provide for an even closer and more successful transatlantic partnership by assuming its share of global responsibilities. United there is no challenge this Alliance cannot meet.

"Opening Statement to the NATO Summit Meeting," NATO Online Library, www.nato.int/docu/speech/1990/s900705a_e.htm.

Discussion Questions

Chapter 1: The Origins and Early Years of the Cold War

1. Caroline Kennedy-Pipe argues that decisions made at the conference among the Allies at Yalta in 1945 helped spawn the Cold War by encouraging (or at least allowing) the division of Europe into two separate spheres of influence. What compromises did both sides make at Yalta that contributed to this division? How does Kennedy-Pipe describe the attitudes with which the three leaders approached negotiations at Yalta?

2. Lynn Boyd Hinds and Theodore Otto Windt Jr. discuss the context and effects of Winston Churchill's famous "Iron Curtain" speech. What do they claim were Churchill goals in making such a strong anti-Communist statement to his American audience? How effective do Hinds and Windt think Churchill ultimately was in accomplishing these goals?

3. Richard Crockatt examines how opposition to communism became the official policy of the United States in the late 1940s as a result of the Truman Doctrine. Describe the various sources that contributed ideas that would become part of the Truman Doctrine. What effect did the Truman Doctrine have on relations between the Soviet Union and the United States?

4. Jonathan M. Weisgall chronicles the use of the atomic bomb as a bargaining chip in the years immediately after World War II. What does Weisgall believe was the intention behind the Operation Crossroads tests? Does his position as an attorney for the islanders displaced by the Bikini Atoll atomic tests hinder his objectivity or does it serve to broaden his historical perspective? Provide specific passages to support your claims.

5. The attitude toward the atomic bomb among the general populace of the United States shifted several times in the first decade of the Cold War, according to Paul Boyer. What factors were most influential in causing these changes? How did the swings in public opinion affect the official U.S. position regarding the use of nuclear weapons?

Chapter 2: Cold War Hot Spots: Confrontation in the Nuclear Age

1. David Rees looks at the Korean War in the context of Truman's policy of containing communism. According to Rees, why did

the United States feel compelled to give extensive military support to the South Koreans in their war against the North Koreans? What did Truman and MacArthur disagree should be the goals of the United States in fighting the Korean War?

2. Stephen J. Whitfield describes the "red scare" that swept the United States in the early 1950s. In Whitfield's opinion, to what extent was fear of the Soviets justified? What motivated fervent anti-Communists such as Joseph McCarthy to root out Communist sympathizers in the United States?

3. Norman Friedman focuses on the superpower showdowns in Berlin and Cuba during the early 1960s. According to Friedman, how were both crises made worse by the superpowers' reliance on exaggerated rhetoric?

4. Carol R. Saivetz and Sylvia Woodby recount the ideological struggle for supremacy between the United States and Soviet Union in the newly independent nations of Africa during the 1960s and 1970s. Why were the two countries so interested in establishing their influence in Africa? How did the two sides attempt to manipulate their respective "client" states and how effective were these attempts generally?

5. What social and military factors does Tom Engelhardt claim were most important in limiting U.S. use of nuclear weapons as part of its policy of containing Soviet expansion? Using specific examples, explain what Engelhardt means by the "victory culture" of the 1950s and discuss how it helped invalidate a nuclear "first strike" by the United States.

6. Spencer R. Weart examines how the notion of deterrence came to be the dominant military strategy of the Cold War by the late 1950s. How did the theory of deterrence, as formulated by Herman Kahn and others, propose to prevent nuclear warfare? What are some of the inherent risks in deterrence policy, according to Weart?

Chapter 3: Cold War II

1. According to H.W. Brands, what brought about the end of détente during the presidency of Jimmy Carter? How much responsibility does Brands place on the Soviets for their actions in Central America and Afghanistan? How and why was Carter's increasingly hostile attitude toward the Soviets affected by internal pressure from anti-Communists such as the Committee on the Present Danger?

2. Fred Halliday compares two prominent periods of superpower rivalry, calling them "Cold War I" (1946–1953) and "Cold War II" (1979–1983). What are some of the important similarities that Halliday notes between these two periods? In what ways did the phases differ and how did these differences affect the superpowers' foreign policy?

3. John Feffer recounts the decline of communism in Eastern Europe in the late 1980s, culminating in the dramatic disintegration of the Eastern bloc in the summer of 1989. How does Feffer say Eastern European countries varied in the transition away from communism?

4. According to David S. Mason, the Soviet Union collapsed as a result of both external and internal pressures. In Mason's view, why did Gorbachev's twin policies of reform—glasnost and perestroika—actually hasten the demise of the USSR?

Chapter 4: Reflections on the Cold War

1. Eric Hobsbawm argues that the term "cold war" is a misnomer, since the two superpowers' main goal for most of its duration was to avoid direct conflict. What support does Hobsbawm provide for his contention that the United States and the Soviet Union both wanted to maintain an atmosphere of conflict but had no actual desire to go to war with one another?

2. Robert Conquest places the blame for the continuation of the Cold War after the mid-1960s directly on the Soviet Union. What evidence does he provide to support his claims that seemingly cooperative gestures such as détente were actually intended by the Soviets to distract attention from their continued desire for greater power and territorial expansion?

3. In Stephen E. Ambrose's view, the U.S. government applied many lessons learned from World War II in conducting the more indirect hostilities of the Cold War. Using specific examples, discuss how the historical example of World War II influenced decision making during the Cold War.

4. Vojtech Mastny contends that the Soviet Union rarely presented an actual military threat to the United States during the Cold War but was nevertheless dangerous because of its leaders' occasionally aggressive rhetoric. How did the Cold War help strengthen Western Europe, in Mastny's view?

Chronology

1917–1921

A revolution and civil war in Russia ends with the Bolshevik faction of Communists gaining power with Lenin as head of state.

1919–1920

The "red scare" in the United States leads to the arrest of more than four thousand alleged Communists by order of Attorney General A. Mitchell Palmer.

1924

January 21—Lenin dies; Joseph Stalin gradually comes to power over several months.

1933

November—The United States officially recognizes the Soviet Union, several years after most other Western nations.

1939

Nazi Germany and the Soviet Union sign a mutual nonaggression pact just before the outbreak of World War II.

1941

June 22—Nazi Germany invades the Soviet Union; the Soviet Union joins the Allies.

1942

September 23—The Manhattan Project to develop an atomic bomb for the United States begins.

December 2—Enrico Fermi achieves a self-sustaining atomic chain reaction, a necessary step toward the development of an atomic bomb.

1943

A Soviet atomic bomb project under Igor Kurchatov begins.

November—The Allied leaders meet at Tehran.

1944

June—The Allies invade occupied France; the Soviets begin a full-scale counter offensive against Germany.

1945

February—The Yalta Conference convenes with Roosevelt, Stalin, and Churchill taking part.

April 12—Roosevelt dies and Truman becomes president.

May 8—Germany surrenders.

July 16—The "Trinity" test at Alamogordo, New Mexico, marks the first successful atomic bomb explosion.

July–August—Truman, Attlee, and Stalin meet at Potsdam.

August 6 and 9—The United States explodes atomic bombs over Hiroshima and Nagasaki.

August 14—Japan surrenders.

1946

February 22—U.S. diplomat George Kennan sends his Long Telegram to Truman from Moscow.

March 5—Churchill gives his Iron Curtain speech.

July—U.S. Operation Crossroads nuclear tests conducted on Bikini atoll.

September—Soviet ambassador Nikolai Novikov sends a telegram to Stalin from Washington.

1947

March 12—The Truman Doctrine is announced in a speech before Congress.

June 5—The Marshall Plan to help rebuild Europe is announced.

July—Kennan elaborates on his telegram in an article published in *Foreign Affairs Quarterly*.

1948

June—The Soviets blockade the western portion of Berlin; British and American planes begin airlifting supplies to the city.

August—Alger Hiss is accused of spying for the Soviets.

1949

May 12—The blockade of West Berlin ends.

July—The North Atlantic Treaty Organization (NATO) is established.

September—The Soviet Union tests its first atomic bomb; the People's Republic of China is established.

1950

January 21—Hiss is convicted of perjury.

February—Senator Joseph McCarthy claims to have a list of "known Communists" working in the State Department.

March—National Security Council Resolution 68 (NSC 68) recommends a nuclear arsenal buildup and aggressive military containment policy toward communism.

June—The Korean War begins.

1952

November 1—The United States detonates a hydrogen bomb at Elugelab atoll.

1953

March 5—Stalin dies and Nikita Khrushchev succeeds him as general secretary. The House Un-American Activities Committee (HUAC), led by McCarthy, begins investigating suspected Communists in the government, the military, and the arts.

June 19—Julius and Ethel Rosenberg are executed as Soviet spies.

July 27—The Korean War ends.

August 14—The Soviet Union successfully tests a hydrogen bomb.

1954

September 7—The Southeast Asia Treaty Organization (SEATO) military alliance is formed.

December 2—McCarthy is censured by the U.S. Senate.

1955

May 14—The Warsaw Pact military alliance is formed.

1956

February 14—Khrushchev gives his "secret speech" at the Twenty-fifth Party Congress denouncing Stalin.

November—The Soviets forcibly put down a Hungarian insurrection.

1957

October 4—The Soviet Union launches *Sputnik*, the first artificial satellite. Both the USSR and the United States successfully test intercontinental ballistic missiles (ICBMs).

1959

January—Communists revolt successfully in Cuba led by Fidel Castro.

July and September—Vice President Richard Nixon visits the USSR, and Khrushchev visits the United States.

1960

May—An American U-2 spy plane is shot down over the USSR; pilot Gary Francis Powers is eventually convicted of spying.

1961

April—The U.S.-sponsored Bay of Pigs invasion fails in Cuba.

August—The Berlin Wall is erected.

1962

October—The United States and Soviet Union nearly come into direct military conflict during the Cuban Missile Crisis.

1963

June 20—A "hot line" between the Kremlin and the White House is established.

June 26—Kennedy visits Berlin.

August 5—The Limited Test-Ban Treaty is signed.

November 22—Kennedy is assassinated, and Lyndon Johnson becomes president.

1964

August 10—The Gulf of Tonkin Resolution allows an increased American military presence in Southeast Asia.

October 15—Khrushchev is ousted and replaced by Leonid Brezhnev and Alexei Kosygin.

1965

July—The first U.S. combat troops arrive in Vietnam.

December 28—China successfully tests its first hydrogen bomb.

1968

American military involvement in Vietnam peaks.

July—Nuclear Non-proliferation Treaty is signed.

April 4 and June 5—Dr. Martin Luther King Jr. and Robert Kennedy are assassinated.

August—The Soviets invade Czechoslovakia to put down the Prague Spring uprising.

November—Richard Nixon is elected president.

1969

March—The United States begins bombing Cambodia in a widening of the war in Southeast Asia. Strategic Arms Limitation Talks (SALT) begin.

1970

February—The Paris Peace Talks begin between the United States and Vietnam.

April 29—The United States invades Cambodia.

1972

February—Nixon visits China.

May—Nixon and Brezhnev sign the Anti-Ballistic Missile (ABM) Treaty and SALT I agreement.

1973

January 27—The Paris Accords establish a cease-fire in Vietnam.

March 29—The last American combat troops leave Vietnam.

September—CIA support helps in the overthrow of Salvador Allende in Chile.

1974

August 8—Nixon resigns from office after the Watergate scandal and is replaced by Gerald Ford.

1975

April 30—Saigon falls and the United States evacuates the embassy.

July 17—U.S. astronauts and Soviet cosmonauts cooperate in the *Apollo-Soyuz* linkage.

August 1—The Helsinki Accords are signed, recognizing the official boundaries of several Eastern European nations in exchange for promises from the Soviets to improve human rights.

1979

June 18—The SALT II agreement is signed by Carter and Brezhnev.

December 28—The Soviet invasion of Afghanistan prompts Carter to call for a U.S. military buildup, thus effectively ending détente.

1980

The United States and its Western allies boycott the Moscow Summer Olympics; Ronald Reagan is elected president on a strong anti-Communist platform.

1981

December 13—Martial law is imposed in Poland in response to the "Solidarity" labor movement actions.

1982

November 10—Brezhnev dies and is replaced by Yuri Andropov. The Strategic Arms Reduction Talks (START) open in Geneva.

1983

March 23—Reagan proposes the Strategic Defense Initiative (SDI, or Star Wars) program.

September 1—Korean Air Lines flight 007 is shot down by a Soviet fighter jet.

1984

February 9—Andropov dies and is replaced by Konstantin Chernenko. The Soviet Union and much of the Eastern bloc boycott the Los Angeles Summer Olympics.

1985

March 10—Chernenko dies and is replaced by Mikhail Gorbachev.
November—Reagan and Gorbachev hold a summit in Geneva.

1986

Gorbachev announces glasnost and perestroika reform policies.
October—Reagan and Gorbachev hold a summit in Reykjavik.

1987

December 8—Reagan and Gorbachev hold a summit in Washington, at which they sign the Intermediate-Range Nuclear Forces (INF) Treaty.

1988

May—Reagan and Gorbachev hold a summit in Moscow.

1989

January—Soviet troops withdraw entirely from Afghanistan.
June—Pro-democracy demonstrations are suppressed with force in China. Numerous East European nations renounce ties with the Soviet Union.
November 9—The Berlin Wall is torn down.
December—Gorbachev and George Bush meet in Malta and declare the Cold War "officially over."

1990

July—The London Declaration by NATO declares an end to the Cold War. Baltic republics begin breaking away from the Soviet Union.

1991

July 31—The START Treaty is signed by Bush and Gorbachev.
August—Hard-line Communists mount an attempted coup against Gorbachev.
December 8—The Commonwealth of Independent States (CIS) is formed.
December 25—Gorbachev resigns.
December 31—The Soviet Union is dissolved.

For Further Research

Books

Gar Alperovitz, *The Decision to Use the Atomic Bomb*. New York: Vintage, 1996.

Michael Barson, *"Better Dead than Red!" A Nostalgic Look at the Golden Years of Russiaphobia, Red-Baiting, and Other Commie Madness*. New York: Hyperion, 1992.

Arnold Beichman, ed., *CNN's Cold War Documentary: Issues and Controversy*. Stanford, CA: Hoover Institution, 2000.

Michael R. Beschloss and Strobe Talbott, *At the Highest Levels: The Inside Story of the End of the Cold War*. Boston: Little, Brown, 1993.

James G. Blight, *The Shattered Crystal Ball: Fear and Learning in the Cuban Missile Crisis*. Lanham, MD: Rowman and Littlefield, 1992.

David Callahan, *Dangerous Capabilities: Paul Nitze and the Cold War*. New York: Harper and Row, 1990.

John Lewis Gaddis, *The United States and the End of the Cold War: Implications, Reconsiderations, Provocations*. Oxford, UK: Oxford University Press, 1994.

Robert M. Gates, *From the Shadows: The Ultimate Insider's Story of Five Presidents and How They Won the Cold War*. New York: Touchstone Books, 1997.

Peter George, *Dr. Strangelove, or How I Learned to Stop Worrying and Love the Bomb*. Oxford, UK: Oxford University Press, 1988.

Mikhail Gorbachev, *Perestroika: New Thinking for Our Country and the World*. New York: HarperCollins, 1987.

Peter Grose, *Operation Rollback: America's Secret War Behind the Iron Curtain*. Boston: Houghton Mifflin, 2000.

Margot Henriksen, *D. Strangelove's America: Society and Culture in the Atomic Age*. Berkeley and Los Angeles: University of California Press, 1997.

Seymour Hersh, *The Dark Side of Camelot*. Boston: Back Bay Books, 1998.

William Hyland, *The Cold War Is Over*. New York: Times Books, 1990.

Jeremy Isaacs and Taylor Downing, *Cold War: An Illustrated History, 1945–1991*. Boston: Little, Brown, 1998.

Chen Jian, *Mao's China and the Cold War*. Chapel Hill: University of North Carolina Press, 2001.

Edward H. Judge and John W. Langdon, eds., *The Cold War: A History Through Documents*. Upper Saddle River, NJ: Prentice-Hall, 1998.

George F. Kennan, *At a Century's Ending: Reflections, 1982–1995*. New York: Norton, 1997.

Robert F. Kennedy, *Thirteen Days: A Memoir of the Cuban Missile Crisis*. New York: Norton, 1999.

Sergei N. Khrushchev, *Nikita Khrushchev and the Creation of a Superpower*. Trans. Shirley Benson. State College: Pennsylvania State University Press, 2001.

Stephen Kotkin, *Armageddon Averted: The Soviet Collapse, 1970–2000*. Oxford, UK: Oxford University Press, 2001.

Walter LaFeber, *America, Russia, and the Cold War, 1945–1996*. 9th ed. New York: McGraw-Hill, 2001.

Derek Leebaert, *The Fifty Year Wound: The True Price of America's Cold War Victory*. Boston: Little, Brown, 2002.

Frederick W. Marks III, *Power and Peace: The Diplomacy of John Foster Dulles*. Westport, CT: Praeger, 1993.

Ernest R. May, ed., *American Cold War Strategy: Interpreting NSC 68*. Boston: St. Martin's, 1993.

Martin J. Medhurst and H.W. Brands, eds., *Critical Reflections on the Cold War: Linking Rhetoric and History*. College Station: Texas A&M University Press, 2000.

David E. Murphy, Sergei A. Kondrashev, and George Bailey, *Berlin: CIA vs. KGB in the Cold War*. New Haven, CT: Yale University Press, 1997.

Paul Nitze, *From Hiroshima to Glasnost: At the Centre of Decision*. London: Weidenfeld and Nicolson, 1989.

Arnold A. Offner, *Another Such Victory: President Truman and the Cold War, 1945–1953*. Stanford, CA: Stanford University Press, 2002.

Ronald E. Powaski, *The Cold War: The United States and the Soviet Union, 1917–1991*. New York: Oxford University Press, 1998.

Ronald Radosh and Joyce Milton, *The Rosenberg File*. New Haven, CT: Yale University Press, 1997.

Peter W. Rodman, *More Precious than Peace: The Cold War and the Struggle for the Third World*. New York: Scribner, 1994.

Ellen Schrecker, *Many Are the Crimes: McCarthyism in America*. Boston: Little, Brown, 1998.

Martin Walker, *The Cold War: A History*. New York: Henry Holt, 1995.

Randall B. Woods and Howard Jones, *Dawning of the Cold War: The United States' Quest for Order*. Athens: University of Georgia Press, 1991.

John W. Young, *Winston Churchill's Last Campaign: Britain and the Cold War, 1951–55*. Oxford, UK: Clarendon, 1996.

Websites

Bulletin of the Atomic Scientists (www.bullatomsci.org).

CNN Interactive—Cold War (www.cnn.com/SPECIALS/cold. war).

Cold War International History Project at the Woodrow Wilson International Center for Scholars (http://cwihp.si.edu).

Cold War Museum (www.coldwar.org).

Journal of Cold War Studies (http://muse.jhu.edu/journals/cws).

National Security Archives at George Washington University (www.gwu.edu/~nsarchiv).

Program in Presidential Rhetoric Speech Archive at Texas A&M University (www.tamu.edu/scom/pres/archive.html).

Index